The German
Democratic
Republic

Other Titles in This Series

943.02 Ger   Main o/o   20.00

3-11-99

Westview Special Studies on the Soviet Union and Eastern Europe

The German Democratic Republic:
A Developed Socialist Society
edited by Lyman H. Legters

The shifting patterns of relationships in Central and Eastern Europe require that students of international relations be well versed in the attitudes and internal structures of the nations involved. Until now, material in English on the German Democratic Republic has consisted primarily of journalistic reminiscences or narrow scholarly treatments. Recognizing the need and responding to it, the authors of this book—leaders in the study of the GDR—present an up-to-date and comprehensive look at the country, focusing on domestic political and social change. The authors are agreed that the GDR is not only here to stay, but is also a rather stable society that can withstand moderate, well-regulated processes of change. They address education, intellectual life, the military, foreign relations, and the economy, as well as the customary subjects of politics and governmental direction.

Lyman H. Legters is professor of Russian and East European studies and chairman of the Program in Social Theory at the University of Washington.

The German Democratic Republic

A Developed Socialist Society

edited by
Lyman H. Legters

Westview Press • Boulder, Colorado

Westview Special Studies on the
Soviet Union and Eastern Europe

Copyright © 1978 by Westview Press, Inc.

Published in 1978 in the United States of America by
   Westview Press, Inc.
   5500 Central Avenue
   Boulder, Colorado 80301
   Frederick A. Praeger, Publisher and Editorial Director

Library of Congress Cataloging in Publication Data
Main entry under title:
The German Democratic Republic.
   (Westview special studies on the Soviet Union and
Eastern Europe)
   Bibliography: p.
   1. Germany, East—Addresses, essays, lectures.
I. Legters, Lyman Howard, 1928-   II. Series.
DD261.G415   943'.1087   77-578
ISBN 0-89158-142-1

Printed and bound in the United States of America

Contents

Preface

Some of the contributors to this volume have suggested to me that they feel academically isolated in their continuing effort to study and interpret contemporary life in the German Democratic Republic. One such discussion of the "loneliness" of the East German specialist took place in Salt Lake City, where some of these papers were first presented at a panel of the Rocky Mountain Association of Slavic Studies in April 1972. My reaction at the time, speaking as one who had sought to stay abreast of East German developments for two decades, was that they did not know what loneliness really was. The very fact that enough scholars could be gathered to staff a session devoted exclusively to the GDR already signified a relative burgeoning of interest in that country. And the ensuing process, set in motion by the high quality of the original papers, of gathering additional contributions to form a book on the GDR of the 1970s has only confirmed my observation. Not only are there many more scholars engaged in producing a much larger volume of scholarship on what was once described as the least-known country of Eastern Europe except Albania; even more important, the skills and critical faculties now being applied to the problem have risen commensurately, as the chapters in this volume demonstrate.

The reasons why scholars and groups of scholars choose to study some topics and neglect others are sometimes accidental. Factors of that sort help to account for the periodically changing fashions of academic attention and are of interest, as such, to sociologists of knowledge, to book review editors, and conceivably to publishers. Those of us who have worked against prevailing fashion for some time by attempting to focus an appropriate measure of attention on the GDR can discuss this kind of academic lore among ourselves—cheerfully if we think that neglect is finally being overcome and angrily if we do not—but there is no reason to burden others with analysis of that sort.

Sometimes, however, the choices of subjects for research and the corresponding neglect of others are not so fortuitous. Sometimes a decision to study or not to study a given topic is symptomatic of more general intellectual currents or attitudes in society at large. And if, as I would suggest is true of the American record of research on the GDR, neglect of an important subject mirrors quite faithfully a distorted view prevailing in our society, then the fact of neglect is no longer merely an item of academic folklore but rather an item of intellectual history and, as such, worthy of examination. If the distortions, fictions, and myths operate simultaneously to account for popular attitudes, official external policies, *and* academic neglect, and especially if the distortions continue to enjoy widespread currency, then it is important to inquire into the sources of misapprehension. At a time when the Western states are finding reasonably graceful ways of establishing diplomatic relations with the GDR, it seems timely to take a fresh look at the country formerly known as East Germany, a geographical designation long presumed to be devoid of lasting significance.

The contributors to this volume are united by, among other attributes, their determination to view the GDR as it is and not according to the wishful expectations of an earlier era. They would not necessarily agree on all points, but, as their respective chapters show, they take the GDR seriously and with a just appreciation of the importance it has in contemporary world politics. In recognition of the primacy of domestic politics—of the principle, that is, that the inner workings of the society and polity will significantly condition that country's place in international affairs—they give the bulk of their attention to developments within the GDR. Although that procedure runs counter to the old habit of treating all of Eastern Europe as a mere extension of policies fashioned in the Kremlin, it seems to me wholly defensible under conditions prevailing now in that part of the world, and especially so for a country that remains terra incognita to most students of the international scene. Our hope for this book is that, in making the GDR a better-known territory, it will also help to dispel some of the outworn myths and distortions.

As in any book of this sort, the contributors have completed their chapters at different times. The result is that some are more up to date than others, but all have been retained because of the pertinence of their analyses, even when particular developments have outrun some of the material covered. Two of the chapters have previously been published: Ludz's in

substantially the same form in *Problems of Communism,*
March-April 1972; Mallinckrodt's in German in a special issue
of *Deutschland Archiv,* 1971. Thanks are owing to both
journals for permission to reprint these essays.

As for the contributors, instead of regarding this enterprise
as a headache to be borne exclusively by the editor, they have
been both amiable and accommodating in bringing the effort
to completion. As editor, I am grateful to all of them.

Lyman H. Legters

The Contributors

THOMAS A. BAYLIS teaches political science at the University of Texas at San Antonio. His book, *The Technical Intelligentsia and the East German Elite,* was published by the University of California Press.

M. DONALD HANCOCK is a professor of political science at the University of Texas and director of the Center for European Studies there; he has been visiting professor at the University of Bielefeld. His study of civil-military relations in the GDR was published in a monograph series at the University of Denver.

KENNETH HANF has his Ph.D. from the University of California at Berkeley in comparative administration and is presently affiliated with the International Institute of Management in West Berlin. He is at the moment working on a study of patterns of local-central relations in the implementation of social policy in the GDR.

ARTHUR M. HANHARDT, JR., is professor of political science at the University of Oregon and author of *The German Democratic Republic* in the Johns Hopkins Press series on Integration and Community Building in Eastern Europe, as well as of many articles on the GDR.

DALE R. HERSPRING holds a Ph.D. in political science from the University of Southern California and is the author of *East German Civil-Military Relations: The Impact of Technology, 1949-1973,* published in 1973 by Praeger, as well as of numerous articles dealing with East European civil-military relations. He is currently a Foreign Service Officer with the Department of State.

MICHAEL KEREN is senior lecturer in economics at the Hebrew University in Jerusalem. A Yale Ph.D. in economics, he has been a visiting fellow at the Institute of International Studies, University of California at Berkeley, and has written several articles on the economy of the GDR.

HENRY KRISCH is an associate professor of political science at the University of Connecticut. He is the author of *German Politics under Soviet Occupation* (Columbia University Press, 1974), and of review articles on German and GDR affairs in *Problems of Communism* and *Studies in Comparative Communism.* He is a contributor to the forthcoming *Handbuch der Aussenpolitik der DDR.*

LYMAN H. LEGTERS is professor of Russian and East European studies and chairman of the Program on Social Theory and Ideology at the University of Washington. His book on *East German Higher Education* will soon be published.

PETER C. LUDZ is now professor of political science at the University of Munich, having been affiliated previously with the Free University Berlin and the University of Bielefeld. He is also director of studies at the Stiftung Wissenschaft und Politik (Ebenhausen/Isar). The M.I.T. Press published the English version of his book *Changing Party Elite in East Germany* in 1972; and his *Two Germanys in One World* appeared under the auspices of the Atlantic Institute for International Affairs in Paris.

ANITA MALLINCKRODT is adjunct associate professor of international affairs at the George Washington University and has authored two books on the GDR: *Propaganda hinter der Mauer* ((Kohlhammer 1971) and *Wer macht die Aussenpolitik der DDR* (Droste 1972). She is coauthor of *Politics in the German Democratic Republic,* published in 1975 by Praeger, and will publish *The International Political Communication of the Two German States: Instrument of International Image-Making,* University of Köln, 1978.

MICHAEL W. OLSZEWSKI is a graduate student in East European Studies at the University of Washington, working on the politics of the GDR under the direction of Professor Lyman Legters.

GREGORY P. SWINT is a graduate student in Interdisciplinary Studies at the University of Oregon and is working on GDR affairs under the direction of Professor Arthur Hanhardt.

The German
Democratic
Republic

1. Introduction: The GDR in Perspective

Lyman H. Legters

Should a latter-day Rip Van Winkle have awakened in the mid-1970s and looked about to assess the international political situation, he might have been more than mildly intrigued by the opening of formal diplomatic relations between the German Democratic Republic and certain Western states, including the United States. When he went into hibernation, East Germany, although formally constituted as a state, had clearly still been in an occupied status. Soviet tanks had cruised the streets of East Berlin only two years before, restoring and maintaining an internal order that East German authorities had allowed to lapse. The regime of that day had tottered and just barely survived to reestablish its control over domestic politics. It was generally understood that the government had no popular mandate, that the Soviet presence was the only effective guarantee of its authority. Even if, by 1955, the Ulbricht government had regained something of its grip on the internal order, the Soviet Union was still its manifest tutor in all policy matters and its master in things touching on international relations.

Yet, as he would have quickly realized, much can happen in two decades. His curiosity about the GDR would soon have revealed to him that this once abject client had transformed itself into one of the paramount industrial powers of Europe

and the world and, as such, into one of the Soviet Union's most
valued trading partners. Had he looked a bit more closely, he
would also have discovered a new sense of confidence, an
awareness of accomplishment and of still more to be accomplished, in the land he had known as occupied East Germany. It
might, then have puzzled him that so many prestigious states
were only just getting around to recognizing the GDR as he
awakened, for plainly the transformation could not have
occurred overnight.

For an explanation of this seeming incongruity, he would
have had to acquaint himself with the intervening history of
Cold War encounter in Central Europe and of the attitudes
accompanying it. And, unhampered by direct experience of the
rhetoric and the illusory perceptions that typified the later
stages of the Cold War, he would have found that actuality had
changed much more rapidly than U.S. perceptions of it. He
would have had to realize that perceptions that were more or
less accurate at one time had taken on a life of their own, that
they had been preserved in artificial divorcement from changing actuality, as fictional or mythological characterizations of
an international political configuration and of a particular
polity that had been outrun by events. Only by grasping the
outworn quality of these perceptions could our modern Rip
Van Winkle begin to understand the interval in which the GDR
had taken on such impressive stature as a modern nation-state
while being simultaneously ignored by the United States.

Having spoken of fiction and mythology as if they were
equally accurate names for our postwar understanding of East
Germany, I should probably admit that our faulty perceptions
were at least understandable for quite some time. Even with
the arrogance conferred by hindsight, we can recognize that
prevailing American attitudes toward East Germany could
hardly have escaped a Cold War coloration. By the nature of
the occupation arrangements, it was inevitable that the Soviet
zone of occupation be seen as an aspect of "the German
problem." Diplomats, the military, popular sentiment, and the
academic world were united in viewing the occupation as a
legitimate, though temporary, transfer of sovereignty, and if
anyone thought of challenging its legitimacy, the challenge had
as much force for the Western occupation powers as for the

Soviet Union. The mounting antagonisms that signaled the outbreak of what we habitually regard as the Cold War merely reinforced prevailing assumptions. Although it was some time before Soviet policy in Germany crystallized into any kind of definite commitment to "sovietization" of the eastern zone of occupation, a community of sentiment emerged relatively swiftly in the West, involving the United States and West Germany most conspicuously, united around the oversimplifications of presumed virtue on one side and imputed villainy on the other.

The formation of an East German state and the gradual restoration of sovereignty that followed formed a pattern of Soviet response, not initiative, actuated almost without exception by developments in the West. By that time, of course, the Soviet Union had consolidated its East European domination (with the important Yugoslav exception), yet East Germany was still seen as part of the German problem, not as a junior member of the Soviet bloc.[1] Reunification was no longer an eventual and unenthusiastically embraced goal of four-power occupation; it had become a political slogan, expressive more of Soviet-American antagonism than of any realistically weighed policy objective. And as the external policies of the Federal Republic and the United States coalesced in the 1950s into a seldom-questioned community of interest, the understandable West German indignation over the country's division became an almost visceral ingredient of American policy as well.

If British and French views managed on the whole to include a few more shadings and subleties, American and West German depictions of the East German situation required only the purest white and the starkest black. Likewise, the Soviet Union, as soon as it adopted a policy of gradually integrating the Soviet Zone of Occupation as a more or less sovereign partner into the East European coalition, tended in the fashion of Cold War rhetoric to portray the German situation in completely polarized terms. For both sides, the future of Germany had become an article of faith and a test of loyalty. In that climate of discourse, symbols became more important than facts: one side celebrated German-Soviet friendship and blamed all difficulties on Western subversion; the other ridi-

culed Ulbricht and made West Berlin the outpost of democracy. The Berlin Blockade was either Soviet expansionism or
self-defense; the airlift was a heroic defense of democracy or
imperialistic interference; the uprising of 1953 was a confirmation of popular repudiation of the regime, or it was a plot
hatched by Western intelligence agencies; and, somewhat later,
the Berlin Wall was either legitimate self-protection or unal-
loyed beastliness.

Symbols partake of facticity, of course, and I have no wish to
suggest that the only legitimate vantage point for viewing this
conflict-ridden situation was one of neutrality. My point is
only to indicate the excess of heat over light in postwar
discourse on the German problem, a surfeit of partisanship
that effectively muted the voices of detached criticism and, in
effect, placed a negative value on scholarly treatment of the
GDR as a permanent feature of the Central European land-
scape. I would not like to argue either that the academic world
is the only source of such detachment and criticism (in fact, a
number of astute journalists were well ahead of most academics in facing the GDR as a real phenomenon) or that the
provision of these is the sole function of higher education. But
the academies are the seats of scholarship and the only social
institutions we have that proclaim a detached quest for truth as
their first order of business. Since, as noted before, we inherit
the literature and many attitudes characteristic of that postwar
discourse and since, in my estimation, the process of demythol-
ogizing is begun but far from complete,[2] it remains pertinent to
ask why the scholarly community was not quicker to see in the
GDR an important and timely subject for investigation.

The cruder kinds of conspiratorial explanation afford little
assistance here. There is no doubt that public agencies engaged
in the funding of scholarly research have an impact on what
happens in the academic world, but I know of no evidence
suggesting that some taboo has excluded East Germany from
the company of favored subjects. Even if it be shown that
public support for research is withheld from projects starting
out from premises antagonistic to current policy, there is ample
evidence that such research can be pursued and published
without public subvention. In any case, there was no clamor

from the academic world, as there has been in other instances, protesting some shortsighted public policy inimical to the study of East Germany. On the contrary, the academic world has been implicated, tacitly perhaps but just as emphatically as the State Department and prevailing popular attitudes, in a habitual stance of ignoring the GDR, of acting as if it were shortly to disappear. One can make a case for a subtler kind of conspiracy, resting it on the recognition that both government and universities are social institutions committed to the status quo. There is of course a status quo in matters of foreign policy and perceptions of international relationships, just as there is in social and economic organization, and it may well be that the academy has, where our perceptions of the GDR are concerned, yielded up its advertised critical detachment in favor of a passive acquiescence in official policy toward the GDR. But even that rings strange when one considers that a wave of revisionist writing on the emotion-laden subject of the Cold War blossomed at a time when East Germany was still virtually terra incognita. Better explanations of the neglect of this subject are to be found, I suggest, in the realm of fortuity: that Germanists concentrated on material that seemed to fit a discernible tradition culminating in West German culture, society, and polity, while East Europeanists were by and large neither trained nor motivated to embrace the GDR within their scholarly purview.[3]

If one is to go beyond the merely accidental factors that allowed the GDR to fall between two stools, the failure lies not in some putative conspiracy in behalf of official policy but in a combined deficiency of insight and conceptualization. We all wore blinders for a time; we all conceived the world of international politics in terms of the prevailing antagonism between the United States and the Soviet Union. And, ironically, the country that was, more than any other of comparable capability and weight in international politics, a creation of what we call the Cold War, had its impressive developmental processes and its rapidly increasing economic and political capacities obscured, shielded from Western view, precisely by the rhetoric of the Cold War.[4]

As I have intimated, the Cold War cast a fearsome shadow

across the postwar years, and few among us had the clear-sightedness to practice critical detachment in the face of deep anxiety. But it seems to me that all explanations of neglect or ignorance—whether applied to scholarship or to diplomacy—cease to excuse as of 1961. The erection and, still more, the Western acceptance, amidst great indignation, of the Berlin Wall are, as I see it, the milestone beyond which no amount of explanation relieves either policy-makers or scholars of responsibility for atavistic, and therefore potentially pernicious, views as to the significance of the GDR. The indignation may, in and of itself, be understandable, in the same sense that a romantic apprehension of the uprising of 1953 was understandable. But it became pernicious whenever it obscured serious reflection on what the event signified. As after 1956 there could no longer be any expectation of direct exertion of Western influence on developments in Eastern Europe, so after 1961 no one could be excused for thinking that the status of East Germany was somehow more fluid, more subject to bargaining, more susceptible of treatment as a juridical exception, than that of any other East European state. Perniciousness in diplomatic terms is not identical with perniciousness in academic terms, and the former may seem more dangerous—or at least more immediate in its consequences. But the two forms are in parallel, in this case at least. A sensible academic reaction would have been to begin immediately to redress the neglect of the GDR as a subject of scholarship. A sensible diplomatic reaction would have been to abandon outworn rhetoric and to begin reorienting policy to the recognition of stable international relationships in Central and Eastern Europe. And it should be evident that two such reactions would have been not only parallel but also mutually reinforcing within the overall climate of opinion in the United States.

It may be too much to ask that a single event prompt radical reassessment of habitual attitudes, but we know that some events have that dramatic potentiality. It was certainly difficult to see the Berlin Wall as anything but an affront, yet it should have reminded us that our conceptions were outmoded. Seen clearly for what it really signified, the Berlin Wall could have prompted a salutary reconsideration of the whole episode we call the "Cold War."

We have given the name "Cold War" to an era in international politics because it was pervasive enough to affect all states and to override any other single feature of diplomacy in this period. But that should not, and in most accounts does not, disguise the facts that it had two preeminent protagonists, the United States and the Soviet Union, and that relations between those two powers formed the main axis of the Cold War. Had the same degree of antagonism obtained between, say, Venezuela and Peru, that conflict could have been labeled a "cold war," but it would certainly not have become the designation for a whole period of global politics. That characteristic flowed, in other words, from the predominance of the two principal actors in the international arena, as did the widespread impact of the conflict on secondary players.

But there is something altogether arbitrary, indeed inexplicable, about singling out an episode starting in 1946 or 1947 as if its antagonistic flavor were without precedent, when its proper context is the history of relations between the United States and the Soviet Union. If that perspective is adopted, then the postwar hostility is much closer to the norm of that history than is the brief period of wartime collaboration and ostensible friendliness. One might instead date the Cold War from 1917, noting the moderation of unfriendliness that occurred in 1933 and the exceptional lifting of hostility, four years in duration, required by the military alliance of World War II. I am not suggesting this as the only possible periodization of the Cold War but simply as one that avoids a distortion of the history of relations between the United States and the Soviet Union. What we are wont to call the "Cold War" thus becomes not an unexpected and arbitrary dismantling of the wartime alliance but a reversion to the habitual pattern of antagonism, in which rapprochement is at best an interlude and at worst a sham even for that brief wartime span.

The lengthening of perspective entails some disadvantages, for example, the difficulty of maintaining that Soviet-American relations dominated international politics before World War II as they did after, but these might not loom as large to another generation as they do to us when we are not yet quite sure that the Cold War is over. The signal advantage of the lengthening process, on the other hand, is the increased possibility that we can identify the salient characteristics of Cold War without fear that the period is so short and so close to us in time that we may be diverted by short-term aberrations. It also has some bearing on the argument between so-called revisionists and antirevisionists, who, partly because they generally fail to question the appropriate timespan for their debate and partly because they fail to ask precisely what distinguishes the Cold War from the alliance that preceded or the so-called détente that has followed, spend their time weighing motives and apportioning blame. Such questions might still have to be asked, but they could, I submit, be "detrivialized" if the subject were better defined.[5]

If we proceed to ask, in this lengthened perspective, what is peculiar about the history of Soviet-American relations, or what is peculiar about the antagonistic norm originating in 1917 as opposed to the ostensible friendliness of wartime and the comparative relaxation of the current accommodation, we are likely to center our attention on a characteristic that is really quite unusual in modern diplomatic history. It might be defined as an expectation on the part of powerful states that other powerful states will yield on fundamental positions without the exertion of military force. That formulation does not of course imply that we know what expectations were actually in the minds of policy-makers on both sides; it signifies rather that they behaved as if their expectations were of that sort. Further, the definition directs attention to the otherwise inexplicable rhetoric that seems in retrospect calculated to mobilize popular sentiment in behalf of military action at times and places where we know that military action was not contemplated. And, by placing the Cold War explicitly in an intermediate zone between conventional diplomatic calculus and practice on the one hand and resort to military force on the other, the formulation also does approximate justice to the principal episodes of Soviet-American relations. All of these, from a half-hearted Western intervention to the rhetoric of brinkmanship and from a global strategy of fostering revolution to the deliberate provocation in Cuba, are united by an expectation that radical alterations in power relationships and in the status of powerful states can be made to occur without application of full-scale military force. That in turn seems to represent essentially the set of circumstances we mean to designate when we speak of the Cold War. It follows, I think, that the notion of cold war can be used to describe a set of unusual circumstances extending further backward in time than 1947 but enclosing the postwar German question in an illuminating, rather that distorting, way.

If this be accepted as a fitting context for viewing the extended postwar encounter of great powers, the German issue, without losing its crucial character, becomes one among several instances in which policies derived from faulty or outmoded perceptions. That may help further to explain our (and Soviet) tardiness in arriving at more moderate expectations and assessments. More importantly, it redirects our attention, minus the distorting prism of a foreshortened notion of cold war, to the strange fact that a modern industrial state could emerge almost unnoticed in Central Europe and also, symptomatically at least, to the real significance of the Berlin Wall. We have known for a long time that East Germany would not just go away and have attempted from time to time to adjust our notion of reunification of the two Germanies to take account of the obvious necessity for reciprocality in any putative solution. But the Wall was a proclamation that the GDR intended to exist in its own right and that it was supported in that intention by an alliance system that had long been impregnable from without; the Wall proclaimed that it did not intend merely to exist as a transitional form leading to some new German constellation. It proclaimed what we might already have known but for our unwarranted notions about the sources of basic change in international politics, namely, that reunification was a wholly outmoded concept. It proclaimed, if anybody had been clear-sightedly attentive, the end of the Cold War.

By that I mean, of course, that the Wall was a signal that fundamental changes in the international order would not come about because we wished for them or set our face against that contemporary actuality of which the GDR was a not insignificant part. It was also a signal that we must acquaint ourselves belatedly with a society that had been ignored as much by academics as by diplomats, as much by German specialists as by East European specialists, as much by humanists as by social scientists. We might have been reminded that Ulbricht was not the buffoon of the cartoonist's wit but one of the postwar period's most adroit heads of state; that an economic miracle had been recorded in East as well as in West Germany; that an ignored economy had become one of the industrial powers of Eastern, and indeed of all of, Europe; that significant German novels and plays and scholarly works were appearing east of the Elbe; in short, that the GDR was a stable, yet also dynamic, society, stumbling over some of its problems and coping with others, irked but not fundamentally threatened by internal discontent, sensitive about its international status but tough-minded about its survival.

The risk entailed by any attempt to correct faulty perceptions is that one may overcorrect. The foregoing account has been aimed at persistent mental habits that have allowed and even encouraged ignorance of the GDR by substituting outworn and emotion-tinged notions for continuing realistic appraisals. It was not meant to suggest that the GDR is some sort of idyllic society exempted from the dislocations and aberrations that afflict all societies in some form or other. The argument does not require that we see the Berlin Wall as an esthetic achievement or that we regard it as anything but a disfigurement of governance and of concourse among peoples, although we must understand the genuine concern about loss of population that gave rise to it. Moral neutrality is not required when border guards shoot down fleeing citizens, though again we must recognize the determination to exist that has led a government to adopt such measures. There is no more reason to overlook the ideological shackling of cultural and intellectual life than there is to ignore brilliant artistic and scholarly achievements when they occur. We need not conceal disgust when morbid anxiety over dissenting opinion leads to the revocation of Wolf Biermann's citizenship, but we should not fail to note the readiness of many artists and some party members to protest the action openly.[6] Similarly, we can be aware of economic failures, disenchantment among youth, and excessive claims for the so-called scientific-technical revolution without supposing that the GDR is about to crumble.

Some of the problems are in certain ways unique to the GDR, to be sure, but it does not follow that the GDR is unique in having problems. The warts and blemishes must not obscure the country's underlying stability or the regime's relatively sure-handed management of the social and economic processes of development. Otherwise, we could not understand the presence of the GDR, as recorded in World Bank statistics for 1974, among the twenty highest ranking nations of the world in both total and per capita gross national product.[7] Neither could we understand the emergence among the population of a measure of pride in East German accomplishments.

The authors of the essays in this volume are certainly not uncritical of failures and shortcomings, but their diverse contributions are united by a clear-sighted, empirically grounded apprehension of the GDR as it is. They are not the first to have broken through the older stereotypes,[8] but they do represent the first scholarly generation to have gained a wide-ranging expertise capable of rendering the GDR terra cognita.

Notes

1. This is of course not to claim for the Soviets any special virtue of forebearance; their reason for being fairly patient about a resolution of the status of East Germany was that they still nursed the hope—dating in fact from 1918—that Germany would be their opening to the West. When they finally settled the GDR's status in the East European bloc, it signified that the hope had evaporated.

2. I have been reminded of the incompleteness by my morning newspaper, one of whose editors is roaming Central Europe and discovering, in what sounds like utter panic, that movement from one part of Berlin to the other is not as simple as a border crossing between Seattle and Vancouver. The resulting dispatches have the ring, but not the substance, of comparable experiences of the first postwar decade.

3. Academic programs of study that developed under the heading of Russia and Eastern Europe during this period were

linked simultaneously to the study of the Soviet Union and its orbit and to the Slavic languages. So long as East Germany was seen primarily as one of the occupation zones and as a facet of a yet-to-be-resolved German question, such programs gave minimal attention to the emerging GDR. The study of planned economies was one of the early breakthroughs whereby the GDR began to receive academic attention on an equal footing with other East European countries, followed by studies of political processes common to the Soviet-dominated states. But even today the GDR is radically underrepresented in these academic programs, and, furthermore, it must be remembered that the whole East European area has only recently emerged from the shadow of Soviet studies. It is sometimes claimed that East German studies suffered because there were no exile scholars—as there were from other East European countries— present on American campuses advancing the study of the GDR; but this is an explanation that fails to explain, for academic organization would have first to have created jobs for such exiles to occupy—even if the exiles had been present to fill them.

4. At least two other countries spring to mind because they were also partitioned as a result of great-power actions after the war: Korea and Vietnam. It may not be very important whether they are of "comparable capability and weight in international politics." What does seem significant, however, is a current wave of scholarly attention to the phenomenon of divided countries, an aspect of comparative studies that may have important consequences in the next few years as the International Studies Association and other academic groups pursue the topic. See Thomas E. Hachey, *The Problem of Partition* (Chicago, 1972); and the *Journal of International Affairs* 27, no. 2, (1973), an issue devoted to "Political Integration of Multi-State Nations," for diverse approaches to this problem.

5. This is not the place to review the voluminous literature generated by the debate over Cold War origins, but much of it is conveniently surveyed in Robert W. Tucker, *The Radical Left and American Foreign Policy* (Baltimore, 1971). To my knowledge, only André Fontaine, *History of the Cold War*

(New York, 1968) adopts a periodization resembling the one I suggest here. In general the debate has suffered from a lack of precision as to the special characteristics that distinguish the Cold War, irrespective of time period considered, from more conventional diplomatic history.

6. *New York Times*, 12 January 1977.

7. *Christian Science Monitor,* 28 January 1977.

8. Welles Hangen *(The Muted Revolution)* was one of the first to depart from stereotypes in talking about East Germany; he was joined subsequently by Jean Edward Smith *(Germany Beyond the Wall)* and David Childs *(East Germany)*. Several of the authors in this book count also as precursors as well, and no mention of the literature on the GDR should overlook Peter C. Ludz, *The Changing Party Elite in East Germany* (Cambridge, Mass.: 1972), although that study in its original form belongs to the much more extensive German body of scholarship.

2. The State in the Developed Socialist Society

Kenneth Hanf

According to its supporters and practitioners, the fundamental advantage of socialism is the possibility it offers for consciously shaping the course of socioeconomic development. It is the socialist state that is to be the primary instrument with which the working class, under the leadership of its Marxist-Leninist party, organizes and directs the construction of the new socialist society. Insofar as the state is a product of a given set of social and economic conditions, as well as an active, creative force in steering social development, the "material content of state power—the nature of its tasks and responsibilities—will be the objective result of the qualitatively new political and economic tasks that characterize a particular phase in the development of socialist society."[1] With each step taken by society along the path toward the ultimate transition to communism, the tasks and procedures of the socialist state will necessarily change, its social base will expand and be strengthened, and the conditions for its effectiveness as well as the modes of its operation will be modified.[2]

Specifically with regard to developments in the German Democratic Republic, it is argued that with the expanded dimensions and the qualitative changes in the national economy, the intensive interlocking of its branches with one another as well as with other areas of social life; with the increased importance of international cooperation and socialist economic integration; and with the growing consciousness of the workers and the importance of their initiative and participation in the direction of social development, the scope of state activity will necessarily expand. At the same time, if the state is to meet the demands being placed upon it, the state apparatus must, it is argued, become more flexible and effective in its operations as well as more sensitive to the needs and views of the citizens, whose energies it must mobilize in pursuit of policy objectives. In this sense, the success of state action in directing the development of socialist society is viewed as depending on the adaptation of its structure, procedures, and the main direction of its activities to the changing nature of its tasks and the conditions under which they must be performed. Thus, insofar as the socioeconomic environment within which the state acts undergoes continuing and increasingly more rapid change, "the perfection of the directive apparatus of the state will be a constant process."[3] Viewed in this way, such institutional changes are seen in the German Democratic Republic as objectively necessary measures aimed at improving the quality of the planning, organizing, and educative activities of the state so that it might better meet its responsibilities for guaranteeing the uniform and balanced direction of the total process of socialist development.

At the Eighth Party Congress of the Socialist Unity Party (SED) in June 1971, during which the primary direction and the economic and social tasks for the new five-year plan period were announced, Erich Honecker sketched the broad contours of such a program for "consolidating the socialist state and improving the quality of its activity." Since that time, a number of measures have been taken to implement this program. Among the most important of these are the Law on the Council of Ministers (October 1972); the Administrative Regulation on Tasks, Rights, and Duties of Socialist Enterprises, Combines, and Associations of Enterprises (March 1973); the Law on Local Assemblies and their Organs (July 1973); and an unpublished resolution of the Council of Ministers regarding the tasks, functions, and procedures of the ministries and other central state organs.[4] The constitutional changes approved by the Volkskammer (People's Chamber) in October 1974 were the formal capstone to many of the developments in the organization of state power that had taken place since the Eighth Party Congress.[5] In particular, these amendments gave constitutional expression to the upgrading of the role of the Council of Ministers as well as to the reduction of the powers and functions exercised by the Council of State (Staatsrat) under Walter Ulbricht.

This series of measures represents the core of a program of institutional reform through which the organization and operations of the state are to be adapted to the demands made upon its directive capacity in fulfilling the various tasks connected with effectively steering socioeconomic processes in this phase of socialist development. Taken together, these laws and other regulations are, in particular, intended to spell out the material content of democratic centralism as the fundamental principle in terms of which the system of state direction and planning is organized in the GDR. By delineating the rights, responsibilities, and powers of the different levels and units of state power, they are supposed to indicate how, concretely, the "unity of central direction" is to be combined with "the self-initiatives of the citizens, their communities, and the local organs of the state."

In this chapter we offer a brief description of some of the more important elements of this further elaboration of the system of democratic centralism in the GDR. No attempt has been made to present an exhaustive, comprehensive treatment of all the changes in the state institutions that have taken place in the period under consideration.[6] On the contrary, the examination of the general nature of these changes is meant to illustrate the main features of the institutional response of advanced socialist systems to the growing complexity and the dynamics of policymaking and implementation in dealing with highly dynamic and interdependent environments.

We begin with a treatment of the long-range policy objectives of the political leadership in the GDR and indicate some of the consequences such a program of socioeconomic development is perceived as having for the functioning of state institutions. We then examine some of the steps taken with regard to state organization at the central and local levels. Here the main focus is upon the mechanisms that have been developed to promote effective cooperation and collaboration among institutional actors at different levels and in the different hierarchies of state direction.

In presenting this material, we initially look at these developments from the perspective of the political leadership in the GDR. In this sense the picture presented here is one that highlights the understandings of the reformers rather than the actual functioning of the system constructed. As a result, the description remains primarily on the level of the formal legal steps taken to realize the objectives laid out by these reformers. Thus, it seldom penetrates to the actual behavior of the various actors involved. Nevertheless, insofar as the initial constraints upon, as well as opportunities for action by, different individuals and groups in this system will be defined by the formal rules and the official distribution of "resources" connected with the particular positions they occupy in the structure, such a description of formal features of the emerging system of democratic centralism does suggest some of the structural factors that will affect and determine actual behavior.

On the basis of the information presented, the chapter concludes with some brief comments on an approach to the analysis of decision-making dynamics in advanced socialist systems, an approach that could, we believe, usefully complement the traditional emphasis on elites at the central level of the party and state apparatuses

The Developed Socialist Society and the Requirements of Effective State Action

Socialism in the GDR is not viewed as an "end state" or as a "finished product" that is reached with the "victory of socialist productive relations." On the contrary, with the completion of the transition from capitalism to socialism and the construction of the foundations of socialist society the GDR is considered to have entered a relatively extended period of comprehensive social and economic development, in the course of which the advantages and driving forces of socialism are to come to complete expression in all areas of social life and during which the conditions for the full unfolding of the "economic laws of socialism," as the basis for a rational and effective economic policy, are to be fulfilled. This period, described as the "shaping of the developed socialist society," is defined in terms of both the "objective processes and tendencies" at work in society and the set of goals and objectives to be met in moving socialism toward communism.

The draft of the new party program, presented for public discussion prior to the Ninth Party Congress in May 1976, lays out the tasks to be performed during the present phase of socialist construction. Its point of departure is the Marxist-Leninist notion of the two phases of a unified communist social formation.[7] During the "first phase of the communist society," the decisive tasks lie in the consolidation of the political power of the working class and the full development of the socialist mode of production. It is from an analysis of the differences in the structures and relationships that exist between the socialist and communist phases and the various measures required to overcome them in preparing society for the ultimate transition to communism that the strategic orientation for the activity of the state and all other organizations in the GDR during the present phase of development is to be derived.[8]

In the report of the Central Committee of the SED to the Eighth Party Congress, Erich Honecker sketched the primary task to be fulfilled in constructing mature socialism. According to Honecker, the long-range social and economic program in terms of which the activity of society is to be organized is aimed at further raising the material and cultural standard of living of the population on the basis of a high rate of development of economic production.[9] Through the application of the advances in science and technology to the organization and processes of the economy, a higher level of effectiveness of economic activity and a greater productivity of labor are to be achieved; the steady growth of material production depends on these. This increase in the material wealth of the society is, in turn, the necessary condition for steady improvement in the living and working conditions of the entire population. At the center of this long-range social and economic policy is the objective of realizing a more immediate and direct relationship between economic production and the satisfaction of the needs of the citizens. Not only is the productive process to take these needs as the point of departure for its activity, i.e., to produce what the citizens "want" or need, but conditions must also be established to ensure that developments in the economic sphere, i.e., increases in the level of production, are felt more quickly and more immediately in the form of improvements in the quality of individual and collective life.

At the same time that increasing emphasis has been placed upon making the "payoffs" of economic progress more direct (in the form of increased quality of life through higher individual consumption and social programs), it is also stressed that the construction of the developed socialist society involves more than merely satisfying the growing material and cultural needs of individuals. There is more to it than making life "more pleasant." On the contrary, it is argued, the primary task represents a program of social change designed to fulfill the preconditions for the transition from socialism to communism. Thus the various individual measures of social policy that have been introduced over the last five years are viewed as a part of a policy directed toward social equality, growing social homogeneity, and the gradual overcoming of the central differences between intellectual and physical labor and between the quality of life in city and country.[10] The shaping of the developed socialist society is not, therefore, seen merely as a quantitative and qualitative increase in material production and a higher level of consumption; it includes creating the social conditions required for attaining the classless and egalitarian society.

It has been repeatedly pointed out in the literature of the GDR that the pursuit of these goals has become an "objective necessity" and their realization "a real possibility" because the country now possesses the productive potential for creating the material wealth on which the continued improvement of the general standard of living depends. At the same time, it is noted, even an economy devoted to the satisfaction of the needs of all citizens cannot distribute more than is produced. For this reason, only the continued, dynamic growth of the economy can provide the resources for what is described as the "most comprehensive social program until now in the history of the GDR."[11] In this sense, the driving force and the principal set of tasks in constructing developed socialism remain the further development of the economic system as the foundation for the continued growth of material production.

This set of social and economic tasks will determine the character of the activity of the state in the GDR. The demands made upon state direction in fulfilling these tasks give rise to the criteria for designing the institutional arrangements for the effective performance of its role. While the present level of social and economic development has created new possibilities for systematic social action in pursuit of the long-range goals of socialism, it has at the same time, it is pointed out, brought new challenges for the system of state direction and planning. The present period of socialist construction is described as one of "extraordinary intensification of the interrelations between the forces of production, the relations of production, and the social superstructure."[12] This manifests itself in the increasingly dynamic and complex character of the processes of social change. In order to deal adequately with the growing number, variety, and complexity of the social and economic problems faced in the development of socialist society, as well as with the high degree of interdependence among these tasks and their solutions, programs for the proportional and balanced development of society as a whole have become an ever more important concern of state activity. The formulation and realization of programs of this nature require, it is repeatedly maintained, the mastery of the complex interrelationships among the various social processes; they require not only that the individual areas of social life be successfully developed in themselves, but also that the correct interrelationships be established between them.[13] Thus, although the term "system" has been dropped from the characterization of the present period of socialist development, it is still argued that society must be viewed and dealt with in terms of the totality of social relationships, in terms of the interdependencies among all spheres of social life.[14] As a result, the "conscious shaping of the dialectical unity of all sides of socialist society" is to move to the center of state directing and planning activities at all levels.[15]

In order to meet these demands on its directive activity, it is felt that the state must, among other things, improve its capacity for the intermeshed and coordinated planning and organizing of the entire process of economic production as well as the conscious shaping of social structures and relationships. This means it will have to develop a more adequate capacity for long-range comprehensive economic and social planning, based on a "society-as-a-whole" perspective, through which the understanding of the systematic nature of social relations can be translated into decisions and policies reflecting as well as acting upon these interdependent processes. In the search for improved institutions and methods for long-range comprehensive economic and social planning, emphasis is to be placed on expanding the time horizon of planning (i.e., the use of long-range plans in addition to those of the traditional one- and five-year variety) and on improving the coordination of plans with different time frames. In this way, it is hoped a firmer framework can be provided (beyond the general prognostic activity presently engaged in) for coordinating short- and intermediate-range decisions with long-run goals and the conditions to be met in achieving them.

In these and other ways, a higher degree of complexity of state plans and planning is to be sought by guaranteeing that the plan and the programmatic measures based on them will be appropriate to the interrelated and interdependent dimensions of the problems and the environment with which they deal. Such planning, it is argued, must be based on more exact calculations and analysis, the timely anticipation and recognition of problems, and an understanding of their consequences for and interrelations with other problem areas and activities of state direction. In addition to more adequate information, the analytical skills for processing it, and a broad perspective on and understanding of the socioeconomic processes to be directed, an effective system of state direction and planning will require an implementation structure capable of ensuring that the activities of the different actors will, in fact, be integrated around the concerted pursuit of plan objectives.

The recent institutional measures introduced in the GDR to "improve the quality" of state direction and planning have, therefore, been taken in recognition of, and in response to, the fact that the goal of balanced development of all sides of social life must be sought under conditions of increasing dynamic complexity and interdependence within and among individual problem areas. Given the nature of this socioeconomic environment and the tasks to be fulfilled, it is argued that state planning and policy must focus on the integration and coordination of the various contributions and actions of individual organs of state power. A political leadership committed to the conscious steering of social and economic development must be able to pursue a "unified state policy"—in the sense that it must be able to concentrate its resources and energies on the achievement of the common "long-range" policy goals that are to be the basis for the actions of the different elements of the state apparatus. At the same time, its policy must be "complex"; each problem, and the measures designed to deal with it, will be increasingly complicated, with ramifications for other issues and programs. At the same time, each problem will be impinged on by developments in these other areas as well. Since the dimensions of the problems and the measures taken for their solution will seldom coincide completely with existing organizational units, with both the expertise and jurisdiction for dealing with them, effective program planning and execution will require the close coordination and integration of the inputs and activities from these individual units of the state.

To be effective, therefore, a system for the direction of long-range socioeconomic development will have to be at once differentiated enough to correspond to the complex and interdependent nature of the problem areas and the solutions they need. This means that the necessary uniformity of action must be based on institutional differentiation, while this division of labor, in terms of function and structure, must be recombined under broader considerations of problem interrelations and general policy objectives. At the present, the attempt is being made in the GDR to develop a system of state direction "that, in its entirety, embodies on all levels and in all areas of social life the unity of the political state power of the working class and its allies."[16]

Given the ideological and practical importance accorded

central decisions in the direction of economic and social development in socialist countries, it is not surprising that the key element in this attempt has been the set of measures taken to strengthen the position of central direction and planning. Underlying such steps is the view that the importance, and ultimately the preeminence, of central decision making are a result of the functional requirements for the effective construction of the developed socialist society as well as a consequence of the political foundation of state power and responsibility.

In the GDR, as in all other socialist states, it is held to be possible, on the basis of the objective requirements and opportunities contained in a given level of social and economic development, to determine what measures are required for the realization of the long-range goals of developed socialism and thus what at any given time is in the interest of society as a whole. This belief both reflects and supports the dominance of the Marxist-Leninist party as the source of all political power and wisdom. A further institutional consequence of this perspective is the dominant role played by the central state decision-makers, who, along with party leaders and on the basis of fundamental party decisions, have the job of translating general policy objectives into action programs that are to be the framework for development at each subsequent level of government. It is through these central determinations and guidelines that unity in fundamental matters is to be guaranteed as the basis for coherent action on the part of "working class and its allies under the leadership of its Marxist-Leninist party." By means of central direction, conditions are to be created for ensuring that, in the course of fulfilling their particular responsibilities, all organization at all levels will make the maximum contribution to the realization of the primary task of socialist development.

At the same time, since these central policies and programs must be realized under "particular conditions" in the different areas of the republic, it is recognized that action programs must be adjusted to local needs and possibilities if they are to be implemented effectively. It is further acknowledged that if the flexibility and responsiveness felt to be necessary for the effective realization of general policy at the local level is to be achieved, the responsibilities of these lower organs of power, for the formulation as well as the implementation of plans and programs, must be increased. In this way, it is argued, conditions are to be created for the more effective mobilization of local resources and the organization of the energies of citizens in pursuit of general policy objectives.

In addition to the arguments advanced in the name of efficiency for the heightened involvement of local decision-makers and the active participation of citizens in the direction and planning of social development at this level, the democratic nature of central decisions themselves is also stressed. In this connection, it is pointed out that "the totally unified character of the organization of the socialist state and of its direction has a fundamentally democratic basis and character.[17] This democratic character, it is pointed out, is rooted in the fact that, with the capture of power by the working class, the state for the first time has become an instrument of majority rule. As a consequence, in terms of its social base and the source of its power, the socialist state is "by definition" democratic. Under socialism the officials of the state are chosen out of the working class and its allies; they are charged with the task of realizing the interest of the majority; and they are accountable to it for the adequate fulfillment of these duties.

The democratic quality of the state in socialism is also seen as a function of the goal it pursues: the interest of the working masses in improving their material and cultural standard of living. In this sense, the activities of the state promote democracy in that, and insofar as, they contribute to the realization of this general objective. Because the socialist state brings to expression the objective interest of the working masses and is the instrument for the realization of this interest, the distinction between the citizen and the state as some power "outside" him and imposed upon him by the ruling class is supposed to disappear.

Resting on this democratic base, the "center" is, therefore, considered to represent the interest of the whole, the general or common objectives toward which social development is to be directed. The policies and programs for the realization of these goals are to provide the common basis on which the contributions of individual actors are to be integrated. Of course, the realization of the necessary "unity of action" is not to be left to chance or the goodwill or insight of the various actors involved. On the contrary, since these separate actions must be coordinated with one another and combined into complex programs if they are not to work at cross-purposes, the ordering "impulse," it is argued, will have to come from above.

Thus, the basic organizational problem connected with the construction of developed socialist society is seen as that of providing institutional arrangements for the conscious planning of social and economic development to ensure that all elements of the state work together to promote the general social interest as specified in the various central plans and programs. The consequent realization of democratic centralism, as the principle in terms of which decisional authority and responsibility is to be distributed among the different levels of state action, will, it is felt, guarantee that central decision serves as the point of departure for the individual actions and decisions of local units. To this end, an integrated, hierarchical system of policy making and implementation has been constructed in the GDR running from the top levels of the SED (the Politburo and the Secretariat of the Central Committee) down through the state and economic apparatuses to the individual members of society in their various activities. At each level, the general parameters and constraints are set within which the activities of the subsequent levels are to be organized in pursuit of the centrally determined objectives. At the same time, the various forms of popular participation in the decision process are supposed to provide channels through which the necessary informational inputs from below can enter into the deliberations of superior decision-makers. Equally important, the active involvement of both local state organs and citizens in the implementation of central plans (and in the monitoring of progress toward the realization of these objectives) is seen as an important means for more effectively mobilizing the energy and initiative of those most immediately affected in meeting their specific responsibilities.

The improvement of central direction and planning, as the overarching or integrating element in the principle of democratic centralism, is viewed as an indispensable precondition for increasing the responsibilities of local units of state power and for widening the opportunities for effective citizen participation in the direction of social development. Only on the basis of central decision, it is argued, is it possible to make sure that the activities of the different individual and collective actors will effectively contribute to the realization of general policy objectives and that their actions will be appropriately integrated into the general processes of economic and social development. Without qualified central direction and planning, therefore, it is held that no framework would exist for the unified action of all elements of the state apparatus. Without this framework, there would be no basis on which to extend local responsiblities and to make individual initiatives more effective.

At any given time, the system of democratic centralism represents the institutional answer given under specific social and economic conditions to the problem of maximizing the uniformity of state operations while at the same time mobilizing the contributions of an institutionally and functionally differentiated system of state direction for the development of effective measures for dealing with the complex problems confronted by the state. Recent legislation and other legal statements, in which the concrete "meaning" of democratic centralism is spelled out for this point in the development of the GDR, have been designed to articulate such a clearly defined division of labor between and within the different levels of state activity as the foundation for a more effective realization of central plan objectives.

The Council of Ministers: Unified Direction of Complex Programs

With the law regulating the rights and duties of the Council of Ministers in the system of state direction and planning, a law passed by the Volkskammer in October 1972, the system of "unified state direction, on the basis of the principle of democratic centralism, presently finds its further concrete expression in the increased responsibility as well as in the extension of the authority of the Council of Ministers."[18] Although "all

organs of the state work to achieve uniform state policy, even
when they do so on different levels and with different tasks,"[19]
it is the Council of Ministers, the keystone in this institutional
edifice, that is to carry the fundamental responsibility for the
"practical direction of the entire work of the state."[20]

According to article 1, paragraph 1 of the law, "the Council
of Ministers is, as an organ of the Volkskammer, the government of the German Democratic Republic." It "works out . . .
the basic principles of the domestic and foreign policy of the
state and directs the uniform implementation of the state
policy of the German Democratic Republic." Although, in contrast to previous legislation, the Council of Ministers is here
referred to as the "government" of the German Democratic
Republic, the system of democratic centralism also determines
its actual position in the decision-making hierarchy. There
is no doubt that the making of "political" decisions, in the
sense of setting the general direction of social development and
making fundamental policy determinations in pursuit of these
goals, is exclusively the activity of the top leaders of the SED:
its Politburo and the Secretariat of its Central Committee. In a
functional sense, in terms of the motive or directive force in the
state as a whole, here is where the "government" is to be found.
To the extent that these general policy determinations of the
party must be filled out in legislation and these measures
implemented, and to the extent that the central party apparatus refrains from concerning itself too deeply with such "details," there is leeway for significant "governing activity" on the
part of the central organs of the state. It is in this more
restricted sense that the Council of Ministers is the government.

Thus, irrespective of what state organ initiates or promul-
gates program decisions, it is clear that the central organs of the
SED are intended to have the decisive influence. The various
decisions and directives of the party leadership are the foundation for all "legislative" and "executive" activity of the government. However, although the final decisions rest with the
party, such determinations are preceded by some not insignificant element of consultation with counterpart state organs. In
addition to the significant overlap between central state and

party leadership—for example, a number of top state officials are, at the same time, members of the party Politburo[21]—the ministries themselves serve as important sources of policy information and suggestions and participate to one extent or another in the ongoing deliberations. A simple rule of thumb for determining the division of responsibility at a given point would suggest that the more basic the matter, the more likely it is that the decision will be made by central party leaders—but with some participation by central state organs. The general responsibility for implementing such decisions rests with the state apparatus—but always in interaction with the corresponding elements of the Central Committee apparatus. The present law does, to be sure, represent a clear institutional "upgrading" of the Council of Ministers. This has occurred, however, in relation to other state organs (in particular vis-à-vis the Council of State) and does not alter the "executive role" of this organ with regard to the concretization and implementation of central party decisions. Nevertheless, within these constraints central state organs play an important role in formulating and deciding upon the plans and other measures on which the activity of the state apparatus rests.

As the linchpin in the system of unified state direction and planning in the GDR, the Council of Ministers is supposed to ensure that the activites of individual organs of state power will be guided by a common perspective on state policy as a whole. Such an appreciation by individual state organs of the total picture, and their own position within it, will, it is hoped, not only guarantee a common point of departure and common objectives, but also provide the basis on which to develop complex solutions to problems that cut across formal jurisdictions and individual program areas.

Perhaps the most important institutional device at the central level for achieving this combination is the designation of the Council of Ministers as a collective deliberating and decision body (article 10, paragraph 1).[22] The collective nature of leadership in the Council of Ministers, combined with the strengthened responsibility of each individual member for the direction of his own area of jurisdiction in line with the decision of the Council, is viewed as an important structural element of democratic centralism.[23] In particular, participation in collective decision making is supposed to provide a common understanding and a sense of heightened responsibility for the decisions on which subsequent actions of individual ministries and other central organs can be based. In this way an institutional and motivational link is to be created for integrating more effectively the making of collective decisions and their implementation. Further, by broadening the flow of information and mobilizing the combined expertise of the central state apparatus for these deliberations, it is expected that the scientific soundness and general quality of such decisions will be increased. In addition, this arrangement is viewed as a device for raising the level of complexity and countering narrow departmental program interests and perspectives in state direction by bringing partial contributions together within the context of broad general policy and coordinating them in the solution of complex problems.

In the relationships between the Council of Ministers (as a collective body) and the ministerial organization (headed by individual members of the council), we find another crucial link in the system of democratic centralism: for, it is pointed out, insofar as the responsibility of the Council of Ministers grows, the role of the ministries in promoting the unified direction of state policy will also grow. As with governments elsewhere, the Council of Ministers depends on the directive apparatus of the various ministries for the bulk of information, expert knowledge, and proposals on which collective deliberations and decisions are based. Program planning in this more concrete sense is the job of the respective ministerial organizations that are, in turn, plugged into their local counterparts. Beyond this, the actual "execution" and day-to-day monitoring and supervision of the implementation of programs and plans at the subsequent levels of state direction are channeled through the directive hierarchies topped by the ministries.

Given this general interdependence between these bodies, it is stressed that improvement of the Council's work depends on, as well as conditions, the quality of ministerial activities. Therefore, the new law calls for increasing the "responsibility of the ministries and other central organs with regard to the scientifically planned development of the sectors and branches in their areas of jurisdiction."[24] To this end, the Council of Ministers subsequently promulgated guiding principles on the tasks and procedures of the ministries. In general, these regulations have been aimed at strengthening the responsibility of the ministers for solving general state tasks, for the effective execution of the decisions of the SED and the government in their areas as well as for the coordinated collaboration with other central organs, and the executive councils of the districts, in preparing and implementing decisions.[25] The coordination of activities among different central organs is considered to be particularly significant in connection with achieving the desired quality of central state direction and planning. Such interaction is important not only for the decisions and activities of the affected areas, but also (since it contributes to a reduction of agenda items for the Council of Ministers by keeping many issues out of this decision arena until the preliminary negotiations and bargaining have been taken care of by the ministries) for other central organs involved. In cases of particular political importance or stickiness, this coordination is extended to include more directly the appropriate units of the central party apparatus, the Secretariat of the Central Committee. Indeed, it may happen that a decision of the Politburo will be necessary before the matter finally is presented to the Council of Ministers for its action.[26] Underlying the law dealing with the Council of Ministers is the structural assumption that the strengthening of central planning and direction and the improving of the work of central organs are preconditions for the "self-responsible" activity of decision-makers at other levels in pursuing the goals of state policy. In the general scheme of things, the Council of Ministers is supposed to concentrate on basic matters of domestic and foreign policy—to explore the implications of party decisions for state activity, to cast these decisions in appropriate form, and to organize the basic thrust of their implementation. Here general state programs are to be mapped out and final decisions made on plans and "legislation." An important function of these collective deliberations is, as we have seen, the coordination of inputs and activities of the different areas of state activity.

Viewed in this way, the activity of the Council of Ministers is designed to set the broad framework for the unified action of the socialist state, action that each successive level of direction is then to fill with concrete detail according to its respective function and responsibilities. In this connection, it has been pointed out that the guiding principle for the Council of Ministers should be that "once a matter has been decided, then the ministries, the directors of other central state organs, and the chairmen of the executive councils in the districts are to be fully responsible for implementing it and for controlling this implementation in their areas."[27] Implied here—and for organs subordinate to those specifically mentioned— is the intention of increasing the direct responsibility of all levels for the execution of the decisions of the SED and the government. Thus, an important objective of the steps taken to fix the position of the Council of Ministers as the apex of the system of state direction has been to ensure that it is able to meet its responsibilities for creating the conditions that enable other state and economic organs to get on with their tasks.

The Local Organs of State Power: Vertical Deconcentration and Territorial Coordination

The preeminence of central decision has been justified by the need for a unified system of state power through which society's energies can be mobilized and concentrated in pursuit of common goals. Thus the initial emphasis of democratic centralism is on the integration of the system of state direction and planning around the making and implementing of central decisions. Uniformity of action, as the means for achieving a concentrated impact in the realization of central policy objectives, does not, however, mean that everywhere, without distinction, the same thing is done. On the contrary, a certain division of labor will of necessity exist, where "in the solution of specific problems and the fulfillment of particular responsibilities, each organ and each functionary works uniformly on the solution of the tasks of the socialist state as a whole."[28] While these activities are to be based on and directed toward the objectives contained in central plans and decisions, it is argued that the goal of uniform state action need not be sought at the expense of reduced activity or responsibility at the different levels of state direction.

A look at the organization of the state in the GDR makes clear that it is indeed a highly differentiated institutional system. Below the central level with the Volkskammer, the Council of Ministers (under whose direction are the various ministries and other central administrative organs), and the Council of State (the collective head of state), the country is divided into fifteen districts (including the capital, Berlin), 214 counties, and approximately 9,000 communes of various sizes. At each of these levels are, in addition to the variety of offices of central agencies, a popular assembly (with its standing commissions), an executive council elected by the assembly, and the different administrative and planning departments through which the council directs and manages development in its territory. These local units interact with a variety of centrally and locally directed production and services enterprises and with a number of mass social organizations.

In view of this high degree of differentiation, it is clear that any system of unified state direction and planning must incorporate a complex division of labor between the levels of state direction and the individual units of state power. The problem faced under these conditions is that of integrating the actions of the separate institutional actors in a way appropriate to the nature of the complex and interdependent problems and tasks faced by the state in running and developing a socialist industrial society. For although the solution of this or that problem can be the focus of the activity of a state organ, the practice of state direction shows that effective problem solving will involve the purposeful and planned cooperation of many individual actors as well as their interaction to one degree or another with citizens and groups in society.

Given these conditions under which effective programs and plans must be formulated and carried out, it is argued that the new and growing responsibilities of the socialist state cannot be met by developing and strengthening the capabilities of central state organs alone. To proceed in this way, it is stressed, would be to miss the important interrelationships that exist between the central and local levels of state power. This means, according to commentators in the GDR, that the stronger and more effective central state planning becomes, the more crucial the planning and directive functions of local state organs will be for the preparation of these central plans as well as for their implementation.[29] In this sense, then, the "further development of the power of the socialist state is inseparably connected with the perfection of the direction and planning by the local organs."[30] It follows from this that one of the "logical steps in the application of democratic centralism lies in the continuous expansion of the role of the local organs in order to consolidate further the power of the working class, to extend without interruption its mass base, and to shape more effectively the exercise of [this] power."[31]

The "objective" reasons for the growing importance of these organs of state power are found in the fact that, as important points of contact between the state and its citizens, they have substantial and growing responsibilities in realizing the social and economic objectives of the present five-year plan. Indeed, as the energies of society as a whole are focused upon the steady increase of the material standard of living of the working population, local organs of state power will play a crucial role in determining the extent to which these tasks will be fulfilled.

The material basis for the realization of the developmental goals of the current, as well as subsequent, five-year plan is, as has been repeatedly stated, the proportionately balanced growth of the national economy. This growth, in turn, will require the correct shaping of the reciprocal relations between sectoral and territorial (regional) processes. The increasing importance of this dimension of economic development is reflected in the growing attention that is being given to the interrelations among decisions and plans concerning social and technical infrastructure, industrial location, economic rationalization, the effectiveness of investments, and the general improvement of living and working conditions in the territories.

Since the shaping of economic and social conditions in the territories both contributes to and is affected by the development of the national economy as a whole, it is pointed out that decisions on matters of fundamental importance in this area cannot be made from the perspective of a single district or sector alone. Therefore, the responsibility for the overall balance and integration of sectoral and territorial considerations is to rest with the Council of Ministers and its central organs. The law dealing with the Council of Ministers makes clear that the direction of the entire activity of the state apparatus by the government includes responsibility for the coordination of sectoral and territorial development. The Council of Ministers is to be responsible for making the basic decisions on which balanced political, economic, and cultural and social development is to rest. Furthermore, the Council of Ministers is also responsible for providing for the necessary cooperation between central and local state organs as well as for ensuring that the concerns of both economic sectors and territorial units are adequately considered in central planning and directive activities. In this connection, the State Planning Commission is supposed to make sure, in working out the plans of the sectors and territories, that the necessary balance between them is achieved and that central tasks are coordinated with the local resources available for their realization. Beyond this, the Council of Ministers is responsible for the guidance and control of the executive councils of the districts as well as for the unified operations of all local executive councils. Of particular importance in this regard is the provision that "the district executive councils be involved in the formulation of such decisions that touch the material, social, and cultural concerns of their areas" (article 1, paragraph 6). In addition, the ministers and the directors of other central state organs are obligated to explain decisions of the party and the Council of Ministers to local assemblies, their executive councils, and the workers, and to discuss and deliberate with them about their implementation. These central officials are also supposed to provide for the effective exchange among local decision-makers of information and ideas drawn from experience in implementing state policy; they are also to evaluate and act upon the suggestions and proposals that come from their meetings with local officials.

By means of such participation by local executive councils in the deliberations of the Council of Ministers as well as in those of the ministries and other central state organs it is expected that "every decision and measure that directly or indirectly touches the local organs of the state will be carefully checked out and coordinated with them."[32] As part of a general revamping of the central planning of territorial development, this procedure is designed to remedy a situation in which the objectives and tasks of sectoral development were first centrally determined and in which, on the basis of these decisions, attempts were then made to bring about some degree of fit between such central determinations and local responsibilities. With the 1972 economic plan, a new start was made in coordinating these factors as early as possible in the planning process. Another important procedural device for ensuring closer involvement of the territories in central decision making have been the so-called complex consultations, which are carried out in the initial preparatory phases of plan formulation among members of the Council of Ministers, district executive councils, and enterprises. These meetings are designed to acquaint all participants with problems connected with the balanced development in their jurisdiction and to deliberate on appropriate courses of action for handling them.

However, no matter how important the role of central direction may be in this regard, cooperation and coordination between economic sectors and territorial development must, in the last analysis, be secured on a continuing basis in the immediate area of responsibility of the local assembly and its organs. Given the strategic role played by the local state organs in securing the conditions for economic production and in mobilizing the collective resources of their areas for improving living and working conditions, recent legislation has sought to strengthen the responsibility and to increase the authority of the local assemblies and their organs for exercising the general coordinating function with regard to all activities in their respective territories. To this end, considerable attention has been devoted to securing the preconditions for the effective performance of this task by spelling out the nature of the directive relations between central and local organs of the state in such a way that local conditions and possibilities can be better utilized and even greater expression given to the variety of methods and forms available at the local level for the fulfillment of general state tasks.

At the same time, commentaries on this legislation make clear that the law fixing the rights and duties of local assemblies and their organs is not to be considered a measure on local self-government. It is, rather, "more directed to putting local assemblies and their organs in a position, on the basis of democratic centralism, to make a broad contribution to the realization of general state policy."[33] In concrete terms, this means that local organs decide "self-responsibility" on all matters of fundamental importance for their territories but do so on the "unshakable basis" of party decisions, laws, and resolutions of the Volkskammer, decisions of the Council of Ministers and of higher popular assemblies and executive councils. Such an arrangement is to ensure that "central state direction and planning will be firmly combined with local initiative and that the point of departure for local decisions . . . will be the . . . policy of the working class and its party."[34] In this sense, the concrete tasks of local assemblies can only be those that are derived from the general social goals. On the basis of these objectives and the interrelations among the various state tasks, local organs are then expected to work out and carry through their particular programs of action.

Thus, "self-responsibility is not autonomy . . . but independent responsibility for the whole" and, as such, is viewed as "creative participation in producing the general will and its realization under the corresponding utilization of local resources."[35] Such self-responsible coordination of territorial development requires that each local level of state direction balance its own area both in terms of itself and within the requirements set by the movement of society as a whole. By tying each level of local responsibility firmly into the general system of vertical direction of socialist development, the law fixing the rights and duties of the different organs of state direction seeks to guarantee that these organs will, individually and in concert, function as part of the total responsibility of the state for the development of the conditions for reaching the level of mature socialist society.

As its elected organ, the executive council is directly responsible to the popular assembly in its particular territory. At the same time, through the system of democratic centralism it is also integrated into the vertical relation joining the different levels. At any point in the system of state power (including the Council of Ministers, over which stand the central party leaders and apparatus as well as the Volkskammer), the organs of the state apparatus are doubly subordinated. With regard to the local executive council, this organ is not only accountable to its popular assembly but is, at the same time, also subordinate to the council of the next higher level. This set of subordinate-superior relations culminates in the responsibility of the Council of Ministers for the guidance and control of the district councils and for the unified functioning of all local executive councils. Double subordination likewise determines the position of the administrative organs of the executive councils. At any given level, these organs, through their directors, are subordinate to the executive council as a whole and to its chairman. They are also responsible and accountable to the counterpart administrative agency on the next higher level.

In the first instance, double subordination is a device for securing the vertical coordination of the activities of all state organs. The tight chain of command from the center down to the communal level is intended to guarantee the uniform direction of state policy. At the same time, as we have noted, the goal of organically connecting central state direction and planning with the increased self-responsible activity of local organs in carrying out their tasks is meant to soften—in the name of efficiency and flexibility—the centralist character of this arrangement. In this regard, it has been repeatedly remarked that a style of direction from the center (or from "above") in ignorance or disregard of local conditions is incompatible with the "spirit" of democratic centralism.

However, it is not enough to prevent central decisionmakers from running roughshod over subordinate organs and their administrative agencies in the territories. Double subordination is also designed to counter tendencies within the different directive hierarchies toward functional (or programmatic) isolation and narrow definition of responsibility. Thus, in its intention, the device of double subordination of executive councils and their administrative units is also viewed as an important means for bringing about the desired balance between territorial and sectoral developments. By tying territorial administrative units to their superiors at the next higher level, an adequate consideration of the interest and requirements of the particular functional or programmatic area is to be guaranteed at each territorial level. On the other hand, the subordination of these administrative units to their respective executive council at the same level is intended to guarantee that the more limited perspectives and interests will be integrated into the all-around social development of the territory. Together with the double subordination of the executive councils as collective directive bodies—which ensures that the territorial direction will be guided by general social state policy as mediated by superior organs—the double subordination of territorial administrative units is the institutional device for integrating general state, territorial, and sectoral developments. In this way this organizational arrangement is to promote the coordination of both the vertical and the horizontal dimensions of state policy within the territories.[36]

Such devices as double subordination and other forms of hierarchical coordination are obviously limited to situations in which those whose behavior is to be influenced stand in a clear relation of subordination to those doing the directing. But hierarchical relations account for only part of the total interaction in which local organs of state power are engaged in the course of guiding and directing the development of their territories. Of particular importance, therefore, in strengthening the position of these local organs in connection with their responsibilities for balanced territorial development are the recent legislative provisions that regulate their relations with those economic units operating in their area of jurisdiction, but not under their direct control.

The heart of the question of balanced territorial development is seen in the rational utilization of all territorial resources and reserves for improving the working and living conditions of the citizens in these areas and for developing the territorial conditions of production most fully. In the pursuit

of both these interrelated objectives, local organs of the state
and economic units are mutually dependent on one another.
The primary responsibility for directing social development in
the individual territories rests, of course, with the local state
organs. The importance of local activity in fulfilling state plan
targets and in realizing general policy objectives is reflected in
the rough figures available regarding expenditures of state
funds: in 1972 approximately two-thirds of all expenditures for
education, 60 percent of those for health and social services, 75
percent for sport and recreation, and almost all monies for the
maintenance and renovation of housing units flowed through
the budgets of local organs of state power.[37] In addition, local
state organs, especially at the district and county levels, have
important capacities under their direction for the production
and supply of consumer goods and services.

At the same time, however, working and living conditions
are shaped by the activities of actors who do not fall under the
direct responsibility of the local organs. In this regard, considerable resources and potential are contained in the plans and
programs of those enterprises not directly subordinate to
them—but that nevertheless have important responsibilities
for employing both their financial and material resources (on
their own and in cooperation with other enterprises and state
organs) in the construction and operation of cultural and social
facilities for plant and community use. Apart from participation in general communal projects, such plant activity might
include, for example, the provision of nursery school or
kindergarten facilities, or the use of plant cafeterias for feeding
schoolchildren. Furthermore, it is clear that the economic
units have an important direct impact on the conditions under
which work is done and thus on the quality of social relations
and the conditions of individual development in the community.

On the other hand, the activities of local organs of state
power are also directly involved in the territorial production in
that they direct and plan essential aspects of the economic
process on which the successful operations of the enterprises
depend. As we have noted, these organs are responsible, in one
way or another, for matters having to do with plant siting,

social and technical infrastructure, and the allocation of manpower. Of course, the reciprocal relation between the territorial economy and the standard of living is also seen in the fact that the level of social and material development affects the quality of the work force and its productivity, while the continued improvement of these general living conditions depends on the level of production achieved by the economy.

It is clear, therefore, that in pursuing the balanced development of all aspects of its territory, the local assembly and its executive council must work closely with all economic units, irrespective of their formal position in the hierarchy of economic direction. In order to facilitate such cooperation, the present law contains provisions designed to promote the effective coordination of the interrelated activities of state organs and the enterprises. At a minimum, such coordination is to involve the exchange of information with regard to ongoing and planned programs so that the various affected parties can plan their actions in light of these activities. Local state organs are also to enter into agreements with economic units with regard to those tasks whose solution can best be pursued through the concentrated use of common financial and material resources. As organs of state power, the local assemblies and their executive councils' local organs are, it is stressed, more than just contractual partners or parties to information exchanges. Thus, the recent legislation emphasized that the success of such coordination cannot be left to the goodwill or discretion of the individual enterprise. Acknowledging that these local organs must be in a position to "force" compliance when all else fails, the new law lays out the legal basis on which relations between the economic sectors and territorial organs are to be shaped.

In the past, the imprecise determination of the role of the local organs vis-à-vis those economic units not under their direct control and the lack of clarity with regard to their authority to influence the behavior of these enterprises led to a situation in which these production units were able to ignore the orders of the local state organs with apparent impunity or, at any rate, with low costs incurred for noncompliance. The new law seeks to remedy this state of affairs by spelling out those situations in which local organs of state power can make demands upon centrally directed—or otherwise non-subordinate—economic organs. The legislation gives, for example, these local organs increased authority for meeting their responsibilities for supervising the activity of these enterprises in the areas of consumer goods production, compliance with manpower plans, and in the fulfillment of programs for economic rationalization. In particular, the local organs have the right to demand the necessary information and data on these matters from the directors of the enterprises. In addition, local assemblies and their executive councils are authorized to make binding decisions regarding the obligations of these plants in connection with the utilization of their resources for improving the working and living conditions in the territory. It has been stressed by commentators in the GDR, however, that such "obligating" should not be allowed to become the main form of the relations between the enterprises and the territorial organs of state power. On the contrary, all energies are to be devoted to shaping these reciprocal relations more effectively through the exchange of information, common deliberations, and the synchronization of projects, contracts, and common planning, so that "binding obligations" become the exception.[38] Thus, although it has been considered important that the local state organs be in a position to make their word stick in their dealings with the economic units in their territories, action is to be taken in close consultation and agreement with those economic units involved. It can be expected, therefore, that where hierarchical authority is lacking and where these enterprises have strong functionally determined loyalties toward their superiors (who can also be important allies), the relations between local state organs and the economic units in their territories will tend to be characterized by a significant degree of negotiation and bargaining as well as by some degree of conflict. Further, it seems apparent that these local organs of state power will only be successful in meeting their coordinating responsibilities and in developing relations of effective cooperation and collaboration with all economic units operating in their area to the extent that they win the support of the superior directive units in the economic chain of command. For even with the new legislation, much of the increased authority and weight of local state decision can only be realized in consultation with, and in some cases only with the approval of, the hierarchic superior of the economic units involved.[39] Thus, in spite of the fact that the local organs act as "organs of state power" in their dealings with the economic decision-makers within their jurisdiction, their effective authority would seem to be limited by the need to work with a set of authorities beyond their immediate hierarchical control.[40]

In addition to strengthening the position of local state organs vis-à-vis all enterprises operating in their territories, the law dealing with the local assemblies and their organs also underscores the increasing importance of "socialist cooperation" between cities and towns in creating the conditions for meeting the goals of economic and social policy. Through more formal collaboration among these local organs it is hoped that obstacles to balanced development can be overcome, namely, those that result from the uneven distribution of population and the fragmented settlement structure of the GDR. At present, 47 percent of the total population lives in towns and small cities with up to 10,000 inhabitants; while of all cities and towns in the GDR, 85 percent have populations under 2,000, and approximately 50 percent number less than 500. Such figures, it is argued, make clear that it is impossible to satisfy the political, economic, social, and cultural needs of the citizens at a level corresponding to the possibilities of socialist production within the existing territorial framework at the local level.[41] Both the limited resources available to individual communes and the scope and complicated nature of the tasks confronted make necessary close cooperation among the units of state power at this level if the standard and style of living in rural areas is to be brought closer to that enjoyed in more populous, urban areas.

Intensified cooperation among those cities and towns sharing geographic proximity and common problems is to make possible the tapping of significant reserves for raising the material and cultural standard of living in these areas. The different associative forms that have been developed provide the organizational framework for such common planning of tasks and the pooling of financial and material resources. Although there are looser forms of cooperation—such as nonbinding consultations and the synchronization of activities—two main institutions have been developed: the more limited in function (but more frequent in use) special purpose association *(Zweckverband)* and the functionally more comprehensive association of communities *(Gemeindeverband)*.

The special purpose association is a form of cooperation in which towns and cities join together to deal with common tasks in particular areas of social life. It is seen as an effective means for concentrating collective effort on a limited problem—for example, the management of a common recreation area or the maintenance of streets in the areas. The association consists of a deliberative body, in which common proposals are worked out for recommendation to the respective popular assemblies of the participating communities and to the enterprise or facilities through which the tasks are carried out. The responsibilities of the association of communities are, on the other hand, more extensive. They are not limited to individual problem areas but are designed to deal with a wide range of matters regarding working and living conditions in the area on the basis of common plans for the development of the member communities. These associations form their own executive councils to direct their affairs and can, at a later stage of development, set up a representative assembly as well. Associations of communities are seen as a form of cooperation that can, over time, lead to the creation of larger, more effective communities. At present there are approximately 250 such associations, encompassing some 21 percent of all cities and towns and about 1.8 million citizens. They exist primarily in rural areas and represent the culmination of a long process of development out of earlier, looser forms of cooperation.[42]

Conclusion: Democratic Centralism and the Dynamics of the Political Process

The institutional changes that have been undertaken in connection with the modernization of the state apparatus in the GDR since 1971 do not represent a sudden or radical departure from the arrangements and procedures for policy making and planning that existed before the Eighth Party Congress of the SED. To be sure they are in some ways closely related to the attempts of the new political leadership around Erich Honecker to consolidate its powers and to adjust the system of state direction and planning to the perceived institutional requirements of the present phase of socialist development. However, even with this changing of the guard and the shifting of accents in policy and programs, policy has remained basically the same, and the long-range goal continues to be that of constructing mature socialism. Likewise, these institutional changes display a basic continuity in relation to the various measures introduced since the late 1960s and serve to consolidate developments already underway.

These changes in the system of state direction and planning are, therefore, part of a continuing effort by the political leadership to adapt state institutions to the tasks they confront and the demands made upon them in constructing a developed socialist society under the conditions of increasing social complexity and dynamic change. These measures have aimed at creating a highly differentiated, yet tightly intermeshed, system of state direction designed to ensure a coordinated and unified movement of all organs of state power toward the attainment of general goals. This system of deconcentrated direction and planning is to serve as the institutional framework for developing and implementing coordinated and complex plans and programs.

In this system, the central organs have been given the responsibility for those basic decisions that, on the basis of the objectives laid out by the SED leadership, define the general direction and measures of state policy. The center, under the direction of the Council of Ministers, is also to organize and control the implementation of this policy in such a way as to guarantee that its decisions are effectively and uniformly carried out throughout the system of state power. Beyond this, the more detailed execution of state policy is to be left to the action of each subsequent level of state direction acting "self-responsibly" within its particular area of jurisdiction and competence. New mechanisms have also been developed—and old ones have been taken more seriously—for channeling the expertise and other informational inputs from local state organs into the decisions of their respective superior levels.

Because of the highly complex economic and social environment within which the state operates and because of the tasks it is called upon to deal with as a result, the importance of mechanisms for developing solutions adequate to highly interdependent problems has increased. As an integral part of the developments resulting from this need for guaranteeing and coordinating the collaborative efforts of many different organs of the state, the specific responsibilities and tasks of subordinate levels of decision making have, of necessity, been expanded.

While recent legislation has underscored the importance of self-responsible action on the part of local state organs and the need to encourage the further development of the initiative and creative energies of citizens and groups in carrying out state policy, all of this is to occur within the constraints set by the primacy of central state decisions. Under such conditions, intervention and control from above can be—and is—justified at any time in the name of unified action for the promotion of the development of society as a whole. What is sought, then, is a clearly articulated system of divided labor in which each organ views itself and acts as a part of a unified system of state direction, the activities of which, in its many parts, are constantly directed toward relating particular actions to the broader goals of state policy. These objectives are to serve as a point of departure for the activities of subordinate levels, which then mobilize their own forces and resources for the realization of their specific tasks within a particular area of responsibility. What these institutional reforms have created, therefore, can be described as a centrally dominated system of deconcentrated policy making and administration.

This examination of the institutional changes made since 1971 has been little more than an overview of the formal measures introduced and an outline of the structures they have created. It should be clear that it cannot, without further examination, be assumed that this system of decision making and planning does in fact work as smoothly as or necessarily in the manner intended by its designers. Nor can it be taken for granted that these institutional arrangements are sufficient to or appropriate for solving the problems confronted by the political leadership in its efforts to steer the general course of social development. Nevertheless, a description of such formal institutional arrangements does provide important information on a crucial element of the "rules of the game" that guide the interactions of the various decision-makers. Without asserting that all actions occur within such formal arenas or that the behavior of such institutions is completely determined by formal rules, we maintain that these structures will still constitute an important set of constraints as well as opportunities defining the initial action space for the different actors. Therefore, while it may not be possible on the basis of the descriptive material presented here to make conclusive statements regarding the actual performance of this system of democratic centralism in action, the information on the general structural conditions of decision making does suggest a useful perspective from which such a "behavioral analysis" could be carried out.

There are a number of points that should distinguish such an analysis from the traditional approaches to the study of the relations between central and local decision-makers in socialist systems. First, it should be clear that recent and continuing efforts to institutionalize a more complex division of function and responsibility as the foundation for the effective realization of central plan objectives at each level of state direction cannot be adequately understood if we examine the organization and dynamics of political decision making in terms of local self-government as this is understood in Western Europe. If we do so, we will come to the not surprising conclusion that democratic centralism, as practiced and intended in the GDR, is not "self-administration" of "local government."

This is surely a fundamental difference between the GDR and Western European countries with regard to the role and position of the local decision making within the general system of state direction. However, this "obvious" fact cannot be the conclusion of our analysis, but rather its point of departure.

Pointing out that political decision making in socialist systems is "different" from that in nonsocialist systems does not, in itself, tell us much about the actual processes through which plans and programs are produced and implemented in the GDR.

No matter how the emerging system of democratic centralism develops and functions in the immediate future, it should be clear from even a formal description of its institutional characteristics that democratic centralism is, in the present period of socialist development, a much more complex, a much more dynamic, set of relationships than has usually been assumed. Normally, in the study of communist systems, the organization of state direction is analyzed in order to show that in such states there is no true decentralization or local self-government, as these terms are understood and used in Western Europe, and to lay bare the mechanisms through which the unitary state works to secure and reinforce the dominance of central party leadership. It is certainly true that central party leadership and, in its name, the central organs of the state are preeminent, both in theory and practice. Nevertheless, to conclude from the undeniable concentration of decision-making power in the hands of central decision-makers that the local units of state are nothing more than instrumental administrative subdivisions, without meaningful decisional impact of their own, would be to prejudge the effectiveness of central hierarchical control and to neglect the impact of the reciprocal relations between central and local actors on both the formulation and implementation of state policy. A more complete picture of the relative "weight" of the different levels of government in their various and complex interactions would require an examination of the increasingly important relations of cooperation and coordination among the different elements of the structurally and functionally differentiated systems of state control. The attempt to strengthen and consolidate the directive capacity of the state in the GDR, by combining stronger central control with more effective deconcentration of responsibility to local organs, has introduced new, dynamic elements into the vertical relationships of democratic centralism. In addition, this hierarchical component has been further complemented—and complicated—by the increasing importance of horizontal relationships at all levels of state direction in the various forms of "socialist cooperation" between state and economic units as well between cities and towns.

There is no denying that this emerging decision system is characterized by two basic realities: the priority of the general social interest, as authoritatively interpreted by the SED; and the predominance of central decision-makers in determining the concrete content of this general interest and the nature of the measures necessary for its realization. These are the fundamental "givens" that set the action space for other actors in the decision process and that give the system its unmistakably "centralist" flavor. However, within these structural constraints there are clear signs of an opening of the decision-making processes of superior organs to participation by the subordinate units. As a result—both intended and perhaps unintended—institutional channels are provided through which individual and group interests are able to enter into the central determinations of the general social interest. Further research will be necessary to establish the extent to which and the modes by which these possibilities for influencing the process of direction and planning from the "bottom up" have introduced an element of de facto articulation and representation of, at least, institutional interests in the setting of policy priorities and the formulation of programs.[43] Further analysis would also be necessary to specify more clearly the nature of the mutual dependencies that have developed among different institutional actors, i.e., the extent to which the performance of the tasks and the responsibilities of any given unit requires or depends upon inputs from others and to which performance itself is a necessary input into the decisions of other institutional actors. It should not be surprising that in such a system of democratic centralism, basic decisional premises and parameters flow from the top to the bottom. However, closer examination of the developing two-way flows of information and influence would surely show that this general framework is not only filled out in concrete detail by subordinate state organs but is itself a product of interactions between the different levels of government.

Of course, there is nothing new in noting that any highly differentiated decision system will require a variety of forms of cooperation and coordination for integrating the different substructures into a functioning whole. It is also true that in the past the activities of the individual state organs in the GDR had to be coordinated and interrelated with one another. However, this integration now occurs under different social conditions and in the context of new political dynamics. Within the decision system we have been describing, it would seem clear that the necessary coordination cannot in the first instance (and certainly not alone) be achieved by means of hierarchical commands emanating from above. Today central decision-makers must come to terms with the de facto influence accruing to local state organs—both by virtue of their "functional" importance in the decision-making process and as a result of the strengthening of their relative position sought by recent institutional changes.

What we are suggesting on the basis of this understanding of the general nature of the structure and dynamics of state decision making in the GDR is that the study of political processes in advanced socialist societies give up its almost singular preoccupation with the central party leadership and its apparatus. Important as these may be, a focus concentrating too heavily on political elites restricts the view too much to the central level of decision making and tends to overemphasize relationships of hierarchical authority between decision levels. In so doing, such an approach neglects the fact that it is at the local level of state direction and in the relationships between the central and local organs of state power that increasingly significant "pieces of political action" are to be found.

Having said this, however, it must be noted, that while we stress the important role of local state organs as active participants in the policy-making and implementing processes, it makes little sense to analyze these relationships among levels of state decision making in terms of more or less local autonomy, or in terms of greater or lesser decentralization or centralization. We are not trying to prove that local decision-makers act in any way "autonomously" or "independently" vis-à-vis central decision-makers. Nor do we argue that they will necessarily be at odds with decisions from the center. (Of course such opposition may in fact occur; the possible conflict between institutional or regional interests and central determinations as well as the mechanisms through which these conflicts are resolved are important questions for subsequent empirical analysis.)

The GDR is, as we have noted, a highly differentiated and complex political system, both in terms of functional specialization and territorial division of labor. At the same time, the goals and objectives of state policy as well as the objective nature of the problems that must be dealt with in moving toward these goals require that the political leadership acknowledge and adapt the system of direction and planning to the necessity of linking together interdependent activities of the individual institutional actors. Under such conditions, we assume that the different elements of the state apparatus will have to work together. At the same time, we cannot take for granted that the central leadership will be able to unite these individual activities behind general system goals. To be sure, the hierarchical element of democratic centralism provides the dominant structural feature of the decision context within which the functionally and territorially differentiated system of decision making is to be integrated. Nevertheless, the analysis of policy and planning processes in the GDR must take as its point of departure the increasingly significant set of decision situations in which problem solving involves the mobilization and coordination of the activities of a number of separate institutional actors under conditions that place effective limits on the ability of central decision-makers to bring about concerted action through hierarchical commands. Thus, without questioning the basic unitary character of the context within which these interactions occur, it is argued here that an analysis of the political dynamics of democratic centralism must examine the various ways in which the GDR has attempted to deal with the problem of horizontal and vertical interdependence, which must be confronted in steering the development of any advanced industrial society.

If we are to proceed in this way, we will need an analytical perspective that "problemitizes" the effectiveness of central direction, one that takes as its point of departure the fact of institutional differentiation and examines the various mechanisms available for rejoining these interdependent sets of activities in line with central intentions and goals. We need, therefore, a perspective that will enable us to place linkages and interrelationships among different levels and decision units in the center of our analytical interests. It would appear, therefore, more useful for future research if it would take as its point of departure an understanding of democratic centralism as a network of organizations with a dominant, but by no means all-powerful, center.

With this perspective, the study of the ongoing attempts in the GDR to develop an appropriate system of state direction with which to steer the construction of developed socialist society provides a challenging opportunity to break out of the confining conceptual models of the past. Such an approach as described here should enable us to appreciate the nature and role of decision making at the local level and its relation to the center, to understand better the dynamics of the system as a whole, and, thus, to draw a more complete picture of the political system of the GDR in this phase of its development.

Notes

1. On this point see, for example, W. Weichelt, *Der sozialistische Staat, Hauptinstrument der Arbeiterklasse zur Gestaltung der sozialistischen Gesellschaft* (Berlin: Staatsverlag der DDR, 1972), p. 17.

2. W. Weichelt, "Das Wesen des sozialistischen Staates," *Staat und Recht* 23, no. 10 (1974): 1632.

3. Weichelt, *Der sozialistische Staat,* p. 27.

4. Gesetz vom 16. Oktober 1972 über den Ministerrat der DDR (GBl. 1, no. 16, p. 253; Gesetz vom 12. Juli 1973 über die örtlichen Volksvertretungen und ihre Organe in der DDR (GBl. 1, no. 32, p. 313); Verordnung vom 28. März 1973 über die Aufgaben, Rechte und Pflichten der VEB, Kombinate und VVB (GBl. 1, no. 15, p. 129) in der Fassung der Änderungsverordnung vom 27. August 1973 (GBl. 1, no. 39, p. 405). Although the guidelines on the tasks and procedures of the ministries have not been published, it is possible to get a

general overview on what is contained in them from M. Benjamin et al., *Funktion, Aufgaben and Arbeitsweisen der Ministerien* (Berlin: Staatsverlag der DDR, 1973).

5. For a brief analysis of these constitutional changes, see Siegfried Mampel, "DDR-Verfassung fortgeschrieben," *Deutschland Archiv* 7, no. 11 (1974): 1152-1157.

6. An overview of changes in the organization of the state since the Eighth Party Congress is given by S. Mampel in "Die staatsrechtliche Entwicklung in der DDR seit dem VIII. Parteitag der SED." *Recht in Ost und West* (1974), pp. 89 ff. For a "definitive" commentary on the GDR constitution from a Western perspective, see Mampel's *Die socialistische Verfassung der DDR. Text und Kommentar* (Frankfurt/ M.: Alfred Metzner Verlag, 1972). A less monumental analysis of the constitutional order is offered by Herwig Roggemann, *Die Verfassung der DDR* (Opladen: Leske Verlag, 1970). A readable general overview of the political system and an analysis of its ideological and social context are provided by Kurt Sontheimer and Wilhelm Bleek, *Die DDR. Politik, Gesellschaft, Wirtschaft* (Hamburg: Hoffmann und Campe, 1972).

7. This discussion of the two phases of communism is taken from an article by W. Kalweit, "Die Einheit der beiden Phasen der kommunistischen Gesellschaftsformation," *Neues Deutschland,* 30 January 1976, p. 3, a contribution to the public discussion of the drafts of documents to be presented at the Ninth Party Congress of the SED.

8. Ibid. In addition to Kalweit's article, *Neues Deutschland* published articles by Otto Reinhold, "Wesen und Merkmale der entwickelten sozialistischen Gesellschaft" (29 January 1976); and Gerhard Schüßler, "Die Rolle des Staates bei der Gestaltung der entwickelten sozialistischen Gesellschaft" (31 January 1976). The authoritative statement regarding the nature of the developed socialist society and the tasks connected with shaping it is contained in section 2 of the draft program of the Socialist Unity Party, "Die Gestaltung der entwickelten sozialistischen Gesellschaft in der Deutschen Demokratischen Republik." For extended treatment of this topic, based on developments in the USSR and the GDR, see the collectively authored *Die entwickelte sozialistische Gesellschaft, Wesen*

und Kriterien—Kritik revisionistischer Konzeptionen (Berlin: Dietz Verlag, 1973).

9. The official statement of this "primary task" *(Hauptaufgabe)* is contained in Erich Honecker, *Bericht des Zentralkomitees an den VIII. Parteitag* (Berlin: Dietz Verlag, 1972) pp. 38-43.

10. Kalweit, "Die Einheit der beiden Phasen," p. 3.

11. Ibid.

12. *Die entwickelte sozialistische Gesellschaft,* p. 72.

13. Reinhold, "Wesen und Merkmale," p. 9.

14. Kurt Hager, *Die entwickelte sozialistische Gesellschaft. Aufgaben der Gesellschaftswissenschaften nach dem VIII. Parteitag der SED* (Berlin: Dietz Verlag, 1972), p. 28.

15. R. Rost, "Zu einigen Problemen der weiteren Vervollkommung der staatlichen Leitung nach dem VIII. Parteitag der SED," *Staat und Recht,* 22, nos. 10/11 (1973): 1649.

16. Ibid.

17. Weichelt, *Der sozialistische Staat,* p. 101.

18. Gerhard Schüßler, "Der demokratische Zentralismus als Grundprinzip der staatlichen Leitung und Planung," *Staat und Recht* 22, no. 1 (1973): 37.

19. Weichelt, *Der sozialistische Staat,* p. 86.

20. Gerhard Schüßler, *Staat und Recht* 21, no. 12 (1972): 1840.

21. For a recent discussion of the interlocking of top state and party positions, as well as of the general strengthening of the party "presence" in the state apparatus, see Heinz Lippmann, "Die personellen Veränderungen in den Machtzentren der SED als Ausdruck kollektiver Führung," *Deutschland Archiv* 6, no. 12 (1973): 1266-1272. For further information on personnel changes in party and state leadership, see also K. W. Friche, "DDR-Führung neu formiert," *Deutschland Archiv* 6, no. 10 (1973): 1009-1012; and F. Oldenburg, "Ost-Berlin wieder auf härterem Kurs," ibid., pp. 1121-1129.

22. The collective nature of leadership, in this sense, is a general principle of organization applied in all areas of social activity in the GDR. As such, it is also repeated in the executive councils at each successive hierarchical level of the state. The arguments regarding its advantages for integrating and coordi-

nating the different contributions to decision making would hold for these councils as well.

23. Gerhard Schüßler, "Zur Entwicklung des demokratischen Zentralismus," *Staat und Recht* 22, nos. 10/11 (1973): 1664.

24. W. Stoph, "Die Lösung der Hauptaufgabe bestimmt die Arbeit der Regierung," *Die staatliche Leitung noch enger mit der Masseninitiative verbinden* (Berlin: Abteilung Presse und Information des Staatsrates der DDR, 1972), p. 10.

25. Ibid, pp. 10-11.

26. Werner Obst, *DDR Wirtschaft, Modell und Wirklichkeit* (Hamburg: Hoffmann und Campe, 1973), p. 160. Although Obst has been critically taken to task for his reasoning and conclusions regarding economic development and prospects in the GDR, his previous activity as an official in the Council of Ministers would seem to lend some credence to his remarks regarding the decision process in this body.

27. Stoph, "Die Lösung der Hauptaufgabe," p. 15.

28. Weichelt, *Der sozialistische Staat,* p. 98.

29. Schüßler, "Zur Entwicklung des demokratischen Zentralismus," p. 1663.

30. Schüßler, "Der demokratische Zentralismus," p. 41.

31. Ibid.

32. Friedrich Ebert, *Der VIII. Parteitag der SED über die Entwicklung der sozialistischen Demokratie. Die Aufgaben zur Erhöhung der Rolle der örtlichen Volksvertretungen* (Berlin: Dietz Verlag, 1973), p. 19.

33. Gerhard Schüßler in *Staat und Recht* 22, no. 4 (1973): 646.

34. G. Schulze et al., *Richtig entscheiden—wirksam kontrollieren* (Berlin: Staatsverlag der DDR, 1972), p. 15.

35. Klaus Sorgenicht et al., *Verfassung der DDR. Dokumente, Kommentar,* 2 vols. (Berlin: Staatsverlag der DDR, 1969), 2: 371.

36. It is helpful, in understanding the function of double subordination in guaranteeing unity of action and at the same time promoting balance in territorial development, to note briefly the range of relationships subsumed under the concept of subordination. An organ can be subordinated to another in

the sense that its actions are based on the decisions of a superior and that these decisions take precedence over those of the subordinate. Subordination can also describe a relationship of responsibility and accountability of one organ to another, in the sense that it reports and accounts for its actions to this superior. In some cases, the superior organ may be authorized to issue binding directives, of one degree of generality or another, to its subordinates and to suspend the decisions of the subordinate if they conflict in some way with higher decisions. Thus subordination can leave more or less room for self-responsible action. As an important institutional device for realizing democratic centralism, double subordination is supposed to help secure an effective coordination of state organs "in the vertical." It is not, however, intended to establish a line of bureaucratic command from the center down to every city and town, thereby restricting the responsibilities of local state organs while isolating central direction from local conditions. On the contrary, double subordination is designed to promote the joint determination and fulfullment of those tasks that are the consequences of the uniform policy of the socialist state. See also Ebert, *Der VIII. Parteitag der SED,* pp. 26-27; and W. Weichelt, in *Staat und Recht* 22, no. 3 (1973): 453.

37. Schulze et al., *Richtig entscheiden* p. 13.

38. Ebert, *Der VIII. Parteitag der SED,* p. 22.

39. For example, "The local assemblies and their executive councils submit suggestions in this regard to the state organs responsible for the direction of the branches and sectors and make binding decisions in agreement with the central state organs responsible for the enterprises, combines, cooperatives, and establishments." Article 4, paragraph 1.

40. A common superior for these hierarchies does, of course, exist in party organization at the particular territorial or next higher level. It should be clear that a full examination of the problems of coordination and conflict resolution touched upon here would have to consider the role of the party apparatus as well.

41. Dieter Hösel and Joachim Misselwitz, "Die Bildung von Gemeindeverbänden—ein Erfordernis der gesellschaftlichen Entwicklung," *Staat und Recht* 21, nos. 10/11 (1972): 1609.

42. Figures from *Neues Deutschland,* 21 April 1974, p. 3.

43. An interesting discussion of the relations between the general social interest and the interests of different collectivities and individual citizens is presented by Siegfried Mampel, "Die Funktion des Rechts bei der Bewältigung von Interessengegensätzen" in a special issue of the *Deutschland Archiv* (1975) on social structure and social planning in the GDR (pp. 69-90). In this piece, Mampel also examines the emerging possibilities for local state organs to participate in the decisions of their superiors.

3. The Rise and Fall of the New Economic System

Michael Keren

The term "economic reform" had wide currency during the 1960s in the economic literature of and about the countries of Eastern Europe. Much of it was, however, fake reform. True, there were two radical attempts at decentralizing the economic system—the Czechoslovak and Hungarian models, which are well known. In all other countries but one, change was evident only on paper but had no counterpart in reality. East Germany, the GDR, was the exception. Here an ambitious attempt at devolution *within* a centralized economy was undertaken, an experiment about which all too little is known, both in and out of the economic profession. This experiment was first called the New Economic System of Planning and Managing the People's Economy (NES) and was later renamed the Economic System of Socialism (EES).[1] The purpose of this chapter is to give a brief outline of the principal mechanism of the NES reform, to explain why it was apparently successful at first, and to analyze the causes for its ultimate failure. Both success and failure require an explanation: success, because an earlier experiment in devolution in neighboring Czechoslovakia had failed;[2] and failure, because it followed success. The argument of this paper is that devolution in a centralized system, a halfway decentralization, can work, if at all, only with reasonable reserves, i.e., with plans that are not too ambitious and taut. When patience ran out in 1968 and a system of priority planning led to taut and unbalanced plans in 1969 and 1970, this was the undoing of the NES. Another centralized system followed, but with somewhat new policies.[3]

The end of the NES coincided with the change in the political guard of the GDR. I cannot help but suggest that causation did not necesarily run from the political to the economic upheaval. I even dare to claim (in the final section of this chapter) that the opposite may have been the case, i.e., that causation may have run the other way. For this venture into the minefield of political analysis, for which an economist is so poorly equipped, I hope to be forgiven.

The NES

Every Soviet-type economy is basically one huge firm, run by a planning hierarchy. The apex of this hierarchy is the State Planning Commission (SPC), headed by its chairman, the managing director. The board of directors is the council of ministers.[4] In principle, all decisions are made at the top and then passed on to the bottom of the hierarchy, the enterprises, which are in direct command of the flows of production and exchange of commodities. However, the top depends, as the basis for decision making, on ever-changing technological information, which only the bottom has. The role of the bottom is to supply the top with this information, often in the form of draft plans, and then to accept the decisions of the top embodied in the final plan. It is this interaction that, in an economic context, is often referred to as "democratic centralism."

The problems of the system lie both in the transfer of information and in the implementation of the commands, the plan. The channels that link top to bottom are too narrow to transfer but a limited amount of information. Therefore the top can never have all relevant information: however, the more reliable and relevant the data it has, the better its decisions can be. Furthermore, how the economy fares depends, in the final analysis, on the enterprises and what they do with the plan. It is in their power to disobey the plan. In the classical system, therefore, incentives are designed to reward adherence to the plan. Nevertheless, if the plan is at all feasible, a fairly wide set of alternatives, not all of them equally desirable, is still open to the enterprise; if it is not feasible, the enterprise has a still wider choice of those parts of the plan it wishes to obey. Furthermore, the target-setting procedure has an influence on the type of information the enterprise wishes to furnish, in documents and in deeds, to its superiors. Basically, if what the plan requires of it will be at least as demanding as what it reveals that it can do, by the information that it relays and through actual production, then it may wish to hide the truth and keep some "hidden reserves." In other words, an incentive system that is tied to plan fulfillment depresses productivity and leads to attempts to get "soft" plans.

The top and its staff, in addition to being short of information, are limited in time and knowledge in their ability to make good consistent decisions for all enterprises. The more they choose to decide at the top, the less attention each decision can receive. Poor decisions of superiors, combined with unsatisfactory obedience by subordinates, provide the "immanent pressure for reform"[5] in developed Soviet-type economies.

Three types of reform have been suggested: the market socialist way of splitting the mammoth firm into many competing parts; the hyper-centralist solution, which aims at improving channels of communication, planning techniques, and the price system so as to improve the workings of the centralized hierarchy; and the Liberman-GDR type, where the hierarchy delegates many decisions to lower organs while trying to pay more attention to the weightier decisions and, in the final analysis, be as much, if not more, in command of economic activity than before.

It was never the aim of the GDR leadership to adopt the market socialist solution of granting enterprises complete freedom to produce what they want, and to sell to and buy from whomever they want. The leadership would wish to keep to itself the right to fix minimum production targets, though it may not be interested in the detailed composition of all output. Furthermore, it would wish to keep a tab on purchases and sales by enterprises. The latter has, by tradition, been the task of the material supply system. Since the proper functioning of interenterprise flows of raw materials and other intermediate products, which is a prerequisite for the proper functioning of the output plan, has been one of the thorniest problems of most Soviet-type economies, material supply has attracted much of the energy of the hierarchy. A basic part of the reforms was to delegate many of the chores of the material supply mechanism to subordinate bodies in the hierarchy, to the VVB's or *Vereinigungen Volkseigener Betriebe* ("industrial associations"), and even to enterprises.[6]

A basic tool of the material supply mechanism is the material balance, which checks whether a given production-cum-final-uses plan is consistent: it is if production covers final uses and intermediate requirements (which, in turn, depend on the production plan).[7] The administration of these balances was, to a very large extent, delegated to VVBs and enterprises. In 1963, nearly a quarter of all balances were balanced by SPC and the tier nearest to it in the hierarchy and less than an eighth by VVBs and enterprises. By 1966 SPC was no longer responsible for balances, and the second tier, that of the ministries, was responsible for less than 4 percent of all balances (whose number had grown in the meantime); the bottom VVB and enterprises were responsible for nearly 90 percent. Delegation went further in 1967. All the 800 or so balances that had the standing of state plan positions were balanced by SPC in 1963. In 1966 enterprises and VVBs were balancing over 70 percent of those plan positions, and though their share fell to some two-thirds in 1967, this was out of a number of plan positions that had fallen to just over a fifth of its former level.[8]

The conditions for delegation are of some interest. Balances for any commodity were to be administered by the lowest rung that was responsible for the great bulk of its production (or consumption), and only such balances could be delegated to enterprises where production (plus imports) covered envisaged demands.[9] Both requirements were to minimize conflicts of interest for the balancer, for having to decide whether he himself or some other enterprise should get the best orders, or to have to choose which user to ration.

This naturally placed a constraint on planning strategy, a constraint that will be encountered again and again: plans could not be so ambitious and taut that most balances would have to be overcommitted. The administration of a seriously overcommitted balance could not be delegated for long (even in the absence of an explicit provision to this effect), because users were bound to appeal against serious cuts in their orders.

The traditional Soviet system limited input orders by means of material input norms. A system operating on rationing by means of norms alone would have been difficult to decentralize: it is inconceivable that every balancer would have to check closely the orders of each of his customers or that an enterprise would have to argue with each of its suppliers whether it had the right to purchase what it ordered. Strict rationing by means of input norms was a natural concomitant of distribution from above.[10] A way had to be found to make customers limit their own volition, and for that a change in the incentive system was necessary: profit, rather than adherence to the plan, had to be the principal performance criterion. If, in addition, there was a desire that both output and input decision will lead to market equilibrium and be more efficient than before, the price system also had to be reformed: both aspects are discussed below.

Another part of devolution was to provide the enterprise and all other parts of the hierarchy with a much wider freedom of action within the assigned production targets. This was closely related to the functioning of the supply mechanism: for any material balance for which no rationing was necessary and for whose output the top had no particular desire (as it had for certain types of machines and defense equipment), neither limits for inputs (i.e., the Russian *fondy* or GDR *Kontingente*)[11] nor detailed output targets had to appear in the plan. Only for commodities for which capacity was insufficient or for those that were so unprofitable that producers had to be forced to produce them (and perhaps consumers hindered from using them)—only for these had production tasks to be provided and, possibly, input limits also imposed. One is again driven to the conclusion that only slack (i.e., not taut) plans, in conjunction with a reasonable structure of prices, can assure that only few balances need receive special mention in enterprise plans. Many of these may then be of commodities in which the top has some special interest.

The greater autonomy of enterprises and VVBs can be seen

in the shrinking detail of the plan and in a shift away from physical indicators. The target of the total volume of ouput, the most important all-encompassing target in pre-NES days, becomes a secondary indicator, with a growing stress towards marketed, rather than produced, output. The detail in the prescription of the bill of goods declines: not all, but only the more important, products and delivery plans to important customers have to appear in the plan. The number of "important" goods has also fallen: one measure for this is the number of plan positions, some 800 before and during the early NES, which fell under 200 in the 1967 plan, when only products of strategic importance were to be included. The labor plan previously had limits on the number of workers' average wages and the wage fund; in 1969/70—only on the wage fund. The mix of indicators related to efficiency changed: instead of cost reduction and labor productivity, we get export profitability and capital productivity!

What was to take the place of orders from above and allotments by the material supply mechanism were interenterprise contacts embodied in contracts. But the contract system had to be strengthened: the signing of contracts had to be freed from the plan, and breaking contracts had to be made costlier. A new Contract Act enacted in 1965 and later amendments to it put some teeth into the contract by increasing the fines and indemnity payments for its breach. Indemnification is important in the context of the incentive system. In the present context, it must be remarked that the contract was made a basis for the balances and the plan, rather than being dependent on them, particularly for those interenterprise flows that represented stable supplying, or "cooperative" (in GDR parlance), relations. In these cases, the signing of long-term contracts was advocated. The latter were made binding on the balancing organs, who had to indemnify the parties if they suffered any loss through the canceling of contracts by superiors of balancers in the plan implementation stage.[12]

Not only the enterprise obtained a degree of independence. The VVBs, the successors of the *Hauptverwaltungen* (the equivalents of the Soviet *glavki*), were put on state accounting and then given the same incentives as enterprises. Having a simple success criterion facilitated the delegation of decisions to them. In fact, the independent VVBs were an aspect of pride in the early NES. This changed after a few years (see below).

Lest it be thought that the hierarchy was going to abdicate its overall control of the economy, it should be clear that the basic number of balances hovered around 6,000 for all those years for which we have information. If anything, it increased from some 5,200 in 1963 to a peak of 6,350 in 1965 and down again to just over 6,000 in 1966 and 1967.[13] This familiar planning cycle of control figures—project plan—national economic plan stayed until 1967. In that year an additional cycle was added, and the names of the stages were changed. Basically, a more aggregated trial plan was to be sent down and countered by plan proposals of the enterprises. Plan tasks were then sent down, a draft plan was sent up again, and the directives of the national economic plan gave the final orders. The aim of adding another round could only have been to add to the consistency of the plan. That it lasted only two years must have been due to the severe pressure it put on the hierarchy: it must have proved almost impossible to squeeze two rounds into the space that formerly housed just one, even if the top of the hierarchy was freed of other tasks (while the bottom was not). The EES Principles for 1969/70[14] left only one round but made provision for selected data on plan intentions to be sent up by the enterprise in a previous year as part of a systematized flow of "economic plan information." Even this was dropped in 1971 and 1972, when the plan drafting methods at large returned to their pre-NES days.

To sum up, the NES delegated many balancing functions and reduced the intervention of the top in enterprise affairs— though it is possible that much of what the top did not prescribe was added by intermediate organs. It is nevertheless likely that in 1968, the heyday of the NES, enterprises were freer than before, since they received fewer directives on the composition of sales than before. One of the reasons this was possible was that by then the price reform had been completed, many bottlenecks had disappeared after years of slack plans, and most bodies in the economy had learned to operate the freer system. But all this "freedom" was within a central plan whose remaining elements received, if anything, more attention than before.

The Incentive System

The pre-1965 incentive system was designed to buttress the plan, in particular, the supply plan. It therefore made most bonuses to leading cadres dependent on the fulfillment of the plan targets, especially that of total output. The first Bonus Fund Decree of the NES[15] in 1964 introduced many of the features that were to remain until the end of the NES: it recommended tying, where possible, the bonus fund to profits or profitability; it introduced an overbidding system that made it profitable to enterprises (and VVBs) to raise and fulfill their main target rather than overfulfill it; and it provided for the reduction of the bonus if certain physical targets were not fulfilled.[16] Although enterprise managers' performance was more closely related to the fulfillment of the physical targets, we have it on indirect evidence that profits played an important role in determining enterprise behavior: in 1965 profits were withdrawn as the preferred success criterion,[17] to be returned only when the price reform was nearing its end in 1966. There would have been no need for this if profits had not induced behavior, the wrong sort of behavior, with an unreformed price system. Here, too, 1968 introduced some changes: up to then the profit target on whose fulfillment the bulk of the bonus fund depended was fixed annually in the plan. For 1969 and 1970, there was no new target, but bonuses were to depend on the increment in profits during these years.[18] This was to weaken the inhibiting effect of the ratchet principle, as far as it referred to the profits target.

Profits as a success criterion were essential for greater latitude to enterprises, because they have as much incentive to save input as to raise output. This the old output-linked incentives did not do. With them, any squandering of inputs would do, as long as output could be raised to its prescribed level. Nevertheless, the NES was also deeply concerned that the plan target should be fulfilled, especially that the output on the supply side of any material balance will be forthcoming. It is here that the strengthened Contract Act comes in.[19] Planned enterprise flows were embodied in contracts, and the violation of any such contract led to expensive indemnities. So that forces majeures, such as balance changes, would not weaken the authority of the contract, balancers and superiors were also made liable to damage caused by contract violation due to operative intervention.[20]

As a result, except when contract fulfillment was exceptionally expensive, the profit motive itself would make enterprises fulfill their quantitative target as embodied in contracts. However, when these targets are high, i.e., in years of taut plans when enterprises are made to sign contracts that may exceed their optimal level of operation, situations may arise where it will pay them to break contracts. Thus, in years of tautness the contract will not be as effective as in years of slack plans, and the authorities will tend to reinforce the authority of the physical target by giving greater weight to target fulfillment than to profits in bonuses to those persons who matter. This is not necessary in years of slack plans, when bonuses tied to profits alone may result in a satisfactory adherence to targets.

The Price System

The more an economy relies on nonhierarchical coordination and depends on the profit motive, the more will its resource allocation be affected by its price system. This is why a price reform was an important plank in the NES Guidelines,[21] as it was in other blueprints for reforms in Eastern Europe. The price reform, begun in 1963 with a revaluation of the capital stock, was the first general overhaul of the price system undertaken in the GDR. The aim was to bring prices in line with average labor costs, not with relative scarcities. The reform was completed by 1967. More interesting experiments started in the later phases of the NES. First came the gradual introduction of the production fund tax, a tax of 6 percent on all capital employed in an enterprise. This interestlike tax replaced part of the production tax, the GDR version of the turnover tax. In 1968 came the introduction of fund-based prices: profits, rather than being a fixed percentage (some 9 percent) of costs, were tied to the "necessary" capital employed in producing any product. Another break with the past was that these prices were to be "dynamic," i.e., to be continually adjusted to changing cost conditions: higher and lower profitability levels were fixed, and whenever costs fell, profits rose to the higher level and prices were to be reduced so as to equate the profit rate to the lower level. If, as was assumed in GDR economic literature, all costs for all products tend to fall over time, this would gradually equate prices to average costs. In addition to the aim of having prices continuously portray costs, this mechanism was designed to spur enterprises to cost reduction. It appears that they had much chance to achieve the opposite.[22]

In keeping with the spirit of the NES, the VVBs were entrusted with the initiation of dynamic price changes. This obviously confronted them with conflicts of interests, and it is doubtful whether delegation could have worked in this area.

The reformed GDR prices were not scarcity prices. Though the decrees on the dynamization of prices[23] made for provisions to take scarcities, or prices of substitutes, into consideration, these were to affect prices only in certain exceptions, and then only upwards. The new prices have, nonetheless, functioned better than their predecessors. But in periods of tautness, which put a high premium on scarce (but changing) bottleneck materials, a rigid price system, which cannot take into account shifting shortages, is of little help in allocation.

The first years of the NES were characterized by slack plans.[24] They were, therefore, the proper environment for an experiment each of whose parts could not have functioned under taut plans. The GDR economy prospered in these years, experiencing a growth rate of some 5 percent per annum. With hardly any growth in the labor force, this was quite respectable, especially after the lean years in the early 1960s, when growth nearly stopped. It was the mid-1960s that started the talk of a "red economic miracle." But then came 1969 and 1970, and with them two taut annual plans, which spelled doom for the NES, though not for economic growth.

The Late NES: Priority Planning and Tautness

One of the aspects of the pre-NES system with which the GDR leadership was least satisfied was long-term planning,[25] i.e., the planning of investments (in the widest sense). Their attempts at improving long-term planning and meshing it with annual planning came with the method of "planning according to structure-determining tasks" of 1968. This was a method of priority planning in two ways: structure-determining tasks had priority both in attention and in allocation.

Priority planning meant that certain groups of products, mainly those that were expected to assure profitable export markets or that would raise the technical level of the whole economy (i.e., in essence save future imports of advanced equipment), would be planned centrally, whereas the planning of most other commodities would be left to their producers. This would make full use of the basic idea of freeing the channels of communication between the bottom and the top of the hierarchy of inessential flows, so that fuller and better information could flow through them concerning those problems that are of fundamental importance and cannot be solved by any one sector alone and so that the limited capacity of the apex be spent deciding, with all relevant information at hand, these same issues. Whether such a division is feasible is impossible to say, because the experiment, as will be seen, has failed—for many reasons, some of which were extraneous to it.

Structure-determining planning was to draw detailed long-term plans for structure-determining products, from research and development through investment, production, and even procurement. Long-term contracts were to be signed for all deliveries of inputs to investment in facilities for, and production of, structure-determining products, and these contracts were to bind balancers and have priority over all other contracts. Code numbers were assigned to priority tasks in order to assure priority in allocation and procurement. However, it proved impossible to plan the whole line of supplies to these priority products, their suppliers, and their suppliers' suppliers. The chain had to be cut somewhere[26]— and those suppliers who were not included in the planning chain were the potential bottlenecks. Such a method of planning produced plans that were by nature unbalanced. It could nevertheless have worked had the planners kept the proportion of resources going to the priority sectors fairly low and had they taken care to buffer up those sectors (intermediate industries) whose products were not included among the structure-determining ones.

At the same time, there was an attempt to devolve planning of investments in nonpriority projects. The tools of delegation were the production fund tax (see above), together with the self-financing of investment and an increase in the authority of banks in investment decisions. Self-financing meant that, rather than receive grants from the state, investments would be financed from enterprise investment funds, supplemented by bank credits. The investment funds would be fed from profits not taken up by other funds (such as the bonus fund) and by the new net profits tax (which, together with the aforementioned production fund tax, replaced the production, or turnover, tax). The net profits tax was designed so as to require some bank financing to implement the investment target of the enterprise. It was the conception of the late NES that the banks, directed by the profitability of the projects in front of them, would allocate their funds among enterprises.[27] I do not believe that a power to override the plan was ever granted the banks, let alone ever exercised by them.

If structure-determining planning proved the undoing of the NES, it was because it led to impatience, to taut plans. The gaze into the crystal ball of the future must have shown how much was wrong with the present (1968/1969) structure and must have led to attempts to raise investment in the new structure of the future. The disdain of the old *Tonnen Ideologie* led to the neglect of intermediate products, the non-structure-determining beneficiaries of the old policy. As a result, priority planning led to taut and unbalanced plans, and this was more than the delicate balance between central control and delegation, on which the NES rested, could stand.

Specific errors of judgment, combined with specific misfortunes, hastened the arrival of the crisis. An area of particular neglect was electric energy. Electric capacity was sometimes short even during mild winters. It was disastrously insufficient in the extremely hard winter of 1969 and even more so in 1970. This forced many breakdowns in production and arrears in contract fulfillment. Construction also suffered from the cold, and many investment projects were delayed. Structure-determining projects received high priority, and remaining projects had to be cut back savagely. Since this remainder was split into a great many individual projects, the result was a great increase in the stock of unfinished investment and a low addition to the capacity of nonpriority sectors, lower even than the low plan target indicated.

The crisis did not affect the growth rate of the net material product: widespread overtime apparently saw to that. Its symptoms were arrears in the fulfillment of contracts, shortages of key intermediates, and an unplanned buildup of inventories, including unfinished investments. These were signs that the machinery of the NES could not cope with the taut plans. Tautness was given up when some 1970 plan targets were cut in September; at the same time it was decided to slacken the 1971-1975 plan. A lower investment target was set, priority was given to investments in electric power and other intermediate sectors that had suffered neglect over the past few years. Still, there was a choice on how to fight the imbalances inherited from the taut years: short of deflation, a return to strict administrative rationing or a freer price system were the alternatives. The former was the choice, the only one acceptable given the political constraints, and with it came the dismantling of the NES.

The Allocation Mechanism

Intervention in enterprise affairs was increased, with a greater weight attached to physical targets of total output, with an increasing number of plan positions, and with a growing use of balance shares, formerly called *Kontingente*, in rationing inputs. The importance of norms increased, with norm reduction targets being put into the plan. Limits on the use of labor, which had been absent for several years, were also put into the plan.

Balancing was recentralized. All state plan positions (their number rose again to the customary level of 800) were to be balanced in the center, i.e., by SPC and the ministries. And the meaning of delegation of balancing was changed when a great importance was attached to the confirmation of balances, a task that seems to have been perfunctory before.[28]

Incentives

On the face of it, profits have maintained their preeminence; in actual fact, a much greater weight is being given to physical indicators. Thus above-plan profits have, apparently, a minute effect on the bonus fund,[29] and a linking of bonus payments to specific tasks, rather than the general year-end bonus of previous decrees, is suggested. The term "profit" is redefined to exclude profits resulting from the violation of plans: this, in effect, may be a vehicle of tying bonuses exclusively to the fulfillment of physical targets.[30]

The substitutes for profits in discouraging the use of inputs are fines and premiums attached directly to the violation of balance directives and to the saving of materials, respectively.

The Price System

Pricing was recentralized: no longer was it entrusted to enterprises or VVBs. The central plan took upon itself the administration of dynamic price reduction; price reduction targets were assigned and disaggregated in the plan just as *fondy* or production tasks were. On the other hand, a wind of change had swept away old precepts on pricing policy. A general dissatisfaction can be discerned, a search for centrally computed scarcity prices. But there seems to be no solution at hand. Thus the return to old centralism is incomplete, and it has more expediency than dogma.

The Ideological Superstructure

A Western observer of the GDR economy, Erdmann, published in 1968 an article entitled "The End of the NES."[31] But 1968 turned out to be the peak of the NES. Was Erdmann mistaken? Is the present chapter a repetition of his cries of "wolf."[32] The answer, I think, is negative. Erdmann, in 1968, was not writing about the actual workings of the system but about the ideas that lay behind it. And these ideas had undergone significant changes between 1963, when the NES was first broached, and 1966, when the NES entered its second stage, and again in 1968. While the reformers became more conservative, more wary of any extreme economic market experiments, practice continued to search for ways of delegating authority in those areas where decentralized decisions were likely to achieve what the central planners wanted.

What were the hopes of the reformers at the inception of the NES? The guidelines for the NES were imbued with the desire to improve the structure of incentives and prices so as to permit indirect, instead of administrative, direction of the economy. In the NES parlance, "economic levers" were to be used in steering the economy in the direction desired by the planners. Behind this basic conception, which did not change until the end of 1970, stands a changing view of the economic system: if the enterprises are relatively free to act to maximize their rewards within the commands they receive, should they be regarded as relatively free agents? Or should they be regarded as bodies whose actions are determined in the plan because the incentive system is used to keep them within the plan? The distinction may be merely semantic, but it may influence the ultimate scope of economic liberalization (if the latter is the appropriate term).[33]

The shift in perception is apparent in the statements of Ulbricht and in the way they were published at different times. In 1964 Ulbricht said that the aim of the NES was to "achieve a certain amount of self-regulation in the economic system on the basis of the plan."[34] The phrase "self-regulation" is striking here. Another mark of the early NES was that VVBs were often referred to as "socialist trusts," i.e., holding companies, in addition to being "organs of economic leadership." Thus at the Sixth Congress of the SED in 1963, Ulbricht said that "the VVBs [must] be turned from an administrative organization into a sort of trust of a socialist type under economic accounting."

The "trust" was the first to disappear. When the Ulbricht speech was published in a collection of his works in 1966, the holding company is replaced by "an organ of economic leadership." The Research Council of the Federal Ministry for Intra-German Relations explains this playing down of the VVB as an independent economic body by the ill effects of "VVB egotism" and profit-maximizing decisions that conflicted with the plan:[35] this was also when profits were temporarily banished from determining the size of the bonus fund. But there must have been an additional reason: the term "socialist concern" smacks of convergence with capitalism and has therefore been taken up with glee (together with "self-regulation") by Western observers. As such, it turned out to be inopportune. It is indeed surprising that "self-regulation" was expunged only in the 1968 second printing of the Ulbricht works: here the whole section of about a page, in which it was contained, disappeared. This time the reason for the change is obvious: 1968 was the year of Czechoslovakia, and everything had to be done to dissociate the GDR system from the Czechoslovak market socialist blueprints. This must have been a principal reason for changing the name from NES to EES. The year 1968 also saw Mittag's attack on the East German economist Kohlmei for suggesting a market-regulated economic system,[36] again reminiscent of the Czechoslovak heresy. There followed a series of articles, both in *Wirtschaftswissenschaft* and *Einheit,* condemning market socialism.

All of these changes, which seemed to signal a return to the old system, signified only a change in the way the NES was seen by insiders and described to outsiders. It was as accurate to emphasize the aspect of strict central planning enforced in the NES by means of the indirect, economic, instruments of the incentive system as to describe it as one in which subsystems were, to a degree, self-regulating.

It so happens that the system itself was also changing at the same time. But it was changing most of the time. As Leptin showed, the NES guidelines can hardly be called blueprints: they contained specific criticism of the ancient regime and were replete with bits of ideas about the new order, so that one could find in the guidelines the seeds of almost any policy or slogan advanced since 1964. But, when launched, the NES reforms were open-ended: they showed the direction of reform, not the exact route.[37] In 1966, with the price reform drawing to its end, profits were reinstated as the main performance indicator, the number of plan positions was reduced, balancing was delegated, new and devolved forms of pricing were introduced, and, on the other hand, a two-round planning method was experimented with. In 1968 priority planning was introduced; it indeed centralized the planning of certain sectors of the economy, but at the same time it aimed at a far-reaching decentralization of the remaining sectors.

The changes of 1970-1971 were different. Here the ideology changed but little. It is not surprising that new slogans were coined or that old slogans were suppressed. True, one would not expect to hear of any market, except in reference to the planned exchanges among socialist producers of commodities. But as for the rest, "democratic centralism," "plan discipline is state discipline"—these are old slogans that do not contradict the spirit of the NES. "Unity of structure policy with proportional development" is new, but only because it is topical. And the phrase "a realistic plan" is nothing new at all. The name EES is rarely, if at all, mentioned; the "economic system" is preferred. The "system of management and planning" has replaced that of "planning and management."[38] But there has been no statement to emphasize the new departures, only a stress on different aspects of the old armory of epithets. In 1970-1971 the policies were radical, the words were not. The adulation of the Soviet Union has always been there, though now it is found in novel contexts of learning from Soviet experience with improved forms of planning. And now there is more of it.[39] In 1970-1971, in contrast to 1968, the policies have changed, the words have not.

The New Directions

The year 1971 brought more than a change in the economic system. It brought a change in the growth strategy—to slack, rather than taut, plans—and in economic policy. It also brought changes of personnel at the top.

The change in economic policy is in the greater attention paid to consumption. It started with the 1971 plan: here consumption was planned to increase, albeit more slowly than in the previous year, while investment was to decline. Except for 1964, when consumption was to increase marginally faster than investment, investment was always planned to increase faster than consumption.[40] In January 1971, barely a month after the promulgation of the plan, came increases in consumers' goods targets, and others followed in September, thus raising the rate of growth of consumption to the accustomed level. Then came the draft of the 1970-1975 Five-Year Plan, which put increases in consumption at the head of the national tasks for the coming half decade. It is the first time a five-year plan has put the rate of increase of consumption above that of investment, this in a country where the proportion of investment in gross material product, though increasing in recent years, has not been particularly high.[41]

While the original 1971 consumption target of a 2.4 percent increase over 1970 may have been determined on its own merit, all other changes were doubtlessly related to the December 1970 events in Poland. These events were also among the reasons for the change of the guard, i.e., the replacement of Ulbricht by Honecker. However, this change should be seen in the context of events on the economic front. Ulbricht was closely identified with the NES, with priority planning, and with the taut plans. He saw the stable foundation of the East German state in the reformed economic system, and he was surely proud of its success. This is why his collected works are entitled *On the New Economic System* or, in a later edition, *On the Economic System of Socialism*. He was therefore to a large extent personally responsible for the events of 1970. As late as January 1971, in his last major economic address, he still sounded the sentiment of what had been the NES in its last phase:

> We should aim to concentrate the decisive part of our investment resources on those fields that are decisive for the structuring of the developed social system of socialism, because that will enable us to implement the scientific-technical revolution.

That was a call for structure-determining tasks when the 1971-1975 Five-Year Plan draft, which was published three months later (two days after his resignation), put the stress on investments in areas neglected by the structure policy. In trying to explain the dilemma confronting the drafters of the 1971 plan, he was, in fact, explaining the grounds for the errors of the 1970 plan and indirectly admitting that he was to blame for them:

If we concentrate insufficient resources on structure-determining projects, we shall not reach fast enough the world level in important areas. If, on the other hand, we concentrate to such an extent that the projects cannot be balanced, then we lead to disproportions and to a slow-down of the rate of development.[42]

Furthermore, it was Gunter Mittag, a technocrat closely associated with Ulbricht, who in the summer of 1970 so clearly expounded the need to continue with the taut plan of 1970.[43]

Had the policies of the late 1960s proved a success, there would have been no reason for Ulbricht to retire. But they did not, and there was clearly a need for new departures in the economic policy. And because of what happened in the East, these new departures acquired a new urgency. A fundamental rethinking of the economic way, the need to learn a new phraseology—these an old and inflexible man may not have found himself up to. He may have decided that the day had come for somebody with a new approach. His successor, Honecker, was a man who had no responsibility for any of the existing economic policies. In this sense, he was the right person to start upon new directions.

The accession of the Honecker team was in many respects novel. Ever since Stalin combined taut, centralized planning with high priority for investments, we have become used to thinking of the reformers' mix as the opposite: slack, decentralized, and consumption-oriented. What we got instead was slack, but centralized, planning, with an orientation toward consumption. Is this a temporary aberration, a transition measure promising a return to either reforms or tautness and high investments once the events of December 1970 have receded into the more distant past or the new team is settled in the saddle?

If we try to look at the Five-Year Plan for the intermediate future, we find no evidence for a planned change. True, the envisaged rates of growth of gross material product are to rise from 4.6 percent in 1972 to 5.5 percent in 1975, but this seems a reaction to the underfulfillment of the 1971 plan: the missing 0.4 percent was apparently shifted to 1975, so that the total planned increase of 29 percent announced in May can be achieved on paper. Investment, a good indicator of impatience, is planned to increase at about the same rate as consumption during the remaining term of the plan. What is going to change, after the imbalances of the taut years are corrected, is the mix of investments and production, again toward final demand sectors and away from intermediate production.[44]

The stress on consumption is here to stay for some time, so it seems. Consumption is rarely referred to except as the *Hauptaufgabe*, the main task, a euphemism that carries political commitment. It is true that the 1973 plan provides for a respectable 6.2 percent growth in sales of consumer goods and a 9 percent growth of investments (both targets slightly underfulfilled). But this faster rate of growth of investments comes after a near stagnation of two years and cannot be seen, therefore, as a reversion of precedence to investment. In 1974 both consumption and investment are to increase at the same rate. So much for policy.

Does the 1973 plan give an indication as to strategy? Is it taut or slack? Here the answer is not easy. On the face of it, the envisaged growth rate of 5.7 percent in gross material product is higher than the rate attained in any year since the late 1950s, though it is not quite as high as that of the plans for 1969 and 1970. Indeed, the actual growth claimed in the fulfillment report was only 5.5 percent. However, a member of the Politburo, Werner Lamberz, declared in October 1972 that the current plan, rather than its fulfillment, will serve as the basis for preparation of the 1973 plan;[45] if the same applies to the published figures of the plan, then the truly planned growth for 1973 was only 5 percent, a more modest target that was actually surpassed. The 1974 target of 5.4 percent is, again, within what was actually surpassed. The planners seem to be wary of any return to tautness. As for the new centralism, if official pronouncements are any indication, it is here to stay. Thus it is the policy that the Plan Methodology, the constitution of the allocation system as it were, is to remain fixed and not change annually.[46] To symbolize this, the methodology for the 1974 plan has been issued in the form of corrigenda to the 1973 methodology.[47] The corrections are 52 pages long, the original methodology, 203 pages; obviously, the changes are many. But the general structure has been maintained.

On the other hand, *Die Wirtschaft* is again full of the old complaints against bureaucratization and the flood of paper. The ills of the old centralized system are showing again. As Leptin says, "if one can . . . state today the NES reform experiment is at its end, this does not say that economic reforms are at their end. The need for reform is still there."[48] But we cannot say whether the new reforms, in progress or yet to come, will be as original and far-reaching as the NES.

Notes

1. Since these terms refer to the same economic system, their initials will be used interchangeably in the following, with preference given to the older name, the NES.

2. J. M. Montias, "The Evolution of the Czechoslovak Economic Model 1949-1961," mimeographed (Yale University, 1962).

3. That the NES has been superseded by the old regime is not generally agreed. For a closer exposition of this assertion, see M. Keren, "The New Economic System in the GDR: an Obituary," *Soviet Studies* 24, no. 4 (April 1973): 554-587. For a counterargument, see Jacob Naor, "How Dead is the GDR New Economic System," ibid. 25, no. 2 (October 1973): 276-283.

4. The analogy could be carried further: all shares of this mammoth firm belonging to the people, are held by proxies, the leadership of the party; here—the Politburo of the SED.

5. Peter Mitzscherling, "Die Wirtschaft der DDR— Bestandsaufnahme und Aussichten," in *Die Wirtschaft Osteuropas zu Beginn der Siebziger Jahre*, ed. Hans-Hermann Höhmann (Stuttgart: Kohlhammer, 1972), p. 97.

6. *Richtlinie für das Neue Ökonomische System der Planung Leitung der Volkswirtschaft* (Berlin: Dietz, 1963), pp. 112 ff. (to be cited as NES Guidelines).

7. This formulation disregards foreign trade and inventories.

8. See Keren, "The New Economic System in the GDR," table 1.

9. Rolf Keilacker, "Voraussetzungen, Bedingungen und Kriterien der Delegierung von Bilanzierungsfunktionen auf Betriebe," *Wirtschaftswissenschaft* 14, no. 10 (October 1966): 1631 f.

10. See Keren, "The New Economic System in the GDR," pp. 557ff, for the reduced importance of rationing in the NES.

11. Renamed "balance shares" *(Bilanzanteile)* when rationing reappeared at the end of the 1960s. See below.

12. "Verordnung über die Aufgaben, Pflichte und Rechte der Betriebsstaats- und Wirtschaftsorgane bei der Bilanzierung materialwirtschaftlicher Prozessen," *Gesetzblatt der DDR,* pt. 2, no. 67 (1968) (to be cited as Balancing Decree 1968); and "Vertragsgesetz" in ibid., pt. 1 (1965).

13. Keren, "The New Economic System in the GDR," p. 560, table 1.

14. "Beschluss über die Grundsatzregelung für Komplex-Massnahmen zur weitere Gestaltung des Öss in der Planung und Wirtschaftsfuhrung für die Jahre 1969 und 1970," *Gesetzblatt der DDR,* pt. 2, no. 66 (1968).

15. See Keren, "The New Economic System in the GDR," for some reservations as to what one can learn from the various decrees on the bonus fund.

16. "Beschluss über die Bildung und Verwendung des einheitlichen Prämienfonds in den volkseigenen und ihnen gleichgestellten Betrieben der Industrie und des Bauwesens und in den VVB im Jahre 1964," *Gesetzblatt der DDR*, pt. 2, no. 10 (1964).

17. Manfred Böttcher, "Where do We Stand with Planning in the NES?" *Eastern European Economics* 6, no. 3 (from *Die Wirschaft,* no. 48, 1965).

18. "Verordnung über die Bildung und Verwendung des Prämienfonds in den volkseigenen und ihnen gleichgestellten Betrieben, volkseigenen Kombinaten, den VVB (Zentrale) und Einrichtungen für die Jahre 1969 und 1970", *Gesetzblatt der DDR,* pt. 2, no. 67 (1968).

19. "Vertragsgesetz."

20. "Vertragsgesetz" and Balancing Decree, 1968.

21. Mitzscherling, "Die Wirtschaft der DDR."

22. A somewhat fuller treatment of this issue can be found

in Michael Keren, "Concentration amid Devolution in East Germany's Reforms," in *Planning and the Market: Economic Reforms in Eastern Europe*, ed. Morris Bornstein (New Haven: Yale University Press, 1973).

23. "Richtlinie zur Einführung des fondsbezogenen Industriepreises und der staatlichen normativen Regelung für die planmässige Senkung von Industriepreisen in den Jahren 1969/1970." *Gesetzblatt der DDR,* pt. 2 (1968), p. 497.

24. Cf. Keren, "The New Economic System in the GDR."

25. "Richtlinie für das Neue Ökonomische System" p. 86.

26. Roland Scheibler et al., *Die Planung nach strukturbestimmenden Erzeugnissen und Erzeugnisgruppen* (Berlin: Verlag Die Wirtschaft, 1968), p. 48.

27. H. Buck, "Umkehr zur administrativen Befehlswirtschaft als Folge nicht behobener Steuerungseffekt der Wirtschaftsreformkonzeption," in Gleitze et al., *Das ökonomische System der DDR nach dem Anfang der siebziger Jahren* (Berlin [West]: Duncker and Humbolt, 1971).

28. Cf. Keren, "The New Economic System in the GDR."

29. Though the law puts a limit of 25 percent, an example in *Ekonomicheskaia Gazeta,* 1972, no. 2, shows a mere 7.3 percent of marginal profits going into the bonus fund.

30. "Finanzierungsrichtlinie für 1971," *Gesetzblatt der DDR,* pt. 2, no. 6 (1971).

31. Kurt Erdmann, "Das Ends des NÖS", *Deutschland Archiv* 1, no. 9 (1968): 998.

32. As Naor, "How Dead is the GDR New Economic System," claims.

33. The following discussion draws extensively on Erdmann, "Das Ende des NÖS"; and on Federal Republic of Germany, Bundesministerium für gesamtdeutsche Fragen, Forschungsbeirat für Fragen der Wiedervereinigung Deutschlands, *Fünfter Tätigkeitsbericht 1965/1969* (Bonn, 1969).

34. *Fünfter Tätigkeitsbercht,* p. 45.

35. Ibid., p. 47.

36. Gunter Mittag, "Meisterung der Ökonomie ist für uns Klassenkampf," *Neues Deutschland,* 27 October 1968.

37. Gert Leptin, "Das NÖS Mitteldeutschlands," in *Wirtschaftsreformen in Osteuropa,* ed. Karl C. Thalheim and Hans

Hermann Höhmann (Köln: Wissenschaft und Politik, 1968).

38. The change of this slogan can be dated. In the draft resolution for the 1971-1975 Plan, *planning* comes first. In the approved resolution, *management* gets precedence. But the English translation, which must have been hastily prepared, keeps the old order: Eighth Congress of the SED, *Directive on the Five-Year Plan for a Development of the National Economy of the GDR 1971-1975* (Dresden, 1971), p. 20.

39. Kurt Erdmann, "Abkehr vom bisherigen Modell des ÖSS," *Deutschland Archiv* 4, no. 8 (August 1971).

40. Cf. Keren, "The New Economic System in the GDR," p. 578.

41. Investments were 23 percent of gross material product in 1970, 18 percent in 1960. *Statistisches Jahrbuch der DDR,* 1971, (Berlin, 1972), p. 42.

42. *Neues Deutschland,* 30 January 1971, p. 5.

43. Ibid., 11 June 1970, p. 3.

44. Cf. the interesting analysis of Peter Mitzscherling in the *Wochenbericht des Deutschen Instituts für Wirtschaftsforschung,* 1971, no. 22, p. 155.

45. *Neues Deutschland,* 13 October 1972. If the consumption and investment target are to be read in the same light, then sales of consumer goods are to increase by 4.2 percent, investment by 8 percent.

46. Cf. H. W. Hüber, "Wie erreichen wir eine höhere Stabilität des Volkswirtschaftsplanes 1971," *Die Wirtschaft,* 27 January 1971, pp. 4-5.

47. *Gesetzblatt der DDR,* Sonderdruck no. 726 of 14 March 1972 and 726/1 of 16 March 1973.

48. Gert Leptin, "Bilanz der Wirtschaftsreform in der DDR," in *Die Wirtschaftsordnungen Österreichs im Wandel,* ed. Hans-Herman Hömann, Michael Kaser, and Karl C. Thalheim (Freiburg: Rombach, 1972), 1:108.

4. Participation and Ideology

Thomas A. Baylis

It is by now a familar idea that one of the marks of political and social modernization is the rapid expansion of citizen participation in public life.[1] Communist societies too, in their mature phases of development, are said to face growing demands for participation; indeed, they may come to require participation in order to function effectively.[2] The development of participatory institutions in such societies, however, cannot be viewed solely as a response to economic need or as the unavoidable concomitant of popular mobilization. It must also be examined in its ideological setting, which provides both justifications for and inhibitions upon the emergence of an authentic "public realm"[3] under communism. In turn, the ambiguity of the ideology in its implications for participation suggests fundamental questions about the nature, distribution, and legitimation of political power.

Richard Lowenthal has argued that a conflict between the goals of economic "development" and ideological "utopia" is characteristic of communist societies.[4] This conflict may be said to have become embodied in the ideology itself, which brings together principles meant to serve the goals of rapid economic modernization with utopian ideals inspired by Marx's vision of the classless society and enriched by the implications for such a society of the Marxist critique of capitalism. Neither the developmental nor the utopian dimen-

sions of ideology exclusively serve any one group or tendency
in communist societies. Party veterans and bureaucrats can
wield both against managers and intellectuals as readily as
reformers and economic rationalizers can employ them against
functionaries. What the proper inferences from an incomplete-
ly described utopia are for contemporary policy is subject to
disagreement, just as are the appropriate means for maximizing economic development. The answers arrived at in both
cases will determine the place accorded by the ideology to
citizen participation under socialism and thus in some measure
its practical implementation.

The ideal of "socialist democracy" is informed by utopian
passages in the Marxian classics and by heroic events in the
history of proletarian struggle: by Marx's imprecise vision of a
cooperative and classless society peopled by men of a new
morality, freed from alienation, masters of their own existence;
by the memory of the Paris Commune as celebrated in Marx's
account of it; by Lenin's insistence that even the revolutionary
dictatorship of the proletariat will be "a *million times* more
democratic than any bourgeois democracy";[5] and by the
spontaneous emergence of workers' soviets in the 1905 and
1917 Russian revolutions. The proclamation of rule by the
working class, while interpreted diversely in practice, occupies
a central position in the Marxian classics; it is at the root of the
syndicalist impulse that has surfaced repeatedly both within
and outside the communist nations. But it is also, given the
vagueness with which "worker" comes to be defined, the source
of a kind of communist populism, whereby the broad masses
are assured that for the first time in human history state power
is truly theirs.

To these syndicalist and populist overtones must be juxta-
posed Leninist organizational doctrines, which do not accommodate participation quite so comfortably. Lenin's insistence
on vanguard control of the revolution and, after the seizure of
power, on the discipline and hierarchy called forth by the
imperatives of political stability and social and economic
development, finds its ideological expression in the doctrines
of democratic centralism, one-man managerial authority, and,
more generally, the "leading role" of the party. All of these

necessarily inhibit the development of genuine participatory institutions, however fervently it may be asserted that vanguard discipline and socialist democracy, through the dialectic, in reality complement one another.

Initially, Lowenthal suggests, communist societies require a type of "mobilization regime" or "dictatorship of development" that seeks to "activate the people in its service" without extending to them the right to advocate their own interests or voice their own opinions.[6] Later, with the expansion of education and communications networks, it proves economically and socially expedient to increase the number of participatory institutions and to broaden their functions in order to deepen the involvement and commitment of their members and thereby reinforce regime legitimacy. It is at this point that the *quality* of participation and its relationship to the utopian promises of the ideology become issues of some political significance. As a degree of economic abundance seems to come within reach, the question of the relationship between the instrumental uses of participation and its substantive place in the emerging classless society is likely to present itself with growing insistence.

A verbal distinction can readily be drawn between two fundamental types of participation—I have labeled them "manipulative" and "influential"[7]—and then used to dismiss communist participatory devices and to applaud those of Western pluralist societies. Yet a moment's reflection should make it clear that *both* types of participation are to be found in *all* societies. Purely "consultative" bodies openly intended to serve as safety valves for discontent or as legitimizing supports for the "real" leader are familiar mechanisms in both public and private organizations in the West, while examples of specialist and even lay groups substantially influencing decisions through their expertise or persistence are far from unknown in communist societies. In some cases, the distinction between manipulative and influential participation may be apparent only to the beholder; it is usually difficult for observers to know reliably whether any particular individual's acts really influenced a given decision, or to agree whether that influence touched on truly significant matters. Over time, participatory institutions may also change their significance; institutions intended by a regime to facilitate popular mobilization and control may establish themselves as centers of genuine influence, while once-influential bodies may be reduced to obedient ciphers, ratifying everything put before them. If the ideological justification and the institutional definition of such bodies is vague and ambiguous, the possibility of a transformation in their functions becomes greater.

This possibility is what makes the study of participation in the German Democratic Republic of special interest to us. In this chapter I will survey the institutions of citizen participation in the GDR against the background of economic and social modernization and that of the official ideological treatment of the problem of socialist democracy. In the final section I will return to the question of the relationship of existing participatory practices to the changing character of communist societies and the image of utopia.

The Theory of Socialist Democracy

Democracy, in the orthodox communist view, is a form of rule whose character is dependent on the class system of a given society; "the question is always: democracy for whom, for which class?"[8] Under socialism, for the first time in human history, "real democracy for the majority of the people" emerges, but it is coupled with dictatorship over "the minority of expropriated exploiters."[9] Socialist democracy is by no means inconsistent with—indeed it requires—the placing of power in the hands of the workers' party, which, following Lenin, has the tasks of *"leading the whole people* to socialism, of directing and organizing the new system, of being the teacher, the guide, the leader of all the working and exploited people in organizing their social life without the bourgeoisie and against the bourgeoisie."[10] Democracy and consciousness building, participation and socialization, are thus all of one piece in the orthodox view. Socialist democracy is also said to be inseparable from planning and organization; "democracy without discipline and responsibility must lead to the squandering of energy and finally to anarchy."[11] Although "real" socialist democracy is repeatedly contrasted to "formal" bourgeois democracy, the forms and claims of the latter retain evident attractiveness in East European polities and influence their structures. In these states constitutional guarantees of citizen rights, the parliamentary structure of national governments, and the procedures of election all resemble their Western counterparts in form, if not in substance or actual function. The ritual often attached to the investiture and pronouncements of the council of ministers, meetings of parliament, and the staging of elections betrays a tacit acknowledgment of the persistent appeal of bourgeois democratic forms, although perhaps only as legitimating devices.

The rhetoric and symbols of citizen rule coexist with those of working-class power. With the overturning of the bourgeois order, legitimacy is presumed to be transferred to the workers, who become collective "socialist owners" of the means of production. As they grow accustomed to their new position as free "subjects" rather than alienated "objects" of history, they assume an ever broader range of social responsibilities, particularly in economic planning and management.[12] The party, as vanguard and embodiment of the will of the working class, by definition assures proletarian dominance while simultaneously tutoring the new rulers so that they may assume their duties more fully and directly. There is no hint that working class rule will ever *replace* party leadership or even that they are conceptually distinct; the two are expected to develop together, in alliance with the reformed sectors of other classes and strata.

Any tension that might be expected to arise between the dual principles of citizen democracy and worker rule is dismissed rhetorically. "Worker" is defined so elastically as to be very nearly a fiction; "workers" often include party functionaries and even members of the intelligentsia with proletarian backgrounds. DDR social statistics combine blue-collar with white-collar employees and treat the collectivized peasantry as an allied, nonantagonistic class whose ideological status is nearly equal to that of the working class proper. In any case, all useful social strata are united under the umbrella term *Werktätige* ("working people"), which is used almost as often and carries nearly as positive an aura as "worker" itself. If the party and its organs are the institutional embodiment of working-class rule, the institutions of government are the locus of citizen demo-cracy. The party, with its "bourgeois" and peasant allies in the "national front," of course staffs and directs the government, and there can in theory be no legitimate antagonism between them.

One may quarrel with the official theory on several counts; the most serious is the uncritical assumption that party rule *is* proletarian rule, that party bureaucracy cannot detach itself from its class base and degenerate into self-perpetuating oligarchy, that the official ideology will always be a sort of general will expressing the true interests of workers and citizens. "Revisionist" Marxist critics of what they term "sta-tist" socialism have differed, insisting that without bourgeois freedoms the assumption of control by a self-interested and bureaucratic party oligarchy is all but unavoidable. They argue that socialist democracy must combine bourgeois liberties with the common ownership of the means of production and the new institutions of workplace democracy it makes possible.[13] The orthodox also tacitly admit the need for synthesis but prefer a limited synthesis of certain bourgeois *forms* with collective ownership and party control. Let us examine, first, the quasi-bourgeois scaffolding of citizen democracy in the GDR and, then, the new institutions of worker and student codetermination.

Institutions of Citizen Participation

Article 21 of the GDR's Constitution proclaims that "every citizen of the German Democratic Republic has the right to participate fully in shaping [*umfassend mitzugestalten*] the political, economic, social, and cultural life of the socialist community and the socialist state. The principle reigns: 'work together, plan together, govern together.'"[14] In practice, governing together includes voting for members of the Volks-kammer and local governmental assemblies (*örtliche Volks-vertretungen*); approving the nomination of candidates for these offices, especially in "voter assemblies"; and serving in such offices or the advisory commissions and committees attached to them. It also includes serving on organs of "social discipline," most notably the "arbitration commissions," the

East German equivalents of comrades' courts. It may include activity in the SED, the "bourgeois" parties, the National Front, and the mass organizations. Informally, it may include participating in public discussions of major legal changes or policy proposals, writing letters to the press, or petitioning local government.

Perhaps the high-water mark of the rhetoric of citizen democracy in the GDR was reached in 1964. Walter Ulbricht, speaking in commemoration of the fifteenth anniversary of the founding of the East German state, declared that the GDR was becoming, in Krushchevian language, a "state of the entire people." He spoke at some length of the "strict assurance of the rights of the individual" and announced that multiple candidacies would be permitted in local elections. A voter dissatisfied with any candidate might strike out his name in favor of an alternate; if more than 50 percent of all voters did likewise, the candidate would be defeated. By the next local election, to be sure, this provision was already nearly moribund: only two of some 185,000 candidates were thus eliminated.[15]

While neither elections nor the voters' assemblies preceding them appear to offer the citizen any real opportunity to influence the choice of officeholders,[16] the very number of elective and appointive local positions provides widespread participation opportunities. Some 200,000 elected representatives, "in their majority tested representatives of the working class," hold office together with nearly a million unpaid members of associated commissions, their *Aktivs,* and committees. Formally, the local assemblies "are to decide on all matters that concern their territory and their citizens," although they are simultaneously expected to carry out the policies of the center.[17] Individual assembly members are expected to be available to their constituents and attentive to their grievances and suggestions; indeed, they may even be charged with "voter assignments" by the voter assemblies, although such assignments must be consistent with party policy.[18] The local council, nominally chosen by the assembly, is claimed to enjoy substantial authority over factories, *Kombinate,* and industrial cooperatives, especially in matters touching upon local working conditions and the production and distribution of consumer goods.[19] But since the councils are simultaneously subordinated to the higher levels of the state bureaucracy as well as to the assemblies *(doppelte Unterstellung)*, their capacity and willingness to respond to local demands remains in doubt. The assemblies, for their part, do not really control the councils and have little decision-making authority, although they serve as a sounding board for citizen dissatisfactions.[20]

Institutions of Worker Participation

It is in the place of work that opportunities for participation take on their greatest ideological significance. The factory, "whose activity is the basis for the creation and accumulation of social wealth,"[21] is viewed as something of a social micro-cosm in which cooperative interpersonal relations and ethical values are nurtured that will gradually be transferred to society at large. In it every worker is said to have a "moral duty ... of creative participation [*Mitwirkung*]" in economic planning and plant leadership.[22] Through his participation, the individual helps to shape his own social environment and furthers his own development as a socialist personality.[23]

The idea of worker participation has had a persistent and seductive appeal throughout Eastern Europe. In the GDR, confronted as it has been by schemes of union codetermination in West Germany and by the workers' councils of Yugoslavia, the question has received repeated attention. Prominent GDR dissidents raised demands for worker control in the crises of 1953 and 1956,[24] and, under pressure of the events in Poland and Hungary in the latter year, the party established "workers' committees" in eighteen selected plants. The committees' functions appear not to have gone much beyond the giving of advice; they were accorded little attention after the 1956 crisis had passed and were entirely dissolved early in 1958.[25]

At present, worker participation is channeled primarily through the trade union (FDGB) and takes essentially three forms.[26] First, there are bodies meant to provide some measure of worker consultation about and influence over plant decision making; these include the trade union unit (BGL) itself, and Permanent Production Advisory Councils, and the (now defunct) Production Committees.[27] Second, there are bodies and groups devoted essentially to production mobilization and technological innovation, falling generally under the rubric of "socialist community work" *(sozialistische Gemeinschaftsarbeit).*[28] Third, there are economic and social "control" bodies, most notably the Workers' and Peasants' Inspectorate *(Arbeiter- und Bauern-Inspektion)* and the quasi-judicial "conflict commissions."[29] Here we will examine only the first and second categories.

In the first category, the most interesting bodies were by all odds the Production Committees, whose elected membership included the "best" workers, technical specialists, and managers as well as representatives of the party, union, and other outside organizations. The plant party secretary served as chairman. The committees served as advisory bodies to the plant director on plan development and fulfillment, technological innovation, and the coordination of other factory groups. The director was obliged to take account of their recommendations and to report disagreements with them to higher organs for resolution.[30] They appear to have offered younger technicians and managers a significant channel of influence over plant decisions, and there were instances, which were sharply condemned, in which the committees attempted to issue directives to management.[31] Such vigorous excesses, together with their perceived encroachment on the functions of the trade unions, may have been responsible for the abolition of the committees in 1972 and their replacement by strengthened Permanent Production Advisory Councils, which are trade union units. While the unions have been told to become more direct spokesmen for worker interests, if necessary against management, they are probably less effective instruments of influence than the committees, especially for the middle managers and intelligentsia. Management is, however, legally obliged to respond to the councils' recommendations.[32]

"Socialist community work" is a term used both as the broad assertion of a general social principle and specifically to refer to those factory groups whose cooperative efforts are organized for the purpose of increasing and rationalizing production and stimulating and implementing technical innovations. They include worker "brigades of socialist labor," and the "work collectives," "research collectives," and innovator brigades, which in varying degrees bring workers and members of the intelligentsia together. Community work in these groups is expressed in part through "socialist competition," which stimulates output and efficiency through self-imposed targets and through the rivalry of groups within the plant and with those outside it.[33] Because these groups are seen as models for new cooperative work relationships and as socialization agencies instilling a new socialist morality, they receive a great deal of attention from party ideologists and instructors of socialist management. Socialist community work, writes one GDR author,

> increasingly is becoming a characteristic mark of socialist work, learning, and life in all areas of the socialist social system and is one of the principal forms in which the convergence of classes and strata in the GDR, the development of the socialist personality, and the creation of the socialist human community takes place. Community work is thus a law of society penetrating all areas of social life under socialism.[34]

To be sure, such bodies do not participate in overall plant decision making; they are meant first of all to facilitate production. Empirical studies by GDR researchers suggest they are useful in technical and production matters, but do little to build consciousness or to inculcate socialist values. Research and development groups tend to include only modest numbers of workers alongside the dominant technical intelligentsia. Elsewhere, participation requirements are often treated "formalistically" and regarded with distrust as a potential hindrance to production and effective economic leadership.[35]

Participation in the Universities

In many ways participatory bodies in East German universities are analogous to those in the factories, although their history is somewhat different. In the traditional German university, the senior faculty enjoyed nearly exclusive academic authority, at least within the institution; it required many years for the SED regime to obtain the desired level of party influence. In 1956 student unrest threatened the very existence of Walter Ulbricht's leadership,[36] and in 1958 Erich Honecker complained that "bourgeois ideology" continued to rule in many parts of the universities.[37] The "Third Universities Reform," undertaken in 1966, sought to reorganize university structures, primarily in order to better integrate them with the needs of the economy, but also to afford some measure of participation to students and other university groups. The reforms were instituted during a period of student agitation for a one-third share in decision-making authority in West German universities. The GDR's participation reforms were directed in part at the West German student audience and in fact seem to have aroused some interest there.[38]

On the level of the university as a whole, "social councils" and "scientific councils" were established, including in their membership students, faculty, employees, representatives of outside economic "contract partners," and party and union functionaries. In each "section"—roughly comparable to an American department—analogous councils were created. In addition there is a large university senate *(Konzil)* and sectional plenary assemblies, both of lesser importance.[39] Student positions on the councils are filled by the official Free German Youth (FDJ), to which nearly all students belong, but which has suffered a decline in prestige and influence in the universities. Apparently it was hoped that both might be revived by associating the FDJ with university governance and encouraging it to act as a more vigorous spokesman for student interests vis-à-vis other components of the university.[40]

The statutes establishing the councils make it clear that their powers are consultative; furthermore, the rector, section direction, party, union, and youth organization nominate all members except the external ones.[41] In accordance with the general "economization" of East German universities, authority is expected to follow the industrial principle of "one-man management" joined to collective consultation.[42] None of this precludes substantial informal influence, of course, particularly if the party believes the rector or section head is ignoring sound advice. Western reports, however, suggest that student interest in the councils is meager.[43]

The Meaning of Participation

Not the least of the attractions of the Marxian utopia has been its promise of human autonomy: bondage to the focus and relations of production and to their political and cultural superstructure is to end, and man is to become "the lord over Nature, his own master—free."[44] It has never been entirely clear, however, what Marxian "freedom" in an advanced socialist society, understood as one based on cooperation and planning, might amount to. Presumably, freedom can only be realized withing a framework of altruistic and cooperative social behavior; it is not the "freedom" of egocentric individualism. The difficulty is that the requisite new morality and new human personality do not emerge spontaneously with the abolition of private property. These must be learned, at least in part, through practice in cooperative and collective ventures; such ventures, it is implied, cannot be permitted to evolve without guidance according to the principles of an advanced, superior ideological consciousness.

Thus participatory institutions in the GDR are seen first of all as means of induction into the values of the emerging socialist order. As such, they must necessarily be subject to the supervision and instruction of the party. Yet as harbingers of the coming classless society they must offer in some degree elements of the autonomy and freedom promised in that society. If all expressions of spontaneity are suppressed, if the manipulation of participatory institutions becomes too manifest, such devices will become—and will be perceived as— a mockery of utopia, not an anticipation of it.

The matter is complicated by the instrumental uses participation is also expected to serve. Participation serves legitimizing functions; it constitutes, as one astute commentator puts it, an "act of demonstrative togetherness" establishing a link between "one's own behavior and the greater common goal."[45] For the purposes of external public relations, GDR participation devices allow the claim to be made that bourgeois citizenship rights *and* worker control have both been realized together in the socialist half of Germany. For the purposes of economic development, the GDR's leaders evidently share the "participation hypothesis": the more participation, or the appearance of it, the happier (or less alienated) the worker, and the greater the output.[46] At the same time, the very high priority placed on production inhibits the extension of participation into those areas where it might be economically damaging; much like their capitalist counterparts, the SED's leaders are convinced that participation should never impinge upon accustomed management prerogatives.

A final instrumental purpose that participatory devices are expected to serve is that of "control." Voters' meetings, Workers' and Peasants' Inspectorates, trade union units, university social councils, and numerous other bodies are all expected to watch over responsible officials, criticize their actions, and call the attention of the party or higher governmental bodies to any mistakes or abuses. They thus serve as a source of leverage over officials on behalf of the regime, but in order to carry out this function they must become loci of some genuine power themselves. It is possible that the control function offers members of these groups a more genuinely "influential" participatory experience than any other.

Given the variety of functions participation is meant to serve and given the ambiguity of the ideology and the diverse requisites of economic development by which participation is conditioned, it is not surprising that GDR rhetoric is not very clear on the proper *limits* of participation in socialist society. "Codetermination," declares an authoritative leadership handbook, "may not be limited to the carrying out of tasks."[47] Another GDR writer remarks, "if socialist society is one in which the 'free development of each is the condition for the free development of all,' then it is part of the nature of socialist democracy that not only the cooperation *(Mitarbeit)* but also the [power of] decision and thus the responsibility of all citizens be expanded systematically and according to plan."[48] But, another source insists, the actual "delegation of full power of decision *(Verfügungsgewalt)* to the employees" would "undermine the social basis of the socialist society" and render rational economic leadership "impossible."[49]

As long as the devices of participation are meant to serve economic and other instrumental uses while simultaneously infusing a bit of Marxian utopia into contemporary GDR socialism, this rhetorical uncertainty is liable to persist. The tenor of most East German discussions of participation is one of cautious ambiguity, and indeed the outburst of discussion of the subject in the late Ulbricht era has given way to less frequent and more pro forma references to it. But the GDR remains a state in which the ideological promise of participation continues to be emphasized and which is full of concrete opportunities for citizens, workers, and students to take part in public life; in that fact lies a substantial potential for political change.

Notes

1. See Samuel P. Huntington, *Political Order in Changing Societies* (New York and London: Yale University Press, 1968), pp. 34-35 and passim.

2. Samuel P. Huntington, "Social and Institutional Dynamics of One-Party Systems," in *Authoritarian Politics in Modern Society,* ed. Samuel P. Huntington and Clement H. Moore (New York: Basic Books, 1970), pp. 38-40; Peter C. Ludz, *The Changing Party Elite in East Germany* (Cambridge, Mass.: MIT Press, 1972), pp. 40-42; Alfred G. Meyer, *The Soviet Political System* (New York: Random House, 1965), pp. 381-384.

3. This term is borrowed, with gratitude, from Kenneth Jowitt.

4. Richard Lowenthal, "Development vs. Utopia in Communist Policy," in *Change in Communist Systems,* ed. Chalmers Johnson (Stanford: Stanford University Press, 1970), pp. 33-116.

5. V. I. Lenin, "The Proletarian Revolution and the Renegade Kautsky," *Selected Works* (New York: International Publishers, 1967) 3: 59.

6. Lowenthal, "Development vs. Utopia," p. 35.

7. "East Gemany: In Quest of Legitimacy," *Problems of Communism* 21, no. 2 (March-April 1972): 46-55. See also Alain Touraine's notion of "dependent participation," which

he attributes to all postindustrial or "programmed" societies. *The Post-Industrial Society* (New York: Random House, 1971), p. 10.

8. *Wörterbuch der marxistisch-leninistischen Soziologie* (Berlin: Dietz Verlag, 1969), p. 93. See also Horst Harmel and Wolfgang Loose, "Arbeiterklasse und sozialistische Demokratie," *Deutsche Zeitschrift für Philosophie* 19, no. 4 (1971): 501-502.

9. *Wörterbuch,* p. 120. See also V. I. Lenin, "The State and Revolution," *Selected Works* 2: 333-334.

10. Lenin, "The State and Revolution," p. 285. See also Willy Wyniger, *Demokratie und Plan in der DDR* (Köln: Pahl-Rugenstein Verlag, 1971), pp. 96-102.

11. Friedrich Ebert, *Der VIII. Parteitag der SED über die Entwicklung der sozialistischen Demokratie. Die Aufgaben zur Erhöhung der Rolle der örtlichen Volksvertretungen* (Berlin: Dietz Verlag, 1973), p. 11.

12. See the account of a highly sympathetic commentator on the East German theory, Wyniger, *Demokratie und Plan,* p. 130; also Rudi Weidig, *Sozialistische Gemeinschaftsarbeit* (Berlin: Dietz Verlag, 1969), pp. 35-37.

13. See Svetozar Stojanovic, *Between Ideals and Reality* (New York: Oxford University Press, 1973), chap. 5.

14. "Wortlaut der neuen Verfassung der DDR," *Deutschland Archiv* 1, no. 5 (May 1968): 107.

15. Hermann Weber and Fred Oldenburg, *25 Jahre SED* (Köln: Verlag Wissenschaft und Politik, 1971), pp. 153-154; *A bis Z: Ein Taschen- und Nachschlagebuch über den anderen Teil Deutschlands* (Bonn: Deutscher Bundes-Verlag, 1969), p. 694. See also Roger E. Kanet, "The Rise and Fall of the 'All-People's State,' " *Soviet Studies* 20, no. 1 (July 1968).

16. See Ernst Richert, *Macht ohne Mandat* (Köln and Opladen: Westdeutscher Verlag, 1963), pp. 200-210.

17. Ebert, *Der VIII. Parteitag,* pp. 16-17.

18. Richert, *Macht ohne Mandat,* pp. 207-209.

19. Ebert, *Der VIII. Parteitag,* pp. 18-22. See also the essay by Kenneth Hanf in this volume.

20. At the Eighth SED Congress, Erich Honecker called for a "heightened" role for the local assemblies, stricter implemen-

tation of their decisions, and a more active *(lebendiger)* accounting of the representative before his constituents. Honecker, *Bericht des Zentralkomitees an den VIII. Parteitag der SED* (Berlin: Dietz Verlag, 1971), pp. 65-66. Following the directive of the Central Committee, a corresponding law was drawn up and enacted on 12 June 1973. See "Gesetz über die örtliche Volksvertretungen and ihre Organe in der Deutschen Demokratischen Republik," *Gesetzblatt* 1, no. 16, p. 313.

21. "Wortlaut der neuen Verfassung der DDR," Article 41, p. 173.

22. *Gesetzbuch der Arbeit*, pt. 2, par. 2, as cited in Wyniger, *Demokratie und Plan,* p. 123.

23. See *Politische Ökonomie des Sozialismus und ihre Anwendung in der DDR* (Berlin: Dietz Verlag, 1969), pp. 212, 365-366, 711-712.

24. See Martin Jänicke, *Der dritte Weg* (Köln: Neuer Deutscher Verlag, 1964), p. 62; Fritz Behrens, "Zum Problem der Ausnützung ökonomischer Gesetze in der Übergangsperiode," in *Zur Ökonomischen Theorie und Politik in der Übergangsperiode,* 3rd Sonderheft, *Wirtschaftswissenschaft* 5 (1957): 125, 128-219, and passim; Fritz Raddatz, "The Case of Wolfgang Harich," *Encounter* 24, no. 2 (February 1965): 91.

25. See Weber and Oldenburg, *25 Jahre SED,* pp. 111, 114, 115; *A bis Z,* p. 31. I am indebted to Professor Melvin Croan for calling my attention to the committees and providing additional information on them.

26. Useful and succinct descriptions of the GDR's institutions of worker participation are provided by Hartmut Zimmerman, "Probleme der Mitbestimmung in der DDR," *Kommunität,* January 1973, pp. 4-18: and Joachim Lieser, "Mitbestimmung in Deutschland," *Deutschland Archiv 5,* no. 1 (January 1972): 31-34.

27. In the large "socialist trusts" (VVBs), which direct all the plants in a particular branch of industry, the comparable body was the "societal council" *(gesellschaftlicher Rat),* which served as an advisory board to the general director.

28. "Socialist teamwork" would be a less awkward translation, but since GDR commentators insist on a sharp distinction between *Gemeinschaftsarbeit,* with its affective and

utopian overtones, and instrumental "teamwork" in the capitalist world, I have avoided using the latter term.

29. These are the factory counterparts of the "arbitration commissions" mentioned above. See Edith Brown Weiss, "The East German Social Courts," *American Journal of Comparative Law* 20 (Spring 1972): 266-289.

30. See *Politische Ökonomie*, pp. 718-719; Lieser, "Mitbestimmung in Deutschland," p. 33; Ludz, *Changing Party Elite*, pp. 166-172; *A bis Z*, p. 498; Zimmerman, "Probleme," p. 14.

31. Hartmut Zimmerman, "Wandlungen der Leitungsstruktur des VEB in soziologischer Sicht," *Deutschland Archiv*, Sonderheft (October 1970), pp. 106-107.

32. Leiser, "Mitbestimmung in Deutschland," p. 31; Zimmermann, "Probleme," p. 14.

33. See *Wörterbuch*, pp. 138-139.

34. Weidig, *Sozialistiche Gemeinschaftsarbeit*, p. 27; see also *Leiter, Kollektiv, Persönlichkeit* (Berlin: Verlag Die Wirtschaft, 1971), 200.

35. See Elke Franke, "Die Zusammenarbeit zwischen den Arbeiter und der Intelligenz im Forschungskollektiv und die Durchsetzung der führenden Rolle der Arbeiterklasse in der Forschung" (Berlin: Dietz Verlag, 1972), pp. 49-50; Weidig, *Sozialistiche Gemeinschaftsarbeit*, pp. 37-41, 167-173; Zimmerman, "Wandlungen," pp. 105-108; Irmhild Rudolph and Erhard Stölting, "Soziale Beziehungen im VEB im Spiegel betriebssoziologischer Forschung in der DDR," *Deutschland Archiv* 3 (October 1970), Sonderheft, pp. 117-119.

36. In November 1956, the SED cadres chief Karl Schirdewan, later purged as the leader of a group seeking to depose Ulbricht, called for the extension of the "right to codetermination" to university students. Weber and Oldenburg, *25 Jahre SED*, p. 111.

37. Honecker, "Aus dem Bericht des Politbüros an das 35. Plenum des Zentralkomitees der SED," *Neues Deutschland*, 2 February 1958, p. 4.

38. See, e.g., Kurt-Christoph Landsberg, "Die dritte Hochschulreform—ein Schritt zum Kommunismus," *Deutschland Archiv* 3 no. 2 (February 1970): pp. 159-161.

39. Joachim Lieser, "Mitbestimmungs- und Autonomie-zeremonien in den deutschen Universitäten," *Deutschland Archiv* 3, no. 6 (June 1970): 598.

40. See Horst Helas, "Die Rolle der Freien Deutschen Jugend an der Karl-Marx-Universität," in Karl-Marx-Universität Leipzig, *Studienführer 1969/70* (Leipzig, 1969), pp. 169-170.

41. Lieser, "Mitbestimmungs- und Autonomiezeremo-nien," pp. 598-599.

42. See "Die Weiterführung der 3. Hochschulreform und die Entwicklung des Hochschulwesens bis 1975. Beschluss des Staatsrates der Deutschen Demokratischen Republic," *Forum* 1969/70. Reprinted in *Deutschland Archiv* 2, no. 5 (May 1969): 509-528. See also my *The Technical Intelligentsia and the East German Elite* (Berkeley: University of California Press, 1974), pp. 36-38.

43. Frank Grätz, "Die Hochschulreform in der DDR—Ergebnisse und Gedanken," *Deutschland Archiv* 4, no. 3 (March 1971): 248-249.

44. Friedrich Engels, "Socialism: Utopian and Scientific," in *The Marx-Engels Reader,* ed. Robert C. Tucker (New York: Norton, 1972), p. 639.

45. Hermann Rudolph, *Die Gesellschaft der DDR—eine Deutsche Möglichkeit?* (München: Piper Verlag, 1972), pp. 32-33.

46. On the "participation hypothesis," see Sidney Verba, *Small Groups and Political Behavior* (Princeton: Princeton University Press, 1961), chaps. 9-10.

47. *Leiter, Kollektiv, Persönlichkeit,* p. 38.

48. Werner Müller, "Das entwickelte gesellschaftliche System des Sozialismus und das Bewusstsein des Menschen," in *Sozialismus und Ideologie,* ed. Werner Müller (Berlin: VEB Deutscher Verlag der Wissenschaften, 1969), p. 39.

49. Harmel and Loose, "Arbeiterklasse," p. 508.

5. Official Nationalism

Henry Krisch

Nationalism, understood as both a goal and an instrument of modern political activity, has been much written about in recent social science literature. Especially in regard to the "Third World," nationalism has become one of the central ordering concepts by which we seek to understand current political trends. Several aspects of this voluminous literature are of special concern to us in connection with GDR policy. For one thing, the subject of these studies is a dynamic aspect of political life rather than an established condition. Thus for Emerson, the nation is a "terminal community,"[1] and Deutsch refers to the "growth of nations," "nation building," and "national development" as three different ways of understanding this process.[2] Second, nationalism is seen as an induced, deliberately cultivated factor, which serves certain interests of a political leadership.[3] Most strikingly, the modern study of nationalism almost invariably stresses nationalism's integrative quality. Regardless of whether this quality is evaluated positively, there is wide agreement that the political function, if not the purpose, of nationalism is, in Silvert's words, to "establish national cohesion across class lines and in response to development-caused class cleavages."[4]

It is misleading, however, to think of nationalism as necessarily a unitary force. The development of national feelings may affect different social groups, different aspects of a

society's life, indeed different phases of an individual's personality quite differently. This is especially true when the dynamic
aspect of nationalism, its development over time, is kept in
mind. Seen alternatively as policy or progress, nationalism
may reflect partial integration of social groups into a polity; it
may appeal to some, but not all, aspects of social and individual development. Daniel Bell, for instance, in his reformulation
of the concept of national character, refers to "five different
elements that are often lumped together": national creed,
national images, national style, national consensus, and modal
personality. Of these, the two most relevant to the GDR
experience are national style ("distinctive ways of meeting the
problems of order and adaptation") and national consensus
(self-conscious attachment to specific group symbols as a
means of group differentiation). (Bell here follows Karl
Deutsch.)[5]

Gebhard Schweigler, in his pioneering comparison of national awareness in the two Germanies, points to four dimensions of national consciousness in terms of commitments to
different objects: cultural values, national symbols, sociopolitical institutions, and "functional roles mediated by the system."[6] As a recent study for the Peace Research Society put it,
"Nation-states are not always unified on the basis of a common
ethnic background and a common culture."[7]

As an indication of how communist nation building may
stress some aspects of social life and, indeed, has apparently
done precisely that in the case of the GDR, and in anticipation
of our argument below, we may cite the judgment of Peter
Ludz, who recently wrote that, in answer to the question of the
existence of a state or national consciousness in the GDR, one
must point to the development of "genuine social norms,
models, and values as well as modes of behavior."[8]

These considerations offset somewhat the problems that the
view of nationalism as consensual community integration
presents for students of communist political life.

Unlike most nationalist leaders, leaders of communist states
are not overtly and explicitly devoted in the first instance to the
achievement of national tasks. (That they may in fact have
their greatest impact in this area is another matter.) Commu-

nist revolutions are far more likely than nationalist revolutions to exacerbate or indeed create serious cleavages. In terms of specific political relationships, Communist parties and their leaders may find their chief competitors to be nationalist movements. In short, for communists, nationalism is a problem to be dealt with rather than a goal to be achieved. Communists usually seek to supplant nationalist modes of community integration with their own.

Of course, there are the well-known cases of "communist nation building," i.e., instances wherein prior processes of nation building were taken over and led to success by communists: China, Yugoslavia, Albania, and North Vietnam are obvious examples. There remains, however, the question of whether the experiment of nation building has ever come out of a prior, communist political process or whether, as Deutsch has stated, "with the possible exception of Outer Mongolia, no new nation-state has been created under communism."[9]

Despite these differences in styles of nation building, there are also points of comparabililty. Although the ideology of a nationalist movement usually binds its adherents to the existence of suppressed and rejected groups, the reality of national building may be quite similar; indeed, the GDR variant of nationalist ideology described below, with its emphasis on the social and conflict-filled nature of emerging nationality, may be closer to the actual process in noncommunist countries than the consensual and unifying myth politically employed. At least one recent GDR author has recognized this, declaring that the traditional hallmarks of nationhood (in this case, in Stalin's "classical" 1913 formulation) need not apply to "nations in the process of becoming, as occurs today most frequently in Africa, or nations involved in a transformation of social character, as today the German."[10]

Are there means available to test the notion of communist nation building? One possible fruitful approach is to consider the cases of the divided nations, especially their communist portions: North Korea, North Vietnam, and the German Democratic Republic. In these cases, the question of disintegration through nationalism arises in a context other than that of a multinational state. To put matters another way, can the integrative function of nationalism, as described by political scientists, be exercised within a larger framework of national disintegration? In the specific case of the German Democratic Republic, a communist political leadership is faced with an existing national community and is seeking to increase the legitimacy and cohesion of their state by appealing to separatist loyalties based not on regional or ethnic grounds, but on socioeconomic and political grounds. The current GDR leadership is not in fact claiming to supplant the existing German social order throughout the German national community, but rather to create feelings and perceptions in the GDR population that will lead to an identification of the community with an extension (or if one will, a contraction) of a particular social order.

Of course, the regimes exercising power in the divided countries may, and usually do, advocate reintegration of the national community on their own terms. Indeed, of the six regimes mentioned (in Germany, Korea, and Vietnam), only the GDR leadership has chosen the path of particularism.[11]

The GDR regime may thus be seen as engaged in an unusual form of nation building. Using Karl Deutsch's three categories of nationalism-as-policy, we may say that the regime's policies over the last half decade represent a form of nation building that it hopes will become national development. These policies are not to be understood as a "growth of the nation," in the sense of a historical process of an emerging, ever more intensive communal self-awareness. Nor, insofar as "national development" involves the "vast, complex, and slow-changing aspects of the actions and expectations of millions of people,"[12] does the current cultivation of GDR nationalism fit into this category. The first reaction of the GDR population to their government's policy may well be an intensified effort to avoid integration into a GDR polity through flight. At least this is one plausible interpretation of the fact that the number of people escaping from the GDR has increased as the consequences of Brandt's *Ostpolitik,* and the GDR's response to it, have become clear.[13] Just as after the signing of the four-power Berlin agreement in 1971, so the signing (December 1972) and ratification (June 1973) of the Basic Treaty between the two

German states have led to more people escaping from the GDR than in the previous year—despite greatly eased facilities for travel between the FRG and GDR.[14] Every process of nation building segregates some elements of the population out and integrates others in. It has been notoriously the case in Germany that each step toward greater demarcation between the fragments of the former nation-state has presented people with immediate pressures to choose. Thus, while some inhabitants of the GDR have responded to policy and circumstance and evinced a greater loyalty to the state (if not the regime), others have been driven to flee.

Thus has been produced the paradoxical situation that the number of refugees increases as travel restrictions are eased and that, generally, people flee the GDR while most evidence indicates increasing acceptance of the regime.[15] It can be argued that the factors usually cited as generating GDR loyalty—career opportunities, improved living standards, pride in shared hardships, resentments toward West Germany—are no more significant than many feelings within a single national community and cannot compare in intensity with more traditional factors, such as common language and social goals. Although the existence of a common language or culture is a disputed issue between the Germanies, the West German government has acknowledged that these ties, if extant, are insufficient and has therefore chosen to stress common historical experiences and a sense of belonging together.[16] But such overwhelmingly subjective factors are precisely those most subject to social control and transformation. The question then arises whether weak and possibly temporary moods and feelings can be transmuted through time and consistent pressure into a national allegiance.

This brings us to the essential element in this matter: the deliberate policy of the GDR leadership. What we are dealing with here is not a societal force but a political decision. The people of the GDR are not transforming their self-understanding from "German" to "citizen of the GDR"; the political leadership has decided to effect this transformation. More precisely, we may say that the GDR has begun to establish parameters of action and expression that may, over a considerable period of time, bring about such a transformation of attitudes.

It will not be argued here that the GDR leadership is free, by virtue of its extensive powers, to confirm or deny a common German nationality at its convenience. Any process of social transformation—nation building not least of all—involves a struggle against certain circumstances as well as utilization of factors conducive to change. As Deutsch and Merritt have put it, "it seems clear that even very powerful governments by themselves cannot manufacture major culture changes," but governments have critical positions and the power to exploit those positions to effect social change, for, as these same authors state further, "governments and communications elites are the managers of public messages about events, selecting out of the mass of competing messages those that they will transmit . . . and those that they will suppress."[17]

For roughly the first twenty years of its existence, the GDR was held up to the German people as one variant on the theme of a common Germany.[18] Although the construction of the Berlin Wall in 1961 began the process of narrowing available alternatives, it was not until 1970-1971 that decisions were taken that amount to a renunciation (by the regime) of all-German ambitions. Previously the contrast between the GDR and the Federal Republic had been drawn so as to depict the GDR as the more worthy expression of the German national community, but the new line is designed to focus the perceptions of the GDR population exclusively on the GDR as an object of "national" loyalties.

The ambiguity of this phase of the regime's appeal is symbolized by some important political statements of the 1960s. In the SED program, adopted at the Sixth Congress in 1963 (but reprinted as valid in a 1971 edition), we read a seemingly unequivocal commitment to all-German goals:[19]

The Socialist Unity Party of Germany remains firmly committed to its goal of restoring that national unity of Germany split by the imperialist Western powers in alliance with German monopolies. Since the days of Marx and Engels, the fight for a united, democratic, and peace-

ful Germany has been part of the traditions of the revolutionary movement of the German workers.

But while "complete restoration of state unity" was proclaimed
as an ultimate goal, a confederation specifically excluding any
diminution of the participants' sovereignty was the only
practical step listed. Moreover, while the program spoke of a
"socialist national culture," the SED's fight on its behalf was
considered to be a "defense of German culture" as such.[20]
Similarly, the new "socialist constitution" adopted in 1968
spoke in its preamble of the people of the GDR being "bur-
dened with the responsibility of showing the entire German
people a way into the future of peace and socialism," and
Article 8 speaks of the eventual unification of Germany on a
socialist basis. It also calls for the establishment of "normal
relations on a basis of equality" between the German states.[21]
The change in attitude since 1968 is shown in a recent discussion of a West German commentary on the 1968 constitution.
We find a typical denial of "any relationship" between even the
earlier 1949 GDR document and either the Weimar or Bonn
constitutions. Furthermore, "with every article of the (1968)
constitution, we differentiate ourselves *(grenzen wir uns ... ab)*
from the imperialist system."[22]

The transition from competition to isolation *(Abgrenzung)*
in the GDR's German policy was brought on by the clear, if as
yet incomplete, settlement of that major heritage of World War
II, the question of the German future. One consequence for the
GDR of the complex of détente policies (FRG *Ostpolitik*,
Soviet-American détente, the Moscow and Warsaw treaties,
and the four-power Berlin agreement) is its involuntary acceptance of the long-run division of Germany. Of course, as the
weaker of the two German states, the GDR has always
had an interest in a certain detachment in intra-German
affairs. The present situation, however, is fundamentally
different from that of the preceding twenty years. The GDR
has lost one of the chief justifications for its existence—
to provide an alternative German future to that offered by
the FRG. Moreover, the population of East Germany can only
with difficulty continue to regard itself as a part of one German

nation, albeit with a special status. These two factors alone suffice to confront the GDR with a major crisis of legitimacy, the nature of which can be expressed as a question: what is the GDR?

The major, although not sole, factor shaping the answers to this question in the immediate future will be the policies of the GDR regime. The regime needs a basic legitimizing idea: it cannot exist for long as a regime based largely on force, but its former role as possible spearhead for Soviet advance in Germany is no longer a feasible one. The present leadership of the GDR has begun to provide its answer: a policy of officially sponsored national consciousness. On the one hand, the regime wishes to transform and intensify the already existing "state consciousness" of its citizens into something like a "national consciousness" by a transvaluation of attitudes toward West Germany. At the same time, it has been dismantling the cautious attempts of Ulbricht's last years to develop a "German socialism" distinct from that of the USSR in particular and of the other communist states in general. Unquestionably, this second policy runs counter to the first. That the GDR leaders felt constrained by their power relationship to the Soviet Union to adopt the second policy is another sign of their weak position in this relationship and of the continuing impact of foreign affairs on the GDR political processes. The logical outcome of this second policy would involve even closer GDR assimilation into the bloc and into the embrace of Soviet policy. Given the increasing strength of nationalist feeling in Eastern and Central Europe, this may not be a very promising policy.

To foster the concept of GDR nationhood, the SED leadership introduced the theme of *Abgrenzung.*The precise definition of this term remains unclear, although the GDR leadership has used it increasingly since 1970.[23] The operative meaning of the term, however, is easier to discern. For one thing, it means that there can be no special character to the relations between the GDR and the FRG based on a supposed common nationality. Speaking to the SED Eighth Congress in June 1971, Erich Honecker declared that[24]

The only relations possible between our socialist GDR and the imperialist FRG are those based on peaceful coexistence corresponding to the rules of international law. Any other kinds of relations can never exist between states with different social orders.

Such statements could be multiplied. Speaking in January 1972 to GDR troops on the Baltic island of Rügen, Honecker declared that it was quite clear that "our republic" and the FRG relate to each other as each of them does to any other third party. The Federal Republic, he declared, is a "foreign country, and an imperialist foreign country at that."[25]

While Honecker's subsequent statements have not always reproduced the sharp tone of the Rügen speech, his position has remained unchanged. Speaking to the Ninth Plenum of the Central Committee in May 1973, Honecker declared that neither of the two German states was a territory *(kein Inland)* of the other.[26] Indeed, while Honecker and other GDR leaders have combined stress on sharp demarcation between the Germanies with offers of fruitful cooperation,[27] they have been concerned to emphasize that the conclusion of the basic treaty between the GDR and FRG has in practice "settled" the German question. Thus Hermann Axen recently declared that "the so-called German question has been definitively settled in accord with the principles of international law."[28] Honecker, stressing that the treaty had established more than a modus vivendi in FRG-GDR relations, declared that anyone construing the existence of "special" intra-German relations was wasting his time.[29] In the opinion of two GDR scholars,[30]

The propagation of such theses as those of the continued existence of unitary *(einheitlich)* German nation and the existence of special intra-German relations . . . serves the aim of hindering . . . the integration of the GDR into the socialist community.

Here we see a related theme: there can be no special intra-German relations because there is not a special framework for them in the shape of a German nation that transcends and encompasses several German states. There can be no unity, declared a GDR radio commentator, "not only because we are separated by borders but mainly because of the different social systems."[31] "Unity of the nation—they [West Germans] say this in order to enlarge the scope of exploitation by German finance capital . . . so-called special relations—in order to subvert the GDR," charged Albert Norden at the celebrations marking the 125th anniversary of the 1848 revolution: for such selfish reasons do they "drivel . . . about joint spiritual and intellectual forces," charged a GDR radio commentator.[32]

The ideological underpinning for this position was provided by Kurt Hager in a major address to a social scientists' conference in Berlin on October 14, 1971.[33] Touching upon the national question, he stressed that it was impossible to ignore its "class character." The nation he declared to be the "unmistakable end product of social development," which for the GDR meant that its essence as a socialist nation could only be understood in connection with the integrative processes of the socialist community of states, which processes would determine the further development of all essential characteristics of the socialist nation.

In the Federal Republic, according to Hager, much use is made of "pan-national demagoguery" and of the notion of the "continuing existence of a unitary German nation. But history has already decided this question." This use of nationalism as an ideological weapon means that the GDR must see to the work of building a "profounder socialist state consciousness" by clarifying the national question along these lines.[34] It seems that some GDR citizens may not be immune to such West German appeals, perhaps because they do not know the horrors of imperialism at first hand. Thus there is a need for works of political education that will put these matters into proper perspective.[35] Consistent with this line is the increasing practice of listing nationalism (as such) as a variant of bourgeois ideology. Hermann Axen spoke of "nationalism and other variants of a hostile ideology," and Honecker referred to "anticommunism, nationalism," and other diversionary tactics.[36]

While Axen's formulation of "two nations" as well as two states is an extreme position within the SED leadership,[37] other statements go almost as far. Albert Norden declared that "one cannot speak of an imaginary 'unity of the nation' at all"[38] having previously denied that the populations of the GDR and FRG share common territory, economy, culture, psychic and moral traits, or even (except as subjectivist error) common emotions.[39]

This denial of a common nationality is accompanied by harshly critical comments on the state of life and culture in the FRG. Thus *Neues Deutschland* has attacked West German society as infested with drug addicts and bank robbers and ruled by accomplices to American criminal aggression in Indochina.[40] This theme, in turn, is related to that of the debasement of the German heritage in the Federal Republic. West German culture suppresses the democratic and humanistic heritage of classical German culture[41] and is reduced to "antihuman excesses . . . late-capitalist nonculture . . . and an Americanized life style." Thus one can no longer speak of a "unitary national culture" in the two German states.[42]

The notion of profound divergence in culture between the two German states is clearly a crucial one for the policy of fostering a separate GDR nationalism. The common German cultural heritage is after all of much longer standing than the seventy-four years of Bismarckian political unity. Common culture is thus a major obstacle to divergent attitudes, and this may account for the often exceptionally shrill tone of GDR comment on this question.[43] It is important to note, however, that a common Germanic cultural heritage has not prevented the formation of separate Swiss and Austrian political consciousnesses and similar phenomena may be found in other cultural traditions, as the SED leadership has pointed out.

In addition to stressing the moral-ethical component of their cultural demarcation from West Germany,[44] the SED leadership has also taken a more aggressive line on the question of common language and culture as an intra-German bond. Axen, in the article already cited, claimed that two German-language states such as the GDR and FRG were *more* distinct "in principle" from one another than, say, West Germany and

Austria, thanks to socioeconomic differences.[45] Norden suggested that emphasis on the German language as a criterion of common nationality came perilously close to Hitler's rationalizations for conquest and declared that, in any case, non-German-speaking miners were closer to the GDR population than West German bankers.[46]

This denigration of the importance of language received the highest party backing when Honecker, in his speech to the Ninth Plenum, discussed at length the implications of a common language.[47] The border between the two German states, he declared,was "drawn not by language or culture, but by the differing and indeed opposed social structures" of the two countries. After citing a number of English-speaking countries, as well as the use of German in Austria and the two German states, and having reviewed the course of German history seen as a history of class struggle, he asserted that

> the fact that the German language is spoken in the two German states and that cultural traditions exist of which the citizens of the GDR as well as the citizens of the FRG can be proud . . . does not necessarily mean that the citizens of Austria, Switzerland, the GDR, and the FRG must be members of one and the same nation. It is known that the term "nation" is applied in different countries in very different ways.

The SED leadership may have taken the line of *Abgrenzung* despite, and not in the absence of, a common culture, partly in recognition of the difficulty in persuading the GDR population that no ties of culture exist. It is intriguing that, in the speech just cited, Honecker spoke openly of "Western mass media, above all FRG radio and television, which everyone here can switch on or off at will."

Abgrenzung may come to mean abandonment of hopes for radical political action in West Germany. A certain resignation concerning revolutionary prospects in the FRG seems to have set in among the SED leaders; thus Abusch, in the article cited above,[48] after repeating the Eighth Congress slogan that the working class will reunite Germany, admits that at the present time, "no one can say how and when" the West German working class will attain power. For the moment, "historical necessity in our decade leads to ever sharper *Abgrenzung* between the ideologies, social systems, and class cultures of the two German states." Logically, therefore, the GDR has disbanded its Secretariat for West German Questions.[49] It seems likely that the SED and its current offspring in West Germany, the Deutche Kommunistische Partei (DKP), will accept the fiction of the DKP as a "new" party and cease to demand the relegalization of the KPD, which has now been banned for over fifteen years.[50]

The current campaign against "social democratism" falls into place here. Although the ultimate hope of a communist Europe has not been given up (as one would not expect it to have been),[51] there is great concern to immunize people and leadership in the GDR and, indeed, in all of Eastern Europe, against the wiles of the Social Democrats,[52] while at the same time recognizing the hold of the SPD on the West German working class—and thus implying poor prospects for a "revolutionary" development in the FRG.[53]

While undertaking national ties, the GDR leadership is not engaged in a policy common to a large number of communist leaders: it has not striven to proclaim its autonomy from Soviet control. The historical record suggests that anti-Russian sentiment would be as easily aroused among Germans as among other East Europeans. Of course, the special background of the GDR as the product of an occupation regime and indeed the continued presence of a large Soviet force may play a role here: the SED leaders have always been careful to emphasize their loyalty to the USSR, including public celebration of the war's end as Liberation Day. Nonetheless, in the last years of Ulbricht's leadership, an attempt was made to stake out a number of distinctive ideological positions: the outcome of this effort would have been the development of a distinctive GDR road to socialism. It would have been a "road" especially well suited to advanced industrial societies—hence, even the Soviet Union might have been called upon to learn from the GDR!

The main items in the Ulbricht list of innovations all related to the nature of the current social and political order in the

GDR.[54] Inasmuch as the idea of a GDR nationalism rests on the social and economic differences between the GDR and West Germany, it would have been very useful had the GDR leaders been able to further dignify the social order by differentiating it from the USSR as well as from the FRG.

Under the Ulbricht scheme, the GDR was described as containing the "developed social system of socialism"; its population had been integrated into a "socialist human community *(Menschengemeinschaft)*"; its successfully completed socialist society was not merely a stage of development antecedent to full communism, but a fairly lengthy, autonomous, and historically significant stage of development. The more orthodox position, as outlined by Hager, calls GDR society the "developed socialist system," stresses the continued leadership role of the working class, and specifies that socialism gradually develops into communism. Without concerning ourselves with the substance of this particular discussion, it is clear that in ideological questions (as in foreign policy and other areas), the GDR has moved closer to the Soviet Union since Ulbricht's downfall.

What this signifies for the attempt to propagate a distinctive GDR nationalism is not wholly clear. Although the reluctance to assert autonomy against the Soviet Union is not the typical pattern of the area, it may not be dictated entirely by the geopolitical situation of the GDR. Given the imperative need to weaken the sense of community with West Germany, the regime may seek to reinforce the economic and social forces favoring loyalty and career advantage in the GDR by redirecting ideological, cultural, and human traffic in the opposite direction (if that last is indeed the significance of the GDR's agreements for easier border crossing to Poland and Czechoslovakia).

Meanwhile, the regime continues to attack the symbols of a common nationality,[55] even while it seeks to socialize a new generation through civics and history teaching that stresses the incompatibility of the two German societies.[56]

A startling indication of this policy is the new GDR citizenship law of October 1972, which effectively expatriates between three and seven million former GDR subjects and their offspring (by in effect replacing immunity from prosecution for "flight from the republic" with deprivation of citizenship).[57]

Of course, the GDR cannot through an act of will escape the comparison with the FRG, and indeed the very self-awareness of its people remains tied to that West German sibling, which, despite everything, is still the standard of measure—whether of achievement or failure.[58] The central issue is, rather, whether the SED leadership can succeed in its effort to redefine the national allegiance of the GDR population so that it derives from social, rather than traditionally "national," categories.

Since the success of such a policy is in part dependent on the passage of time and the maintenance of roughly similar circumstances during that time, it makes more sense to list and evaluate the favorable and obstructing factors involved, rather than to attempt an outright prediction.

The passage of time also involves the passing of generations. To the extent that the regime confronts presently held and undesirable attitudes that it wishes to remove, the coming to power of new generations would seem to be a point in the regime's favor.[59] With time, what is today a novel psychic orientation or a slightly disquieting behavior pattern becomes an accepted norm. There is surely nothing inevitable about this process, but such things do in fact happen.

Moreover, the party leadership is determined to achieve these results and will continue to be so determined, since the success of the policy of official nationalism is in their own interest. In addition to its control over the style and content of the arts and communications media, the regime has established a large-scale educational system of high quality, in and through which, in part, an effective process of political socialization of GDR children takes place.[60] Here again, the regime gains strength with time.

What are the negative factors involved? To begin with, while behavior can be enforced in the absence of supporting attitudes, it is safer in the long run to have the two converge. Changing attitudes, however, is a slow and difficult task, especially in the area of national culture. Nowhere surely is it as difficult as in Germany, where the past is reinforced by a multitude of personal, cultural, and historical reminders.

Ironically, the very success the GDR has thus far achieved as a state has led it into a policy of freer visits—which will in turn make it more difficult to pursue a successful *Abgrenzung* effort.[61] The heightened campaign against bourgeois ideology, above all against "social democratism," is a response to this, as is the system of special prohibitions for middle- and high-rank officials receiving Western guests.

Insofar as identification with the regime rests upon the GDR's economic success, there exists a clear danger that any economic setback, especially a decline in living standards, could seriously and adversely affect loyalty to the GDR. The familiar proposition that democracy in West Germany depends for acceptance on a continued "economic miracle" is applicable in its own terms to the GDR as well.[62]

Finally, and in this connection perhaps most importantly, the history of the confrontation between nationalism and socialism in this century does not inspire confidence in the GDR regime's prospects. Under the aegis of a multitude of regimes, with such communist regimes as those of Yugoslavia and the USSR itself prominent among them, national feeling is experiencing a universal resurgence. The official nationalism of the GDR must compete with memories of past glories and grievances and with dreams of united power, and these are not easily dealt with. The leadership in East Berlin was fortunate when it had in office in Bonn a chancellor who could say that "a good German cannot be a nationalist."[63]

In the past three years the main lines of development described above have been strengthened and extended. The determination of the regime to differentiate the GDR from West Germany and to redirect the GDR's international transactions toward Eastern Europe (and particularly toward the Soviet Union) has intensified. This policy has found its chief formal expression in the revisions of the GDR Constitution in October 1974, in the treaty with the Soviet Union of October 1975, and in the SED program adopted in May 1976.

At the same time, however, the problematical nature of the GDR population's response to this strenuous effort at fostering national consciousness in the GDR must remain as much of a puzzle and problem to the leadership as ever.[64] Moreover, the external factors of West German attitudes and GDR economic performance have not both remained propitious. Although the Schmidt government's greater concentration on domestic and Western policy, together with West German economic difficulties, may have somewhat dimmed the allure of the Federal Republic, the GDR's own economic difficulties endanger the regime's chief legitimacy-building device. These difficulties stem chiefly from general inflation and the particular rise in the prices of raw materials. Unfortunately, a major aspect of the Honecker regime's economic improvement has been allowing imports from the West, and this has resulted in an enormous indebtedness to the industrialized Western world. Worse yet, price rises have had to be negotiated with the GDR's chief trading partner, the USSR; this in turn runs counter to the main line of GDR policy justification: the benefits of close ties to the Soviet Union.[65]

The East Berlin leadership has been determined to impose generally its view that "the German question is closed." In a typical statement of this position, GDR Foreign Minister Oskar Fischer, speaking to the Volkskammer in December 1975, remarked that only hostility to détente could explain "loud assertions that there continues to be a so-called open German question or a supposedly existing single German nation. . . . History has long since decided the national question. In the GDR the socialist German nation is developing, a whole historical epoch ahead of the bourgeois nation in the FRG."[66] It has become apparent that in the view of the GDR leadership, the German question is to be considered closed not only with respect to international and inter-German relations, but also for the GDR population itself. For this purpose, the GDR has stressed the "socialist way of life" as a distinguishing criterion for a society and national community in the GDR different from that in West Germany. The draft program of the SED, while not directly linking this "way of life" to the emergence of a socialist nation in the GDR, clearly implies that this way of life is the substantive content of that "transformation of the nation" that is asserted to have taken place.[67]

This *Abgrenzung* between the German states was formally and symbolically strengthened by the constitutional changes of October 1974.[68] Although undertaken for various reasons, including the ongoing dilution of the Ulbricht heritage in the GDR and SED, the new national provisions are among the most striking features of the amended text. For example, the preamble, which formerly stated that the people of the GDR bore "the responsibility of showing the whole German nation a way into a future of peace and socialism," now declares that the people of the GDR have bestowed a constitution upon themselves "in continuation of the revolutionary traditions of the German working class" and in conformity with historical laws. Article 1 formerly declared the GDR to be a "socialist state of the German nation," but the GDR has now become a "socialist state of workers and peasants." A lengthy passage in Article 8, which pledged the GDR and its citizens to strive to overcome the division of the German nation by the imperialists and to further the step-by-step reconciliation of the two Germanies and their ultimate unification on the basis of democracy and socialism—all this has simply been eliminated. The new text was accompanied by an official decision to make October 7 (the GDR founding anniversary) the formal national holiday.

This emphasis on *Abgrenzung* may have evoked troubled reactions among the GDR population.[69] It certainly raised some perplexing questions as to the national identity of GDR citizens: what were the objective and external characteristics signifying the existence of a "GDR nation?" In response to this, Honecker, in his speech to the Thirteenth CC SED Plenum in December 1974, asserted that the "overwhelming majority" of GDR citizens (*Staatsbürger*) were German by nationality.[70]

A lengthy historical-ideological excursus on this question appeared in *Neues Deutschland* in February 1975.[71] The authors elaborated on Honecker's remarks that German ethnic traits had their origins in the early Middle Ages. Extending the Hager thesis of the nation as a class-determined, historically shaped phenomenon, they traced the various centripetal and centrifugal developments of German history, showing how the long and difficult process of nation building in the German lands had been shaped by political and ultimately productive factors.[72] Today, in the GDR, a social transformation from capitalism to socialism has taken place: "it is impossible to build a socialist society without simultaneously transforming the capitalist nation into a socialist nation." Gradually, the existence of socialist social forces, by changing the way of life of the population, will produce changes in the ethnic traits that we consider to be "German."

These themes have been continued and expanded in the SED program. The program's authors were careful to claim for the GDR's "socialist national culture . . . the careful cultivation and assimilation of all the humanistic and progressive cultural achievements of the past. The GDR's socialist culture is indebted to the rich legacy created throughout the entire history of the German people."[73] On the other hand, the text stresses at several points the importance of assimilation into GDR culture of internationalist, and especially Soviet (and other "socialist"), cultural goods. As we shall see, this is part of the extraordinary integration of GDR and Soviet values and policies generally.

According to the program, the "characteristic features" of the "socialist German nation . . . in the GDR" are being "formed by the working class." Although at one point the text presents the frequently employed paraphrase of Marx to the effect that in socialism the proletariat "constitutes itself" as the nation, this program qualifies this point by asserting that the proletariat, as the "leading force in socialist society . . . is at the same time heading the socialist nation." The other external markings of this socialist nation are that "it comprises the people in the territory of the GDR," has a sovereign socialist state, a socialist and developing economy, and a Marxist-Leninist ideology.

As was pointed out by the Ludz team's authors in writing the section on nationalism for the 1974 "Materials for a Report on the State of the Nation," every political elite stresses those characteristics of nationhood that consolidate its own power.[74] Thus, the SED stresses essentially the hallmarks of its own political rule as also constituting the national community of the GDR. What further measures the regime may take to operationalize these social-economic-ideological traits of nationhood remains to be seen. One may speculate that such concepts could provide the rationale for further restrictions on the import of West German cultural materials into the GDR and heavier sanctions against those GDR artists and writers who are prominently published in West Gemany. It may be noted in this connection that Honecker has interpreted the Helsinki accords to declare inadmissible the impact of West German mass media on the internal affairs of the GDR: witness the angry GDR denials of West German stories concerning price rises for Soviet goods imported by the GDR.[75]

The other side of *Abgrenzung* to the West has always been closer relations with the East, especially the USSR. This trend has become even more pronounced over the past years. For example, the draft SED program declares that the socialist nation in the GDR is "an inseparable part of the community of socialist nations," and it speaks of the "systematic convergence of the socialist nations in all fields of social life," a convergence to which is linked the flourishing of the socialist nation in the GDR. The closeness of ties to the USSR is evident also in the economic sphere. Within COMECON, the GDR is the Soviet Union's chief trading partner (23 percent in 1974) and is the second largest (after the USSR) trading partner for all other COMECON members. Moreover, GDR trade with the Soviet Union increasingly involves manufactured goods and industrially sophisticated machinery.[76]

There have been two symbolic and substantive high points to this relationship in recent years. First was the unusual, and in fact solitary, prominence accorded Brezhnev at the GDR's twenty-fifth anniversary celebrations in October 1974. One year later came the new Soviet-GDR treaty.[77] The most important passages of this pact (for this topic) are, first, the declaration in the preamble that future Soviet-GDR relations will "serve the further convergence *(Annäherung)* of the socialist nations," and that both sides pledge to take "necessary measures" to protect "the historic achievements of socialism" (i.e., the Brezhnev Doctrine). Moreover, there is a passage in Article 8 that suggests that military obligation of the GDR under this treaty (as opposed to the Warsaw Pact) will not be limited to Europe.

The closer ties to the Soviet Union may be a confession of failure in fostering GDR nationalism, akin to the "good Europeanism" of West Germans in the 1950s,[78] but it might better be seen as an attempt to give alternative substance to a "GDR nationalism" now that the oft-trumpeted "all German" mission has been relegated to a distant perspective. Following up on the measures along these lines noted above, the most recent GDR pronouncements place little weight on possible socialist revolution in West Germany. Honecker declared the prospects for West German socialism to be "a matter for the future,"[79] and Alfred Kosing has pointed out that the question of whether, should a socialist nation arise in the FRG after a revolution, a united socialist state would then be possible, can be answered neither positively nor negatively at this time. "Many things are possible about which it is fruitless to speculate." After all, and quoting Lenin, Marxism is based on the actual and not on the possible.[80]

This ambiguity about relations with the West Germans persists despite all brave pronouncements to the contrary. It is true that the movement of people across the GDR borders— both from West Germany and from West Berlin—has attained a high and constant level. There are clearly special agreements regulating a special flow of persons here—no matter how "normal" the GDR leaders would like to have relations with Bonn appear to be. At the same time, and repeatedly since 1971, there have been problems and disputes concerning travel to and from the GDR. The recent trials of persons accused of helping to arrange or carry out illegal escapes from the GDR and the controversy over the aroused West German reaction to these trials indicate how "abnormal" East–West German relations are.[81] These ties may only be a lingering reflection of the fact that over a third of the West Germans have relatives or acquaintances in the GDR and that these ties have not had time to become attenuated.[82] It may also be that not even the GDR leadership, let alone the people, "normally" contrasts GDR socioeconomic conditions with the East European countries—it is always the Federal Republic that, even in rejection and severance of ties, continues to be the "other" by contrast with which the GDR's own identity is established. This basic fact is at one and the same time the greatest obstacle to the propagation of an "official nationalism" in the GDR and an indication of the difficulty of such a program.

Notes

1. Rupert Emerson, *From Empire to Nation* (Boston: Beacon Press, 1962), pp. 95-96.

2. Karl W. Deutsch, "Nation Building and National Development: Some Issues for Political Research," in *Nation Building,* ed. Karl W. Deutsch and William J. Foltz (New York: Atherton Press, 1966), p. 3.

3. For a cogent example, see the "hypothesis" of K.H. Silvert in his "Conclusions," *Expectant Peoples,* ed. K. H. Silvert (New York: Random House, 1963), p. 441.

4. K. H. Silvert, "The Strategy of the Study of Nationalism," in Silvert, *Expectant Peoples,* pp. 25-27.

5. Daniel Bell, "National Character Revisited: A Proposal for Renegotiating the Concept," in *The Study of Personality: An Interdisciplinary Appraisal,* ed. Edward Norbeck et al. (New York: Holt, Rinehart, and Winston, 1968), pp. 118-120.

6. Gerhard L. Schweigler, "National Consciousness in a Divided Germany," (Ph. D. diss., Harvard University, 1972), p. 369.

7. Daniel Katz, Herbert C. Kelman, and Vasso Vassiliou, "A Comparative Approach to the Study of Nationalism," Papers of the Peace Research Society, no. 14, the Ann Arbor Conference, 1969, p. 1.

8. Peter C. Ludz, "Die soziologische Analyse der DDR-Gesellschaft," in *Wissenschaft und Gesellschaft in der DDR,* ed. Peter C. Ludz (Munich: Carl Hanser Verlag, 1971), p. 21.

9. Deutsch and Foltz, *Nation Building,* p. xviii.

10. Quoted from a 1966 article by P. A. Steiniger in Dietmar Kreusel, *Nation und Vaterland in der Militärpresse der DDR* (Stuttgart: Seewald, 1971), p. 90.

11. Recent GDR press accounts of North Korean policy omit mention of Pyongyang's demands for Korean unification. See Hans Lindemann, "Ost-Berlins Reisediplomatie,"

Deutschland Archiv 6, no. 6 (June 1973): 620.

12. Deutsch, "Nation Building and National Development," p. 3.

13. During 1971, 5,843 persons fled to West from the GDR, 832 of them across guarded land frontiers. See Karl-Heinz Janssen, "Statistik der Unmenschlichkeit," *Die Zeit,* 18 January 1972, p. 4; Ellen Lentz, "More East Germans Flee to West Since Berlin Accord," *New York Times,* 7 November 1971.

14. The final ratification of the Basic Treaty seems to have been a signal for a fresh wave of escape attempts and, in fact, of the emergence of high-priced specialists prepared to take advantage of the eased controls over the Berlin access routes to "contract" for refugees. See "Refugee Set-Up Stirs Germanys," *New York Times,* 9 August 1973; "East Germans Threaten Berlin Routes," *New York Times,* 11 August 1973.
Germans Threaten Berlin Routes," *New York Times,* 11 August 1973.

15. The most comprehensive survey of East German attitudes is in Schweigler, "National Consciousness in a Divided Germany," esp. pp. 156-176. See also the survey of journalists' and travelers' accounts on pp. 136ff. A recent example is Joachim Nawrocki, "Honecker tut etwas für die kleinen Leute," *Die Zeit,* 18 May 1973. See also Gebhard Schweigler, "The Development of National Consciousness in the German Democratic Republic" (Paper presented to the 1973 meetings, American Political Science Association, September 7, 1973).

16. For the emphasis on economic achievement and hurt pride in East German attitudes, see, for example, Hildegard Baumgart, ed., *Briefe aus einem anderen Land. Briefe aus der DDR.* (Hamburg: Hoffmann und Campr, 1971). The classic statement of the West German position on this matter is by Willy Brandt, *Bericht der Bundesregierung über die Lage der Nation im gespaltenen Deutschland, January 14, 1970* (Bonn: Bundesministerium für Innerdeutsche Beziehungen, 1970), p. 5.

17. Karl W. Deutsch and Richard L. Merritt, "Effects of Events on National and International Images," in *International Behavior: A Social-Psychological Analysis,* ed. Herbert C. Kelman (New York: Holt, Rinehart, and Winston, 1965),

pp. 170, 137.

18. For a summary of earlier SED policy on the national question, see Fritz Kopp, *Kurs auf ganz Deutschland?* (Stuttgart: Seewald Verlag, 1965).

19. *Programm der Sozialistischen Einheitspartei Deutschlands,* 7th ed. (Berlin: Dietz Verlag, 1971), pp. 57-59.

20. Ibid., pp. 134-136.

21. *Verfassung der Deutschen Demokratischen Republik* (Berlin: Staatsverlag der DDR, 1968), p. 13.

22. Wolfgang Bernet, "Antikommunismus in westdeutschen Publikationen über der Verfassung der DDR," *Staat und Recht* 20 no. 12 (1971): 1908.

23. See for example, Stoph's speech on the twenty-first anniversary of the GDR in October 1970, wherein he declared that "in view of the contradictions between the [two countries'] state and social systems, there takes place unavoidably an objective process of withdrawal *(Abgrenzung)* rather than of assimilation *(Annäherung).*" *Neues Deutschland,* 7 October 1970, p. 3.

24. *Neues Deutschland,* 16 June 1971, p. 4. See also Marlies Jansen, "Deutschlandpolitik und VIII. Parteitag," *Deutschland Archiv* 4, no. 8 (August 1971): 805-815.

25. "Der Sozialismus gewann an Starke—der Frieden ist sicherer geworden," *Neues Deutschland,* 7 January 1972, p. 3.

26. Erich Honecker, "Zügig voran bei der weiteren Verwirklichung der Beschlüsse des VIII. Parteitages der SED," *Neues Deutschland,* 29 May 1973.

27. Thus Honecker in his speech to the FDGB (trade union) congress, *Neues Deutschland,* 28 June 1972. See also Honecker's interview with *Neues Deutschland* on foreign policy questions (7 June 1972). In his interview with C. S. Sulzberger of the *New York Times (Neues Deutschland,* 25 November 1973), Honecker, as in his speech at Sofia the previous spring, once again used the Brandt-Wehner expression *Nebeneinander,* to describe useful, if cool, relations.

28. Hermann Axen, "Zwei Staaten—Zwei Nationen," in *Horizont,* 1973, no. 12, cited in *Deutschland Archiv* 6, no. 4 (April 1973): 414-416.

29. Honecker, "Zügig voran"; see Friedrich Ebert, "Frieden

erhalten ist Inhalt unseres Kampfes," *Neues Deutschland,* 14 January 1973, wherein Ebert denies future possibilities of *peaceful* changes in GDR-FRG borders.

30. Horst Luther and Rolf Schonefeld, "Sozialistische Rechtsentwicklung der DDR im Zerrspiegel Bonner Ostforschung," *Staat und Recht* 20, no. 12 (1971) 1897-1898.

31. Domestic service of 20 January 1972, as cited in Foreign Broadcast Information Service, *Daily Report,* 2, 15 (21 January 1972), E1-2.

32. Norden speech from Voice of the GDR domestic service in German, 19 March 1973, in FBIS *Daily Report: Eastern Europe* 2, 54 (20 March 1973), E10; the commentary, ibid., E11.

33. Kurt Hager, "Die entwickelte sozialistische Gesellschaft (Aufgaben der Gesellschaftswissenschaften nach dem VIII. Parteitag der SED)," *Einheit* 26, no. 11, (1971): 1203-1242, esp. 1228-1231.

34. Ibid., p. 1230.

35. Helmut Meier, "Geschichtsbewusstsein in der Systemauseinandersetzung," in *Geschichtsebewusstsein und sozialistische Gesellschaft,* ed. Helmut Meier and Walter Schmidt (Berlin: Dietz Verlag, 1970), p. 69.

36. Axen, "Zwei Staaten"; Honecker in speech to FDGB, ibid.

37. Axen, "Zwei Staaten."

38. *Neues Deutschland,* 20 March 1973.

39. "Albert Norden zum Begriff Nation," *Deutschland Archiv* 5, no. 11 (November 1972): 1223-1224. Norden was speaking to SED cadre classes.

40. See the issues of 4 and 5 January 1972, p. 2.

41. Manfred Naumann, "Das Erbe und die sozialistische *Kultur,"* *Einheit* 26, no. 3 (1971):306.

42. Alexander Abusch, "Kunst, Kultur und Lebensweise in unserem sozialistischen deutschen Nationalstatt (Gedanken uber die Kulturdiskussion zum VIII. Parteitag)," *Einheit* 26, no. 6 (1971): 730.

43. Manfred Feist, "Autorität der DDR wächst trots imperialistischer Manöver," *Einheit* 26 no. 9 (1971): 1000, is enraged over a proposal to have GDR-FRG cultural centers abroad support one another's work. See also the works cited in

the two preceding notes.

44. Peter C. Ludz, "Zum Begriff der 'Nation' in der Sicht der SED-Wandlungen und politische Bedeutung," *Deutschland Archiv* 5, no. 1 (January 1972): 26.

45. Axen, "Zwei Staaten."

46. "Albert Norden zum Begriff der Nation."

47. Honecker, "Zügig voran."

48. Abusch, "Kunst, Kultur und Lebensweise," p. 731.

49. "Inhalt entleert," *Der Spiegel,* 12 July 1971, p. 30.

50. Karl Wilhelm Fricker, "Das Ende der KPD," *Deutschland Archiv* 4, no. 11 (November 1971): 1124-1126. The longtime head of the illegal KPD, Max Reimann, has joined the DKP and become its honorary chairman.

51. In Honecker's Ninth Plenum speech, he declared that the "future will reveal how the European peoples will shape their coexistence when Western Europe, including the FRG, has entered the path toward socialism." Honecker, "Zügig voran."

52. For a typical ideological discourse on this subject by the SED's leading ideological spokesman, see Kurt Hager, "Das 'Manifest der Kommunistischen Partei' und der revolutionäre Weltprozess," *Neues Deutschland,* 16 March 1973, esp. p. 5; see also Friedrich Richter and Vera Wrona, "Ideologie des Sozialdemokratismus in der Gegenwart," *Einheit* 27, no. 2 (February 1972): 221-227; and Heinz Timmerman, "Was wollen die West-Kommunisten?" *Deutschland Archiv* 6, no. 6 (June 1973): 609-615.

53. Ekkehart Liebermann, "Systemtragende Parteien und politisches Herrschaftssystem in der BRD-Widersprüche und aktuelle Tendenzen," *Staat und Recht* 22, no. 4 (March 1973): 583-601.

54. For this topic, see, in part, Honecker's report to the SED Eighth Congress, *Neues Deutschland,* 16 June 1971, pp. 3-5; Kurt Seliger, "Das obligatorische Sowjetmodell," *Deutschland Archiv* 4, no, 10 (October 1971): 1068-1070; Hans-Dietrich Sander, "Das Ende der Ära Ulbricht," *Deutschland Archiv* 4, no. 12 (December 1971): 1240-1244; Hager, "Das 'Manifest,'" passim; Ilse Spittmann, "Die 9. Tagung . . . ," *Deutschland Archiv* 6, no. 6 (June 1973): 567-568.

55. Ilse Spittmann, "Honecker und die nationale Frage," *Deutschland Archiv* 5, no. 1 (January 1972): 1-2. A leading GDR social science establishment, the Deutsche Akademie der Staats- und Rechtswissenschaft "Walter Ulbricht" lost both the opening adjective and closing name—thus being subjected to *Abgrenzung* and "de-Ulbrichtization" in one operation.

56. Richard Merritt has written that "it nonetheless seems reasonable to expect that these varying images [of Germany in history textbooks] are contributing their bit to a growing psychic distance between East and West . . . Germans." Richard L. Merritt, "Perspectives on History in Divided Germany," in *Public Opinion and Historians: Interdisciplinary Perspectives,* ed. Melvin Small (Detroit: Wayne State University Press, 1970), p. 174. In a survey of GDR civics texts, Horst Müller found them to nurture the conviction that the GDR is an essentially separate and superior German state. See Horst Müller, "Die Entwicklung Deutschlands seit 1945 in den Schulbüchern der DDR," in Ludz, *Wissenschaft und Gesellschaft,* pp. 285-314.

57. The text of the law may be found in *Deutschland Archiv* 5, no. 11 (November 1972): 1221; the figures are in ibid, p. 1140.

58. Kurt Sontheimer, "Der Wille zur Einheit," *Die Zeit,* 24 October 1972.

59. Ernst Richert, *Die DDR-Elite oder unsere Partner von Morgen?* (Hamburg: Rowohlt, 1968), p. 10, writes of an "unprejudiced, untraumatized younger generation [which] . . . has no memories of an all-German past."

60. See Arthur M. Hanhardt, Jr., "Political Socialization in the German Democratic Republic," *Societas* 1, no. 2 (Spring 1971): 101-121.

61. According to official GDR figures *(Neues Deutschland,* 25 July 1973), over 4 million persons from the FRG and West Berlin visited the GDR in the first seven months of the year; of this total, almost half were from West Berlin itself. During these same months, slightly more than 800,000 GDR citizens traveled westward, roughly 500,000 to the Federal Republic and the remainder to West Berlin. It should be remembered that when the Basic Treaty comes into force, inhabitants of selected border districts along both sides of the GDR-FRG

frontier will be able to make day-visits across the border.

62. For a discussion of recent economic difficulties, see Hans-Dieter Schulz, "Neues NÖSPL nötig," *Deutschland Archiv* 5, no.11 (November 1972): 1134-1137.

63. The quotation is from Willy Brandt's speech accepting the Nobel Peace Prize, 11 December 1971. See Willy Brandt, *Peace* (Bonn-Godesburg: Verlag Neue Gesellschaft, 1971), p. 142.

64. Dettmar Cramer has speculated that this uncertainty helps to account for the regime's fondness for conducting its own opinion surveys. See Dettmar Cramer, *Deutschland nach dem Grundvertrag* (Bonn: Verlag Bonn Aktuell, 1973), p. 49.

65. Horst Lambrecht, "Aussenhandel der DDR 1974," *Deutschland Archiv* 8, no.8 (August 1974): 852-855; Hans-Dieter Schulz, "Zu schön um wahr zu sein," ibid, pp. 826-837; idem "Bremsen für den Konsum. Haupttendenzen des neuen Fünfjahresplan," ibid. 8, no.11 (November 1975): 900-903.

66. Oskar Fischer, "Festes Fundament für die Gegenwart und die Zukunft," *Neues Deutschland,* 6/7 December 1975, p. 3.

67. All citations from and references to the draft program in this essay are based on the translation published in FBIS *Daily Report: Eastern Europe,* 2, 15 (22 January 1976), E1-E36. See also Joachim Nawrocki, "Honecker streicht Ulbrichts Utopien," *Die Zeit,* 30 January 1976, p. 4.

68. The constitutional changes are in *Neues Deutschland,* 28 September 1974, p. 2. A useful synoptic presentation of the old and new texts is in *Deutschland Archiv* 7, no. 11 (November 1974): 1188-1224.

69. The authoritative article cited in note 8 speaks of "frequent misunderstandings arising specifically from the confusion of nation and nationality." I take this to be a cautious reference to possibly widespread doubt and disagreement as to the direction of *Abgrenzung*.

70. *Neues Deutschland,* 13 December 1974, p. 4.

71. Alfred Kosing and Walter Schmidt, "Nation und Nationalität in der DDR," *Neues Deutschland,* 15/16 February 1975, p. 10.

72. For example, the authors compare the separation of the German-Swiss and Dutch peoples from the common German stock and contrast the continuity of the German language in Switzerland to the rise of a separate Dutch vernacular in the Netherlands.

73. Apparently, selective use can be made of other strands of the German past. Thus the army pocket calendar marks the birth and death dates of Scharnhorst, Gneisenau, and Stein, as well as the Battle of the Nations (Leipzig, 1813). *NVA-Kalender 1976* (Berlin: Militär-Verlag der DDR, 1975).

74. *Nation: Aus den Materialien zum Bericht zur Lage der Nation 1974* (Bonn: Bundes-Ministerium für innerdeutsche Beziehungen, 1975), p. 75.

75. "Helsinke und wir (Interview . . . mit Erich Honecker . . .)," *Neues Deutschland,* 6 August 1975, p. 3. For the role of Western media in raising unwarranted economic expectations, see Werner Lamberz, "Ideologische Arbeit für das Feld der Wirtschaft," *Einheit* 30, no. 8 (August 1975): 826-837.

76. See Honecker's report to the fifteenth CC SED Plenum in *Neues Deutschland,* 4/5 October 1975, pp. 3-5.

77. The text of the USSR-GDR Treaty is in *Neues Deutschland,* 8 October 1975, p. 1.

78. Ilse Spittmann, "Das 15. ZK-Plenum und der neue Vertrag mit Moskau," *Deutschland Archiv* 8, no. 11 (November 1975): 1124.

79. In *Neues Deutschland,* 13 December 1974, p. 4.

80. Alfred Kosing's article in the February 1975 issue of *Deutsche Zeitschrift für Philosophie,* quoted in Ulrich Neuhäuser-Wespy, "Nation neuen Typs," *Deutsche Studien* 13, no. 52, (December 1975): 336. See also ibid., p. 360.

81. See the statement of the Bonn government's spokesman, Klaus Boelling, as reported in *Relay from Bonn* 7, no. 11 (January 27, 1976): 1.

82. *Nation, Aus den Materialien,* p. 77.

6. Intellectuals and System Change

M. Donald Hancock

With the declared transition to an advanced socialist society at the Seventh Party Congress of the Socialist Unity Party (SED) in 1967, the German Democratic Republic embarked on an uncharted future. From 1945 through most of the sixties, East German leaders could draw on the Soviet models of "system building" and "system management"[1] in implementing successive stages of socialist transformation. In contrast, the SED's present goal to achieve developed socialism raises "new theoretical questions"[2] that underscore the indeterminateness of future system change in the GDR.

Assuming increased functional importance in the unfolding of advanced socialist society is the East German *Intelligenz*—who are authoritatively defined as members of "a social group" who "professionally engage primarily in mental labor and as a rule possess an advanced education."[3] Among such persons, those who come closest to approximating the ideal Western intellectual norm of "sensitive, inquiring, curious, creative minds"[4] are the GDR's scientific, cultural, and to a lesser extent, technical elites. Official recognition of their socioeconomic and political significance dates from early postwar initiatives by the SED to promote a "comprehensive democratic renewal of science and higher education."[5] By "cleansing" and reforming the educational system in the former Soviet zone of occupation, communist leaders sought the recruitment of an ideologically conscious intelligentsia whose task was to serve "the people" rather than "the Junkers and imperialists" of previous regimes.[6] This objective was ostensibly achieved by the mid-1960s, when Walter Ulbricht declared that "the scientist, the artist, the technician, and the engineer are now firmly integrated within the working-class community."[7]

Contemporary efforts to attain advanced socialism in the GDR confront the nation's intelligentsia with a series of contradictory expectations that raise fundamental questions about future socialist society. In the absence of an adequate theory of advanced socialist change, party leaders have called on intellectuals to intensify their efforts to explore "the qualitatively new manifestations of social development."[8] In addition to more general sociopolitical functions, the SED has assigned natural and social scientists the specific tasks of undertaking technical and theoretical innovations to achieve sustained improvements in both the level and quality of material production, and formulating long-range socioeconomic forecasts that can serve as a basis for implementing rational system transformation. The objective of such studies, as one of their practitioners has declared, is "to comprehend, plan, and achieve according to plan the necessary and possible development of the social system of socialism . . . in all its dimensions."[9] Writers and artists, meanwhile, are urged to contribute to the further development of "socialist consciousness" and a "high level of education and culture"[10] by creatively communicating the "contemporary reality, problems, feelings, and thoughts" of the working masses.[11]

In executing these assignments, East German intellectuals have experienced anew the tension between state authority and the autonomous imperatives of science and the humanities, a tension that has characterized the progress of civilization throughout modern times. At issue is not the ideological conflict between the SED leadership and representatives of the traditional (bourgeois) German intelligentsia that characterized the initial decade of the GDR's consolidation. This conflict largely resolved itself through the emigration of dissident intellectuals to the Federal Republic of Germany and the physical closure of the East German regime in August 1961.

Instead, the demands, proposed reforms, and literary contributions of the new socialist intelligentsia reveal a continuing struggle to redefine politics and culture in terms of the prevailing Marxist-Leninist belief system.

To the extent that intellectuals are assuming an increasingly active role in determining guidelines for planned system change in the GDR, the question inevitably arises of whether a new meritocracy—basing its knowledge and vision of the future on the principles of scientific Marxism—can assert itself vis-à-vis SED policy architects. Given the conscious articulation of the *scientific* premises of Marxism-Leninism, is the GDR (as well as other advanced socialist states) more likely than Western pluralist democracies to regard intellectual institutions and organized knowledge as the paramount source of social innovation—a trend that Daniel Bell and others have defined as the central feature of postindustrial society?[12]

In attempting tentative answers to these questions, I shall explore the political status of East German intellectuals and their participatory-creative-functions as coalition partners of the SED. The chapter begins with an assessment of the GDR's transition to advanced socialism and concludes with an overview of the limits of intellectual conformity. My major concern is with the role of social and natural scientists as those members of the GDR intelligentsia most relevant to policy making, although I include references to cultural intellectuals where appropriate.

Transition to Advanced Socialism

When delegates to the SED's Seventh Party Congress in 1967 applauded Ulbricht's central address on "the formation of the advanced social system of socialism,"[13] they affirmed an historic milestone in East Germany's continuing development. Active system change had been initiated in accordance with the Marxist-Leninist model of centralized socialism during the initial postwar phase of antifascist-democratic reform and had yielded throughout the 1950s and 1960s both quantitative and qualitative increments in the capacity of national leaders to implement policies efficiently and to manage an increasingly complex industrial economy. Successive party congresses

defined these stages of socialist modernization as the "creation
of the foundations of socialism" (1951-1957), the "expansion of
the economic basis and institutionalization of socialist relations of production" (1958-1962), and after 1963 the "comprehensive construction of socialism." The latter period was
divided in turn into two phases: the "new economic system of
planning and management" (1963-1967), and after 1967, a
second stage of the new economic system of planning and
management.

Looking beyond existing economic, social, and political
relations in the GDR, Ulbricht outlined at the Seventh Party
Congress three principal objectives of active change under
advanced socialism:[14]

1. further progress toward socialist democracy, which Ulbricht defined as the "growing and increasingly effective
   participation of workers" at their place of employment
   (including such forums as production committees)
2. the "permeation of all spheres of social life by socialist
   ideology"
3. "the continued improvement of the working and living
   conditions of the citizens"

Progress toward attaining these goals was possible, Ulbricht
claimed, because of the victory of socialist relations of production on the East German republic. "Now the objective economic laws of socialism can be fully ... implemented," he declared.
"Now, for the first time, the science of the political economy of
socialism and the other economic sciences can [be used to]
analyze *the reality* of advanced socialist relations of production and to draw the necessary conclusions indicating the next
steps into the future."[15] With a rhetorical flourish of the sort
that some Western observers claim helped cost him his position
as first secretary of the SED four years later,[16] Ulbricht
described that future in terms of a "GDR model" of an
"advanced socialist industrial state that in fraternal cooperation with the Soviet Union and the other allied socialist
countries will achieve the socialist community of man and
master the scientific-technical revolution."[17]

Lacking in both Ulbricht's pronouncements and those of leading SED theorists under Erich Honecker's subsequent tutelage, however, is a concrete definition of the advanced socialist industrial state. For example, Kurt Hager—Politburo member in charge of culture in the GDR—has equated "advanced socialist society" with such labels as "the comprehensive construction of socialism," "the advanced social system of socialism," and "mature or developed socialism."[18] In terms of system change, Hager has characterized the transition to advanced socialism as the balanced development "of all areas of social life . . . in correct proportion to each other."[19] But, like Ulbricht's catalog of general objectives, Hager's statement of future priorities remains substantively vague: "the further development of socialist democracy, a well-functioning system of public assistance for the workers, and a high cultural level at places of work."[20]

Such vagueness reveals the absence of a concrete SED image of the future. Largely for want of an authoritative Marxist-Leninist blueprint of communist society, either in terms of classical Marxist ideology or a Soviet precedent, East German leaders have been reticent to articulate a coherent theory of the advanced socialist state or system change under advanced socialism. For political reasons they cannot outdistance their Soviet colleagues in ideological innovations, even if they might have cause to do so in light of the GDR's economic and social achievements. Moreover, consistent with the orthodox Marxist insistence on the scientific principles of socialism, SED ideologues deliberately eschew abstract utopian thought. At most they can conceptualize the advanced socialist system, as Honecker did at the Eighth Party Congress in 1971, as a nebulous threshold to ultimate communism: "on the basis of the development of socialist means of production and their material-technical foundation, socialist society is evolving gradually into communism."[21]

Yet GDR leaders simultaneously need pragmatic guidelines for policy decisions and implementation. Committed as they are to a conscious program of active system change, they are compelled to contemplate the country's intermediate future. Comprehensive economic plans, as they are regularly formulated and implemented in the GDR, necessitate a theoretical sense of what is desirable and attainable, criteria of efficiency, and projections of system performance. In short, planning the future requires expertise, just as parallel efforts to develop socialist values demand the collaboration of teachers, writers, and artists. And therein lies the sociopolitical significance of the GDR's creative intelligentsia—as innovators of system change and guardians of ideological consciousness.

The Sociopolitical Roles of the GDR Intelligentsia

The innovative-educational functions of the East German intelligentsia derive from both the high status accorded intellectuals by Marxist ideologues and the imperatives of the SED's coordinated strategy of socialist transformation. In the first instance, orthodox Marxists have traditionally celebrated intellectuals—even apart from their knowledge and creativity—because of their historical contributions to the development of Marxist-Leninist tenets and socialist consciousness among the masses. As the successor organization to the Communist Party of Germany (KPD) of the Weimar Republic and the years of exile during the Third Reich, the SED can claim with national pride direct ideological lineage not only from the original authors of classical Marxism but also from such early radical socialists as August Bebel, Rosa Luxemburg, and Karl Liebknecht. In the second case, Ulbricht and his party cohorts deliberately cultivated from 1945 onward the recruitment of a reliable cadre of intellectuals—in science and industry, academics, and the arts—as a necessary support for system survival and growth. The successive stages of economic and sociopolitical development have further enhanced the functional importance of the new socialist intelligentsia.

The SED has assigned four central tasks to the nation's intellectuals, tasks that in combination with the representative, advisory, and creative roles they perform within state and society define their principal leverage on processes of system change. The first of these is the party's general *ideological* exhortation to cultural elites, social scientists, and philosophers to share in the further development of "the social consciousness of all workers and [the attainment] of a high level of education and culture corresponding to the demands of socialist society."[22] To this general ideological-cultural mission, GDR leaders add the more specific assignment of *educating management cadres*—who are defined as "persons who on the basis of their political and expert knowledge and talents are qualified and directed to lead other people in attaining assigned tasks."[23] In accordance with the objectives of advanced socialism endorsed at the Seventh Party Congress, such functional or technical experts are expected in turn to help provide "exact scientific leadership of all social processes."[24]

The scientific-technological revolution imposes the third and most concrete requirement on East German intellectuals, particularly natural scientists and technical innovators, namely, the *direct translation of scientific knowledge into material production*. This function accrues from the elevation of science as a "direct productive resource" with the attainment of advanced industrial society. By this, regime spokesmen mean that the diffusion of scientific standards and methods throughout all areas of production has signaled a synthesis of science and production:[25]

> Through its rapid pace of development, science is [now] in the position to create a scientific sequence of production. Thus science changes from a potential to a direct productive force. This process occurs in two ways: first, science becomes objectivized in new means and kinds of production as well as in modern technology; second, the qualifications of the producers are steadily improved, and their employees become increasingly imbued with scientific knowledge.

The emergence of science as a direct productive resource requires of scientific and technical leaders, Ulbricht declared at the Seventh Party Congress, "the unity of basic and applied research and the mastery of the most modern technological processes for the application of scientific knowledge in production."[26]

Fourth, and closely related to the mastery of the scientific-technological revolution, is the SED's assignment for intellectuals to engage in *intermediate and long-range forecasts of system change*. Even before the Seventh Congress, party leaders had directed social scientists and philosophers to help "develop the scientific foundations of a *total prognosis* of the developed social system of socialism in the GDR."[27] After 1967 such efforts were intensified, with the Research Council of the GDR—a group of approximately 120 scientists who advise the Ministry of Science and Technology on basic scientific, technological, and economic questions—assuming the leading role as institutionalized coordinator for socioeconomic forecasting within the East German scientific community. The Research Council has declared that its most important task is "to formulate from forecasts of developmental tendencies in science and technology comprehensive long-term objectives as well as tasks that can be immediately realized, in order that the forecasts can fruitfully serve—through the use of modern data techniques—important economic decisions."[28]

As the council's assertion indicates, the principal purpose of prognostic activities is thus to provide a direct policy aid for party and administrative officials in planning the future. "It is not the actual task of a forecast to predict what *will be* in the future,"a spokesman for the Research Council has emphasized, "but rather what *can* be, in order to conclude what *should* be. In this support for making decisions for the conscious shaping of the future lies the central value of a forecast."[29] In executing these multiple ideological, educational, productive, and forecasting functions, members of the intelligentsia have diverse means at their disposal to influence policy and economic decisions (and hence the evolving pattern of system change) as well as the public consciousness. The most pro forma channel is the proportional allocation of seats to intellectuals on both national and local levels of government. Between 1960 and 1971, the official number of intellectuals among the 400 members of the Volkskammer increased from 36 (9 percent) to 101 (20.2 percent). Among 2,840 delegates serving in the GDR's fifteen regional assemblies in 1971, nearly two-thirds (1,676) claimed a completed university or advanced vocational education.[30] More important than symbolic representation, of course, is the access natural and social scientists and technical elites enjoy to executive decision bodies at the apex of the party and state administrative structures. Prominent social scientists and philosophers serve the SED directly through the various sections and institutes of the party's Central Committee— among them Otto Reinhold, head of the Institute for the Social Sciences; Günter Heyden, director of the Institute for Marxism-Leninism; and Hanna Wolf, head of the Party Academy "Karl Marx." The advisory role of their natural science colleagues on the Research Council of the GDR has already been cited. Lesser academic figures play an indirect advisory role on budgetary, research, and other matters as members of specialized councils organized within the various disciplines. Examples include the Council for Historical Sciences and the Scientific Council for Philosophical Research.[31]

In the sphere of material production, natural scientists and technical experts have joined forces with industrial managers to establish a number of "industrial combinations" that integrate in a single industrial enterprise research activities, technical preparations for production, and production itself.[32] An immediate result of these and other efforts to "objectivize" science in industry, Honecker reported to the Central Committee in 1973, was the translation of 6,000 inventions and technical improvements into finished production since 1971 alone.[33]

Finally, educational and cultural elites command substantial resources to implement their assigned objectives. State expenditures for higher education rose from 1,453,454 Marks in 1961 to 2,145,748 in 1970, accommodating an increase in the number of university students from 112,926 to 138,666.[34] Educational facilities will continue to receive priority funding in years ahead as university personnel strive to meet the SED goal of expanding by over 250 percent the number of industrial personnel with advanced scientific-technological training by the 1980s.[35] Government subsidies to cultural activities— including the performing arts as well as radio and television— predictably comprise a less substantial share of the annual budget than funds for education but nevertheless permit standards of excellence that even casual visitors to East Berlin can readily appreciate.[36]

But what is the system effect of the multiple tasks performed by East Germany's scientific and cultural leaders? What are their images of the future, and can the latter serve as autonomous guidelines for the further development of mature socialism? Does the intelligentsia potentially comprise a scientific-managerial meritocracy that could seriously challenge the present ideological ascendancy of the SED? Answers to these questions must be sought in the tension between official system norms and the behavior of East German intellectuals. Characterizing this relation are mutual constraints—of ideological partisanship and political power on the one hand and functional dependence on the other.

Constraints of Partisanship and Power

As in all spheres of socioeconomic life, intellectual activity is subject to the imperative of doctrinal loyalty. In essence this means affirmation of the ideological tenets of orthodox Marxism-Leninism as they have been authoritatively defined and implemented by Soviet leaders, the SED, and other nonrevisionist parties within the socialist international community. Such tenets, or basic metatheoretical assumptions about man and his universe, include belief in the primacy of material factors (including modes of production and property-class relations) in determining consciousness, social structures, and the course of history; the unity of theory and action in the progressive attainment of socialism; the legitimacy of the Communist party's claim to leadership as the organized "vanguard of the proletariat"; and the moral perfectibility of socialist man.

In all facets of intellectual activity, these tenets impose explicit demands of partisanship *(Parteilichkeit),* which is defined as political consciousness or "insight into political relations [and] the advocacy of progressive social values."[37] Consistent with the underlying assumptions of Marxism-Leninism, such advocacy is equated with both the objective class interests of the proletariat and scientific objectivity. As an orthodox spokesman for proletarian partisanship has succinctly claimed:[38]

Dialectical materialism is the world-view of socialism—the first social order in the history of mankind that has been erected on scientific foundation. Under socialism there can be no contradiction between science and class interests, since the ruling class is the working class, which represents the interests of the entire society. For the first time science under socialism can develop fully and freely. Under socialism the essence of science—its humanistic impulse—encounters no restrictive class interests and ideologies.

Thus science and proletarian partisanship are considered a "dialectical unity" fused by the subjective certainty that what Heyden calls the "political truth" of Marxist-Leninist epistemology is objectively and morally binding on the intellectual community. For GDR intellectuals, in short, proletarian partisanship—in alleged contrast to bourgeois partisanship[39]—rests on explicit consciousness of "for whom and in whose interests [scientific knowledge] is utilized."[40]

To insure that such insights are in fact binding in all facets of scientific and cultural activity, the SED maintains authoritative ideological standards through a conscious alliance policy *(Bündnispolitik)* with the nation's intelligentsia. Far from being a classless society (which will occur only with the transition from mature socialism to communism), the GDR, in the eyes of its ideological-political leadership, is composed of two distinct classes—the workers and the peasants—and "other social strata." Among the latter is the intelligentsia. While some intellectuals may be considered workers, not all workers are intellectuals—hence the sociopolitical distinction between workers as a class and intellectuals as a social group.

During his final years as first secretary of the SED, Ulbricht had been inclined to minimize such differences. Citing the growing unity of the populace, Ulbricht described the working class as encompassing "no longer principally those who are physically engaged in the productive process" but increasingly persons involved in both "physical and mental activity. . . . The decisive characteristic [of this developmental tendency] is that the percentage of mental labor—embracing productive-mental activity in the economy as well as participation in the leadership of the state and society—is rapidly increasing."[41] Since Ulbricht's fall, however, party spokesmen have adopted a less sanguine position. In his assessment of the role of social scientists in an advanced socialist society, for instance, Hager emphasizes the contrasting relation of workers and intellectuals to the productive process:[42]

> The working class is the best organized class and is more closely bound to social property [than other strata]. Through its physical and mental labor in industry, construction, transportation, mail service, communications, agriculture, and other areas, [the working class] creates the largest share of material values. [In contrast] the intelligentsia is structurally heterogeneous. It includes workers with university and vocational training as well as members who are employed in spheres relatively far removed from major production.

As long as these class-group differences are claimed to exist, the SED will maintain its so-called alliance policy with other social groups, whereby the organized working class joins "in the first instance with the working peasantry, then with the intelligentsia, and then with other workers"[43] to maintain its political hegemony. Accordingly, the constraint of proletarian partisanship is reinforced by the constraint of political subordination in defining formal limits to intellectual innovation.

Yet within the strictures of official norms and established authority relations, the intelligentsia is by no means powerless, for the capacity of party leaders to plan realistic production goals and fulfill their domestic and international economic obligations is dependent to a large degree on the qualitative success with which the nation's intellectuals discharge their overlapping ideological, educational, scientific-technological, and forecasting tasks. That "socialism needs science to triumph"[44] imposes functional constraints on leadership choices, and those constraints afford the intellectual community a discernible, if marginal, autonomy of independent action. The advocates of system reform and creative ideological consciousness have been able to utilize this margin to state their case for alternative visions of change under advanced socialism.

The Limits of Conformity

If proletarian partisanship excludes competing ideological paradigms of authority relations and patterns of system change, its emphasis on advocacy and "progressive social values" simultaneously opens vistas of innovative and hence nonconformist intellectual thought within the prevailing belief system of Marxism-Leninism. The SED explicitly recognizes this potential, even if party leaders have proved intolerant in their response to some of its consequences. As the party program proclaims, "In scientific work in all areas, comradely, open, and fundamental discussion of all controversial issues is the prerequisite for recognizing objective truth." Similarly, Hager exhorts intellectuals to engage in open discussions over differences of opinion as an "indispensable element of scientific knowledge."[45] He continues:[46]

We do not progress if certain research results and publications are viewed a priori as taboo or it becomes customary not to discuss certain publications. That would mean suffocating the scientific dialogue. We fully defend the unity and purity of Marxism-Leninism, but that does not mean that no discussion can or should occur about various open questions.

Given this mandate, as it were, scientists and writers have proceeded to stake intellectual claims outside the prevailing orthodoxy of established party doctrines. They are not representative of the East German intellectual community as a whole, most of whose members perform their professional functions with inconspicuous loyalty, but their visibility in the indigenous scientific-cultural debate and foreign commentaries assures them an importance beyond their limited numbers. Among them are alleged revisionists and some cyberneticists as well as subtle critics (such as the dramatist Ulrich Plenzdorf) and imaginative social forecasters. Each category embodies a different image of East German reality and prescriptions for the future and may be briefly characterized as follows.

Most removed in time and potential effect on future system change are the "traditional" revisionists, who in retrospect can be considered East Germany's most distinct counter intellectual elite. In contrast to dissident bourgeois intellectuals, most of whom emigrated to West Germany or abroad, the so-called revisionists sought during the early to mid-1950s to formulate alternative strategies of *socialist* transformation. They included independent-minded humanist academics such as the philosopher Ernst Bloch and followers of the Hungarian Marxist, Georg Lukäcs, as well as activist partisans of a "humanistic renewal movement" within the SED itself (known as the "Harich-Gruppe").[47] A third subcategory encompassed Robert Havemann and other natural scientists who attempted unsuccessfully during the "physicists' strife" of 1953-1956 to gain SED endorsement of their theses that Marxism-Leninism could be reconciled with the experimental methods and conditional truths associated with modern positivism.

More recently, a second group of intellectual nonconformists has emerged, a group whose vision of socialism differs less in philosophical principle from that of the SED than in the advocacy of explicit means to sustain further progress toward advanced socialist society. They include academics and technical-industrial leaders who propagate in both theory and practice greater subsystem autonomy and more rational criteria of material production. To the first category belong cyberneticists such as Georg Klaus and Uwe-Jens Heuer.[48] Taking his cue from party recognition in the late 1950s of the importance of computer technology and cybernetic concepts for rationalizing planning mechanisms and public administration, Klaus proceeded in a series of articles and books published in the 1960s to spell out the philosophical implications of cybernetics under mature socialism. On a descriptive-analytical level he has attempted to restate Marxist-Leninist categories in "more precise mathematical-logical principles,"[49] and in policy terms he has advocated the self-regulation of economic processes and social-administrative subsystems. Klaus's advocacy of a successive reduction in the power of the centralized party and state apparatus has been elaborated by his social scientist colleague, Heuer, who has formulated a comprehensive blueprint of subsystem autonomy in the GDR. In propagating a vision of socialist democracy as an "open society," Heuer has emphasized the importance of participatory citizen rights:[50]

> Belonging necessarily to the organization of the socialist social system are relative self-regulation and the self-organization of subsystems. Self-organization in the social area means, in the final analysis, making one's own decisions. This right of decisions concerning one's own affairs, whether individually or collectively exercised, is a necessary condition for the development of the socialist personality.

Intellectual images of autonomous economic and administrative units are mirrored in the reality of the structural-managerial transformation that has accompanied the implementation of the new economic system of planning since 1963. As in the other advanced socialist industrial societies, the introduction of the performance criterion as the central measure of economic productivity has encouraged the diffusion of ideal norms of pragmatism and efficiency among the nation's managerial-technical intelligentsia. Aggressively promoted by what Ludz terms the "new elite social group"[51] of top managers in the day-to-day operation of the economy as well as longer-term plans for development, such norms point toward the institutionalization of a socialist rational-legal order that would significantly undercut the present authority of ideological generalists within the SED.

Criticism of both SED orthodoxy and mindless materialism is a third variant of intellectual nonconformity exemplified by the writing of Plenzdord, Volker Braun, and various other contemporary East German authors. Apparently speaking to the emotional needs of many citizens (measured by the public response to their works), Plenzdorf and Braun have depicted characters whose malaise in the face of the relative security and affluence of advance socialism represents critical reflection on the existing system but provides no explicit image of a more desirable future. The central figures in Plenzdorf's suggestive novel and screenplay, *Die neuen Leiden des jungen W.,* and Braun's *Die Kipper* are both outsiders, unable (or unwilling) to integrate themselves into present-day society. As a result the first dies recklessly, and the second revolts, each affirming in his nonconforming lifestyle an individualism that contemporary regime norms cannot comfortably accommodate.

In contrast to the preceding variants of counter or critical intellectual consciousness, a fourth area of nonconformity encompasses efforts by academics to fulfill the SED's assignment of system forecasting. Illustrative of such initiatives is a collection of eight essays on socialist "futurology"—the product of consultations by members of the Philosophy Section of the German Academy of Sciences—under the editorship of the director of the Institute for Marxism-Leninism.[52] In this case, intellectual nonconformity is measured not by critical distance to present society but by intellectual labors at the frontier of the synthesis between Marxist theory and action.

Characterizing this preliminary attempt by East German academics to define the scope and purpose of socialist forecasting are four basic declared objectives: (1) to formulate total system forecasts rather than partial predictions of subsystem performance, (2) to provide prescriptive guidelines for the "all-around development of . . . socialist man," (3) to help clarify policy decisions on the basis of more exact substantive knowledge about international trends in science and technology and more rapid techniques to process such information, and (4) *"to devise a theory of the growth of socialist society for the completion of socialism."*[53] It is the latter point that qualifies the system forecasters as intellectual nonconformists, for aspirations to join Marxist and empirical theory reveal a struggle even by orthodox members of the new socialist intelligentsia to devise alternative images of the future. This struggle will not necessarily be limited to the conventional categories of Marxist-Leninist epistemology if GDR futurologists take seriously one of the contributors' assertions that forecasting theory "must proceed from the assumption of an infinite and dynamic world. Only in such an infinite world can many gradations exist of the possible (the probable), the accidental and the necessary, independence and commitment. Only in such a world is there freedom and reponsibility."[54]

Conclusion: A New Symbiosis?

To a considerable degree, the SED's response to intellectual nonconformity has been predictable. When party leaders have perceived intellectual concepts and behavior as potential threats to the SED's hegemony, they have resorted to various disciplinary measures. A common pattern in the early years of the republic was arrest (as with Harich and his party supporters) or the threat of arrest, which in Bloch's case prompted voluntary exile to the Federal Republic. But as the SED leadership has gained in legitimacy and confidence, it has not only chosen less blunt instruments of coercion but has become increasingly tolerant of persons displaying critical distance to the regime. Rebuked for his revisionist excesses, Heuer lost his teaching position at Humboldt University in the East German captial but was promptly appointed to a research post at the Central Institute for Social Economic Management. There, "under the watchful eye of the SED and to a certain extent isolated," Ludz observes, Heuer "can . . . still develop his own ideas further."[55] Others have been subjected only to relatively mild reprimands by party spokesmen. Hager, for instance, has rebuked the author of an article on cybernetics in a publication of the Technical University in Dresden for relegating ideology as a "subsystem" to the same level as the "material subsystem," "energy subsystem," and the "information subsystem": "Such observations may be useful for cybernetics or data analysis, but from the point of view of historical materialism and the political economy of socialism they constitute a denial of a class-conscious evaluation of socialist enterprises and their activities."[56] At the apex of the party hierarchy, Honecker has singled out Plenzdorf and (by implication) Braun for portraying "loneliness and the isolation of people in society"[57] but otherwise refrained from ordering overt action against them.

Such criticisms are wholly in harmony with the SED's injunction for intellectuals themselves to engage in "creative differences of opinion"[58] and hence cannot be interpreted as a leadership demand for unrelieved conformity. On the contrary, the SED's willingness to tolerate and thus implicitly encourage Plenzdorf and others indicates a growing respect for the intelligentsia. In a more positive sense, SED endorsement of the loyal nonconformists—the system forecasters— underscores the extent to which the GDR leadership has become actively dependent on the intellectual community (as in the mastery of the scientific-technical revolution) to help plan and implement advanced socialism.

To return to the general questions raised in the introduction to this chapter, the SED's functional dependence on the nation's intelligentsia nevertheless does not signal the rise of an intellectual meritocracy that can *displace* the party's claim to preeminence. In the first place, the East German intelligentsia is far too fragmented among specialized academic disciplines and technical skills to comprise an integrated group with a common political consciousness. Moreover, intellectuals are presumably sufficiently astute Marxists not to conceive of their relation to political authorities in dichotomous terms. Whatever tensions may exist between political elites and intellectuals, both groups are joined in a common affirmation of institutionalized socialism. Thus they comprise a leadership *community* with overlapping values, interests, and, to some extent, membership.

But if displacement is an inappropriate concept, symbiosis is not. Increased SED reliance on the technical and social counsel of intellectuals suggests that organized knowledge will become an increasingly pronounced feature of mature socialism— thereby fulfilling Bell's criterion of postindustrial society at least as much as in advanced Western nations. Given this prospect, the interesting speculative question concerning the GDR's longer-range future is whether the new symbiosis will result in the intellectualization of the Socialist Unity Party, leading in time to an historically unprecedented synthesis of power and ideas in postindustrial socialist society.

Notes

1. Alfred Meyer describes Stalinism as the "system-building" phase of communism and post-Stalinism (revisionism) as a shift toward "system management." Meyer, "Authori-

ty in Communist Political Systems," in *Political Leadership in Industrialized Societies. Studies in Comparative Analysis,* ed. Lewis J. Edinger (New York: John Wiley & Sons, 1967).

2. The phrase is from an article in *Pravda* noting that the "transition to the stage of developed socialist society is to be seen as a general problem of the socialist countries, at least within Europe, posing new theoretical questions." Quoted in Günter Heyden, ed., *Gesellschaftsprognostik. Probleme einer neuen Wissenschaft* (Berlin: VEB Deutscher Verlag der Wissenschaften, 1968), p. 147. In a similar vein, First Party Secretary Erich Honecker declared that "the theoretical activity of the party must be raised to a higher level because the development of advanced socialist society in the GDR continually raises new theoretical questions." *Protokoll der Verhandlungen des VIII. Parteitages der sozialistischen Einheitspartei Deutschlands 15. bis 19. Juni 1971* (Berlin: Dietz Verlag, 1971), 1: 110

3. Wörterbuch der marxistisch-leninistischen Soziologie (Köln and Opladen: Westdeutscher Verlag, 1969), p. 225.

4. Edward Shils, "The Intellectuals and the Powers: Some Perspectives for Comparative Analysis," *Comparative Studies in Society and History* 1, no. 1 (1958).

5. Kurt Hager, "Partei und Wissenschaft," *Einheit* 21, no. 4 (April 1966): 440.

6. Otto Grotewohl, *Im Kampf um die einzige Deutsche Demokratische Republik. Reden und Aufsätze aus den Jahren 1945-1953* (Berlin: Dietz Verlag, 1954), 1: 541.

7. Statement before the Volkskammer on 1 December 1967. Reprinted in Lothar Lippmann and Hans Dietrich Moschütz, eds., *Das System der sozialistischen Gesellschafts- und Staatsordnung in der Deutschen Demokratischen Republik. Dokumente* (Berlin: Staatsverlag der DDR, 1969), p. 91.

8. Kurt Hager, *Die entwickelte sozialistische Gesellschaft. Aufgaben der Gesellschaftswissenschaften nach dem VIII. Parteitag der SED* (Berlin: Dietz Verlag, 1972), p. 7.

9. Herbert Edeling, "Über die Möglichkeit gesamtgesellschaftlicher Prognose moderner Produktivkräfte bei der Gestaltung des entwickelten gesellschaftlichen Systems des Socialismus in der DDR," in Heyden, *Gesellschaftsprog-*

notistik, p. 9.

10. "Die Aufgaben der SED auf dem Gebiet der Ideologie, Erziehung, Bildung und Kultur," in the *Programm der Sozialistischen Einheitspartei Deutschlands.* Reprinted in *Dokumente,* p. 43.

11. Honecker, speech at the Eighth Party Congress in 1971, published in *Protokoll des VIII. Parteitages,* p. 94.

12. Daniel Bell, in his introduction to Herman Kahn and Anthony Wiener, *Toward the Year 2000* (New York: Macmillan Co., 1967), p. xxvii; as well as in his more recent *The Coming of Post-Industrial Society: A Venture in Social Forecasting* (New York: Basic Books, 1973).

13. Ulbricht's address "Zur Gestaltung des entwickelten gesellschaftlichen Systems des Sozialismus in der Deutschen Demokratischen Republik," is reprinted in *Dokumente,* pp. 277-286.

14. Ibid., p. 279.

15. Ibid., p. 280.

16. Carola Stern, for one, has maintained that Ulbricht's ambition to establish the GDR as an exemplary system of the "socialist community of man" was a principal factor leading to his apparently forced resignation as first secretary in April 1971. Stern, "Abbruch eines Denkmals," *Zeit Magazin,* June 1973, no. 27 pp. 2, 4-7, 18.

17. Ulbricht, "Die Bedeutung des Perspektivplanes 1971/1975 für die Gestaltung des gesellschaftlichen Systems des Socialismus in der Deutschen Demokratischen Republik," speech at a session of the Perspective Planning Commission of the Politburo of the Central Committee of the SED on 26 September 1968. Published in *Dokumente,* p. 320.

18. Hager, *Die entwickelte sozialistische Gesellschaft,* p. 25.

19. Ibid.

20. Ibid., pp. 26-27.

21. *Protokoll des VIII. Parteitages,* p. 110.

22. *SED Programm,* reprinted in *Dokumente,* p. 43.

23. Richard Herber and Herbert Jung, *Kaderarbeit im System sozialistischer Führungstätigkeit* (Berlin: Staatsverlag der Deutschen Demokratischen Republik, 1968), p. 11.

24. Ibid., p. 9.

25. *Sonntag,* 21 September 1969, p. 5.

26. Quoted in *Dokumente,* p. 308.

27. Heyden, *Gesellschaftsprognostik,* p. 7.

28. "Willenserklärung des Forschungsrates der Deutschen Demokratischen Republik anlässlich des 20. Jahrestages der Gründing der Deutschen Demokratischen Republik," *Neues Deutschland,* 4 October 1969, p. 6.

29. Max Steenbeck, "Forschung im Sozialismus," speech at a plenary session of the Research Council, reprinted in *Sonntag,* 21 September 1969, p. 4.

30. *Statistisches Jahrbuch der Deutschen Demokratischen Republik, 1972,* pp. 493-494.

31. Hagen, *Die entwickelte sozialistische Gesellschaft,* p. 75.

32. *Dokumente,* p. 471.

33. *Neues Deutschland,* 29 May 1973.

34. *Statistisches Jahrbuch der Deutschen Demokratischen Republik, 1971,* pp. 317, 382.

35. Peter Christian Ludz, *The German Democratic Republic from the Sixties to the Seventies: A Socio-Political Analysis* (Cambridge, Mass.: Center for International Affairs, 1970), p. 17.

36. State support for art and culture in 1970 totaled 341,834 Marks. *Statistisches Jahrbuch 1971,* p. 317.

37. Siegfried Schiemann, "Parteilichkeit und Wissenschaftlichkeit," Institut für Gesellschaftswissenschaften beim ZK der SED, *Sozialismus und Intelligenz. Erfahrungen aus der Zusammenarbeit zwischen Arbeitern und Angehörigen der Intelligenz* (Berlin: Dietz Verlag, 1960), p. 58.

38. Ibid., p. 64.

39. Lobkowicz has observed on bourgeois partisanship: "Westernintellectuals usually consider this notion of partisanship . . . false. Against the Marxist-Leninist conception of politically engaged science, [Westerners] uphold a science that seeks truth and only the truth and in no way is bound to political affirmation or a political movement. Western scholars are seldom aware how tenuous their position is and how difficult it is to defend it against the communist accusation that their ostensible objectivity is only a particular and a capricious form of bourgeois partisanship." Quoted in Wolfgang

Görlich, *Geist und Macht in der DDR* (Olten and Freiburg im Breisgau: Walter-Verlag, 1968), p. 191.

40. Schiemann, "Parteilichkeit und Wissenschaftlichkeit."

41. Ulbricht, "Die Bedeutung des Perspektivplanes 1971/1975," *Dokumente,* p. 317.

42. Hager, *Die entwickelte socialistische Gesellschaft,* p. 20.

43. Ibid., p. 22.

44. Karl-Heinz Schumeister, "Die Deutsche Demokratische Republik—Heimat der Intelligenz," *Pädagogik,* 1961, p. 784.

45. Hager, *Die entwickelte sozialistische Gesellschaft,* p. 22.

46. Ibid., p. 70.

47. For a comprehensive discussion of the humanist revisionists, see Görlitz, *Geist und Macht in der DDR,* pp. 53-56.

48. My discussion of the cyberneticists is based on Ludz, *The German Democratic Republic,* pp. 58-60; and his much more detailed *Parteielite im Wandel* (Köln and Opladen: Westdeutscher Verlag, 1968), pp. 295-322.

49. Ludz, *Parteielite,* p. 299.

50. Quoted in ibid., p. 321.

51. Ludz, *The German Democratic Republic,* p. 21.

52. Heyden, *Gesellschaftsprognostik.*

53. Edeling, in ibid., pp. 10-32. Italics added.

54. Siegfried Grundmann, "Prognose als philosophische Kategorie," in ibid., p. 46.

55. Ludz, *The German Democratic Republic,* p. 59.

56. Hager, *Die entwickelte sozialistische Gesellschaft,* p. 56.

57. Honecker, report of the Politburo at the ninth meeting of the Central Committee in May 1973.

58. Hager, *Die entwickelte sozialistische Gesellschaft,* p. 71.

7. Literature and Political Culture

Arthur M. Hanhardt, Jr.,
and Gregory P. Swint

Over the past decade and a half, several efforts have been made to assess the state of German political culture in the Federal Republic of Germany (FRG) and the German Democratic Republic (GDR). Among the most important studies made in the early 1960s, little more than fifteen years after the end of World War II, was Almond and Verba's *The Civic Culture* (1963).[1]

Almond and Verba compared the results of their survey in the FRG with the other four of their five-nation study and found a culture of "political detachment and subject competence," in which the traumatic history of Germany was mirrored. Participation tended to be formal, and knowledge and communication, passive. Moreover, "Germans tend[ed] to be satisfied with the performance of their government, but to lack a more general attachment to the system on the symbolic level."[2]

Two years later Verba's "Germany: The Remaking of a Political Culture" appeared.[3] This was a thoughtful and reflective look at the "civic culture" and other data. The characterization of "political detachment and subject competence" was no longer to be found, and the difficulties and ambiguities surrounding any effort at divining the German political culture were given their due. Along the way Verba raised three questions that we shall return to at a later point:

one question has to do with the level of democracy Germany has attained or will attain in the future, the extent to which there are diffusion of political power and guarantees of basic freedoms. Another question deals with the stability of German democracy, the extent to which the current pattern of German democratic government has a potentiality for survivial. Thus, in connection with the first question we ask how likely it is to last. There is a third question that also deserves separate consideration: if German democracy does not survive, what is the likelihood that it will be replaced by the extreme form of government created in the 1930s rather than by some more conservative and limited authoritarian system?[4]

In his conclusion, Verba finally got around to a crucial issue in any discussion of the political culture of either Germany. He said:

On the one hand the division of Germany plays a salutary role in the support of democratic attitudes by acting as an insulator against Communism within West Germany, by giving the West Germans a sense of unity, and perhaps by removing from West Germany some of the politically more authoritarian sections. On the other hand the carefully cultivated tentativeness of the present Bonn Republic may inhibit the development of a strong sense of commitment to the system. Above all, the fact that such a basic political cultural question as the identity of the nation remains unresolved introduces a great potential volatility into the German political culture. The development of German political attitudes in the past fifteen years or so would lead to a prediction of continued political commitment rather than to a prediction of a return to the radical shifts in the past from extreme detachment to extreme commitment. The reactions to the highly salient political events of recent years suggest the validity of the prediction. The Berlin wall, the Eichmann trial, and above all the affair of *Der Spiegel* have led to an increased awareness and interest in politics, but not to a radical change in the kinds of demands placed on the system. Yet, while the nation remains divided, the volatility will remain.[5]

We reproduce these long quotations because they contain ideas and observations that deserve revisitation, updating, and expansion. Events have generally supported the expectation of "continued political restraint and the gradual development of a more balanced political commitment." One is reminded of the economic crisis of the mid-1960s, the violence of radical student politics of the 1968-1973 period, an apparent resurgence of neo-Nazism in 1969, and the change of governmental control from the CDU/CSU to the SPD/FDP coalition. None of these events materially damaged the liberal democratic order in the FRG.

International developments since the publication of Verba's essay have intervened to reduce some of the tentativeness that Verba felt emanating from the unresolved identity and boundary issues. These matters were important factors in FRG-GDR politics and were much debated under the rubric of "the German question." However, the treaty between the FRG and the Soviet Union of August 1970, the Quadripartite Agreement on Berlin of September 1971, and the Treaty on the Basis of Relations Between The Federal Republic of Germany and The German Democratic Republic of December 1972—all aspects of Chancellor Brandt's *Ostpolitik*—went a long way toward diminishing uncertainties between two distinct and now rather permanent German states. Of course some ambiguities remain, but at nowhere near the level of significance they had when Verba was writing nearly eleven years ago.

It is interesting and characteristic that neither Almond nor Verba mentions East Germany. The GDR was beyond the pale, outside the limits set to their investigations of democratic systems.

Yet as the "Soviet Zone of Germany" became the so-called GDR and was eventually more or less recognized by the FRG and the United States (but not officially until 1974), more questions about the "state" of the communist East were being asked. The answers were not easily come by. Suspicious of the capitalist West and defensively secretive, the GDR until the late 1960s and early 1970s was virtually terra incognita, even among communist systems.

The turning point in Western academic concern with the GDR came with the publication of Peter C. Ludz's *Studien und Materialien zur Soziologie der DDR* in 1964. There followed a broadening flow of studies from the FRG, studies that attempted to arrive at a more objective understanding and analysis of the GDR from the perspective of a liberal-democratic order. (That this was followed by a highly critical literature from a Marxist perspective is an interesting sidelight that we mention only in passing.)

Later in the 1960s, a hearty band of *"DDRologen"* set out to find a U.S. road to the GDR. We think here of Thomas Baylis, Melvin Croan, Kenneth Hanf, Arthur Hanhardt, Henry Krisch, Lyman Legters, Anita Mallinckrodt, and Jean Edward Smith among very few others who published in the United States on the GDR.

The roads proved to be many and rock-strewn. The pathway Hanhardt chose was closely related to the political culture–political socialization approach of Verba. In trying to examine the process of "Political Socialization in the German Democratic Republic,"[6] a systematic effort was made to evaluate social science data from the GDR relating to the concept of the socialist personality.

The "new socialist man" was to exhibit personality traits that accorded as closely as possible with an ideal that greatly lacked in specificity. Let one example stand for several:

> The Socialist personality is the embodiment of the unity of the theoretical and the practical. It is characterized by the inseparable unity of the scientific world view of dialectical materialism, Socialist morality and social-political action in the construction and strengthening of socialist society.[7]

Joining empirical data to that kind of conception proved hazardous. Incomplete data, spotty coverage, and primitive research methodology and technique all complicated the task. Finally, no doubt as a result of a shift in research priorities, investigations of youth socialization were deemphasized. When the journal *Jugendforschung* [Research on Youth] ceased publication in the early 1970s, an era ended.

At much the same time, John Starrels's investigation of socialization turned to other sources than research on youth (as in his "The Political Culture of the German Democratic Republic"[8]), and Gebhard Schweigler undertook a comprehensive survey of the national consciousness of both the FRG and the GDR.[9]

Starrels examined some of the empirical data relating to the cognitive, affective, and evaluative aspects of Almond and Verba's definition of political culture. Consonant with the findings of others, Starrels concluded that the level of cognition or information about the GDR among its citizenry is high and that this cognitive level is particularly high in the case of young people. Moreover, Starrels found that "cognitive orientations toward politics apparently have a weak relationship with questions relating to the GDR's position toward West Germany," suggesting that the sources of GDR identity are turning inward in a positive internal sense rather than in contrast to the FRG.[10] This finding has implications for the integration of the GDR, inasmuch as internal sources of identification are generally assumed to be stronger than those imposed from without or derived from others.

With regard to the affective aspect of political culture in the GDR, Starrels concludes that "since the early 1960s, when the regime launched an ambitious program of administrative reform and economic modernization, growing numbers of East German adults have been developing positive affective orientations toward the polity."[11] Again this finding squares with those of numerous other studies, both U.S. and West German.

When it comes to the evaluative aspect of the GDR political culture, Starrels gives up, citing a lack of hard data and "the relative newness of East German social and political institutions [which] would make even the best informed analysis suspect."[12] As we shall attempt to show later, this is one of the points at which literary evidence might be helpful. As we shall hope to demonstrate in our discussion of the Writing Worker Movement and more recent literary developments, evaluative judgments do show through in GDR novels and plays.

Turning now to Schweigler's *Nationalbewusstsein in der BRD und der DDR* [National Consciousness in the FRG and the GDR],[13] we find the best effort to date to assess the state of what might broadly be called the political cultures of the FRG and GDR, although Schweigler does not make wide use of that term. Schweigler also has to deal with the problems of incomparable data and material not well designed for generalization. Nonetheless, he has amassed such a wealth of data that central tendencies do stand out. These tendencies indicate that distinct political identifications as well as belief and value systems have developed and are developing in the FRG *and* the GDR.

From these changes in the two Germanys, Schweigler goes on to conclude that

> A reversal of this development, returning to an all-German national consciousness that could result in a demand for the reunification of Germany does not seem very probable, since we are dealing here with change processes affecting whole societies and which may not in themselves be reversible.[14]

In other words, once a nation-state has disintegrated under the conditions of post–World War II Germany, the parts cannot be reintegrated. For it is in the restructuring of belief systems through socialization and other means that new political cultures arise from the fragments of what once were national units.[15]

We have thus arrived at the theme of this chapter. Our model is simple and familiar. Through means such as political education, coercion, propaganda, and peer, legal, and psychological influence, people acquire belief systems about their social and political environments. The means vary from the spontaneous and private to the public and coercive. Likewise, the content might vary to conform to a variety of ideals or goals for polity and society. In dealing with postwar Germany, we are studying institutionally very different systems that have been directed toward varying goals. We have suggested in passing that these are the liberal-democratic in the case of the FRG and communism (or stages of socialism) in the GDR.

In moving toward the goals of a communist system, the GDR has encountered problems relating to internal and international integration. In this connection Stephanie Neuman, in the introduction to her *National Political Integration and the International Political Environment: A Study of Small States and Segmented Societies,* has been helpful in viewing integration

> as a measure not of social homogeneity but of the ability of a political unit to conduct its important and necessary business without disaffecting large bodies of its constituents (so that they are no longer willing to have their affairs regulated by or to participate in that particular system). The focus, then, is upon (a) the role various internal institutions, such as the government, the economy, the educational system, religion, etc., play in alienating or accommodating important parts of the population; and (b) the impact international events and forces have upon these processes.[16]

By turning (or returning) the attention of integration studies to the capacity of a polity to govern itself effectively, Neuman has helped at least some of us political scientists to keep our perspective as we look at and interpret data not normally within our ken. After all, we are concerned with the business of government and what governments do to conduct their business with at least the minimum necessary support of its citizenry. The government of the GDR has used many devices to influence belief structures to accord with the values of a socialist polity—in part to reduce the number of actually and potentially disaffected. The competition of Western influences and Soviet models in the GDR has been an acute problem for the GDR leadership. The attractions of the West and residual German suspicion of and distaste for the USSR have presented an imposing challenge.

In reviewing the literature above, we have indicated that we share the view that distinct and separately integrative political cultures are developing in the two Germanies. In what follows, we shall examine one of the means used during an earlier phase of GDR history to influence political belief systems among adults: the Writing Worker Movement of 1959 to 1964. We shall then attempt an analysis of the role and impact that literature has had on the formation of a GDR political culture, including a brief look at the current literary scene. Finally we shall return to the three questions Verba asked of the FRG as a framework for drawing some conclusions about the GDR today.

The Writing Worker Movement: A Case Study

Our purpose here is to describe and assess the role of authors and literature as agents of integrative socialization in the GDR. The Writing Worker Movement was a facet of a comprehensive cultural policy that emerged from the conference at Bitterfeld in April 1959; it provides an excellent example of an attempt to use authors and literature as a means of inculcating the population with political values and modes of behavior deemed essential to the further socialist integration of society.

As a tool of political socialization, the writing worker was to assist in the development of the socialist personality, whose propagation would both facilitate and reflect the integration of society. To achieve this end, the Writing Worker Movement focused on a series of goals, the combined realization of which would facilitate integration. In summary form, these goals were four in number:

1. The discovery and development of fresh working-class talent. The resulting new cadre would become the next generation of GDR writers, whose partisan literary orientation would prove valuable in the achievement of a socialist political culture.

2. The utilization of the Writing Worker Movement as an educational tool. Through literary efforts focused on the problems confronting the socialist worker in his day-to-day tasks, the movement was to provide the citizenry with a means of understanding the realities, goals, and obliga-

tions involved in the construction of socialism. Thus the movement would serve as a vehicle through which an appropriate socialist consciousness was implanted in the population while reinforcing popular identification with the goals of the regime.

3. The heightened awareness of and appreciation for the socialist national culture of the GDR through the movement. The Writing Worker Movement was to aid the acceleration of a popular mass culture in which the entire population could actively participate, thus encouraging and facilitating the propagation of a national cultural identity.

4. The use of the Writing Worker Movement as an example of the potentialities of the socialist personality in a socialist society. Such an example was to provide an internal source of integration, which, when held up to the position of the West German laborer, would provide an additional impulse toward identification and integration.

A focal point in the implementation of the above goals of the Writing Worker Movement were the Circles of Writing Workers. These circles, concentrated in the factories and agricultural cooperatives, were established under the auspices of the Free German Workers' Federation (FDGB), the German Writers' Federation (DSB), and representatives of the Socialist Unity Party (SED). Once a Circle of Writing Workers had been established, it was the duty of these professionals to recruit workers from the ranks of the Brigades of Labor into which factory and farm workers had been organized. Each circle was then to receive material assistance and ideological guidance from party, union, and cultural functionaries. The interaction between writing worker and officials provided both discipline and direction to the circles.[17]

The paramount task of the professional leadership was to provide the correct political-ideological orientation within the Circles of Writing Workers. This was done by insuring that the literary product of a circle focused on an appropriate theme and used the required format. As a result of this, the literature of the writing workers tended toward uniformity, building on the foundations of socialist realism and in content dealing with the precepts of socialist work, learning, and, most importantly, socialist morality.[18]

In practice, the responsibilities for assisting writing workers were delegated among the different functionaries and professionals according to their specialties. For instance, political orientation was given over to the FDGB representatives, while matters of literary form and execution were left to the professional writers and instructors.[19]

Beyond the close professional and political guidance, several ancillary programs were introduced to assist the writing workers. These programs were found at academic institutions as well as the factories and farms. The Leipzig Institute for Literature, for example, initiated a year-long seminar for the most promising writing workers from surrounding districts. Similarly, the district Houses of People's Culture organized weekend seminars for writing workers in the spring of 1960. These seminars provided encouragement, aid, and instruction.[20]

Through Works Academies *(Betriebsakademien)* and representatives of the German Writers' Federation, evening courses for writing workers were elaborated in which novice writers could receive political orientation and literary inspiration.[21] By bringing the program to the people with personal attention, it was hoped that the writing worker would be inculcated with sufficient "partisan truth" *(parteiliche Wahrheit)* to answer in a positive manner the questions posed by the poet laureate of the GDR, Johannes R. Becher:

1. Who are you, you who write?
2. What do you want? For whom do you write?[22]

In addition to the vertical communication between writing workers and the cultural and political functionaries, horizontal interaction among Writing Worker Circles was encouraged. Agitprop groups and amateur cabarets visited each other. Experiences among circles were exchanged. This was deemed necessary in order to instill a fuller appreciation for the many facets of factory life and socialist construction among the participants. Broader experience, it was hoped, would also forestall "one-sided" literary perspectives among the workers and their products.[23]

Writing Worker Circles were also encouraged to assist in writing agitprop texts and manuals. It was felt that writing workers, possessed of well-rounded knowledge of factory life, would be in a position to suggest needed changes in factory regimen or to voice informed criticism of negligent officials.[24]

Within the circles, care was taken in selecting the literary medium most appropriate to these novice writers. As a rule, writing workers were encouraged to begin with less demanding literary genres. It was suggested by the authorities that the circles begin with notices and articles and then progress to skits, portraits, and short stories. Finally the more demanding forms of poetry, drama, and the novel were to be attempted.[25] The fundamental literary vehicle adopted by the the circles was the Brigade Diary *(Brigadetagebuch)*.

The Brigade Diaries, written by the collective efforts of factory "Brigades of Socialist Labor" or the Circles of Writing Workers, were designed to focus on the conflicts and difficulties encountered by workers in their struggle to build socialism. Literary treatment of these themes was expected to reveal the dialectical process of workers becoming true socialist personalities:

> The Brigade Diaries mirror the conflicts and developments of people engaged in the construction of socialism. They thereby aid the self-education of the working class and help form the new man in the socialist epoch. Thereby the Brigade Diaries become documents of the battle of the working class for the victory of socialism.[26]

These diaries were therefore viewed as consciousness builders, serving to instill desired values in both the writing workers and their working-class audience. The authorities who had promoted the Brigade Diaries were not under the illusion that these diaries would be considered literature in the sense of, say, drama or poetry. That was not the point. Rather, the diaries presented the direct personal experiences of workers, experiences and perceptions that were of immense potential use to both the political functionaries and professional writers.

Indeed, a contemporary and hostile West German critic went so far as to suggest that the diaries were the cradle of a new socialist literature.[27] In the official view of the SED:

> Many workers were first made fully aware of the meaningful changes that had occured in their thought and behavior and in their attitudes toward work and socialist property in the sense of the bases of socialist morality and ethics since their brigade had obligated them to work, learn and live socialistically.[28]

The value of the Brigade Diaries did not end with the diaries themselves. They also lent themselves as the foundation for several other artistic endeavors. A few examples will demonstrate the adaptability of the diaries.

Brigade Diaries were used by artists who provided illustrations. Drama circles borrowed portions or complete diaries for presentation on the stage, while agitprop groups seized the diaries for overt propaganda purposes, brandishing them as examples of the artistic and creative powers emanating from the brigades. Elsewhere diaries were put to music or adapted for film. Finally the diaries were used as subjects of literary competition among brigades of workers striving to earn the honorary title of "Brigade of Socialist Labor."[29]

Along with the Brigade Diaries, writing workers were encouraged to submit articles for publication in factory newspapers and weeklies. Special emphasis was placed on pieces dealing with basic economic and political problems arising within the factory. With special sections or supplements reserved for the writing workers, a ready-made vehicle for the dissemination of writing worker literature was available and used.

In addition, writing workers were urged to participate in other journalistic endeavors. Particular stress was placed on the desirability of having writing workers serve as "People's Correspondents" *(Volkskorrespondenten)* for the local and regional press.[30] The duties of these correspondents involved coverage of events occuring in factories, farm collectives, and residential areas. In this work a close relationship between the People's Correspondents and the League of German Journalists (*Verband der Deutschen Journalisten*) was established to insure an active exchange between the socialist press and writing workers.[31]

In order to develop the potential of the Writing Worker Movement as effectively as possible, several publishing outlets in addition to local and factory newspapers were made available with the goal of broadening the movement's audience. Among the most active publishers of writing worker material was the trade union federation house, "FDGB-Verlag Tribüne," which published several Brigade Diaries in book form. The "Mitteldeutscher Verlag Halle" presented an anthology of movement literature.[32]

With the press and large publishing houses providing for broad distribution and quality production of outstanding examples of workers' literature, the SED leadership could point to a considerable output from the Writing Worker Movement. The GDR example was presented to other socialist countries as a model.

In the years between the Bitterfeld Conference of 1959 and the second convocation in the spring of 1964, a major trend can be delineated, one that had a subtle, but definite, impact on the Writing Worker Movement. This trend involved the increasing priority given to the use of authors and literature as weapons of propaganda directed at West Germany.

Regarding the increased emphasis placed on literature as propaganda, this shift in priorities reflected a similar adjustment not only in the broader cultural policy, but also in the approach of the SED toward the task of integrating East German society. The Bitterfeld blueprint was not discarded— there was no particular need to, since it had already contained a strong element of cultural propaganda. This element of Bitterfeld had been viewed as a double-edged sword. On one side, literature was to provide an internal sense of identification by setting appropriate examples of socialist practice in real life situations. The other side was meant to propagate a partisan image of socialist society as something worth defending against real or imagined incursions, threats, and outright attacks by the aggressive forces of Western capitalism.

The construction of the Berlin Wall in August 1961 and the consequent need for the SED to justify its action led to the mobilization of the full resources of party and state to turn the event into a source of internal identification and integration. On the economic front, this meant moving into the reforms known collectively as the "New Economic System," which, in its initial phase, led to economic decentralization. Although the New Economic System was soon recalled, it did usher in a period of increasing prosperity for the GDR citizen. For many of these people, the sealing of the Berlin border was in itself reason enough for them to make their peace with a now thoroughly established political system.

This coming to terms with the GDR was strongly encouraged by the authors and literature of the GDR. We need only mention in passing the novel by Christa Wolf, *Der geteilte Himmel,* as an outstanding example of efforts to place the division of Germany into a perspective meaningful even to the critical GDR reader.[33]

Direction to the literary establishment and the writing workers came in a series of statements by SED leaders. In a combined meeting of the Politburo of the SED with the Presidium of the SED Council of Ministers and "Writers and Artists," the Minister of Culture, Kurt Hager, reacted to the Wall and West Germany:

> By securing our state boundary an end has been made to the imperialistic plans for aggression and revenge against the GDR and the other socialist countries. The Sixth Party Congress [of the SED] made it clear that a reunification with West German imperialism and militarism is not possible since the national question in Germany is a question of class—a question of which class determines the history of the nation. There can be only one perspective for the whole of Germany: the victory of socialism.[34]

Although the Writing Worker Movement was but a small part of the cultural effort in the GDR, it was nonetheless affected by the factors just mentioned. The writing worker was repeatedly encouraged to wield his or her pen as a weapon against the reaction of West Germany. These efforts purported to raise the consciousness of the writing worker and his audience, informing them of the threat posed by the West and the need to get on with the task of constructing socialism in the GDR:

> our writing workers should use the pen as a weapon against militarism and preparations for war and to reveal the machinations of militarists and imperialists in West Germany. They should help appeal to all the working class—including the workers in West Germany—in order to strengthen the grand front of the forces of peace, so that militarism in West Germany will be restrained and so that democratic conditions will be established there as well.[35]

Before attempting to gauge the success of the Writing Worker Movement as a means of inculcating GDR citizens with political values and patterns of behavior, consideration must be given to factors relevant to any discussion of political socialization. In the first place, the Writing Worker Program was directed at adults, not children. Whereas children are less likely to have developed well-defined frames of reference and are therefore amenable to socialization processes, adults do possess established behavior patterns and political values reflecting accumulated experience. In the GDR, this is particularly significant given the fact that a large number of adults were born and raised in a Germany whose political culture contrasted sharply with that being established in the GDR. Given this situation, only limited success could be expected of socialization efforts among adults.

Second, political socialization is meant to instill new attitudes that will lead to changed patterns of behavior. However, it is one thing to press upon a person's mind the precepts of socialist morality; it is quite another to believe that person will behave according to those precepts. There is a kind of uncertainty principle at work here. It is possible to delineate the goals of socialization (as in the characterization of the socialist personality). And, up to a point, behavior can be described. To attribute the latter to the former or (more difficult yet) to indicate the way minds change is virtually impossible.

Finally, consideration must be given to the place of literature in comparison with other agents of political socialization. As indicated above, this is a difficult relationship to assess. Certainly one of the classical functions of literature is to teach, and the Writing Worker literature is nothing if not didactic. Yet when compared to education itself as an activity and institution, literature takes its place as but part of a larger process. We must also take into account the socializing influence of the economic system in the GDR (as elsewhere). The increasing prosperity of the GDR and its citizenry has been an extremely important factor in encouraging alignment with the political system. It would seem safe to assume that material well-being and financial security might provide a stronger source of internal identification with the associated political system than even the most moving piece of literature.

The foregoing considerations frustrate efforts aimed at assessing the impact of the Writing Worker Movement in achieving its fundamental purpose, the development of socialist personalities. Perhaps we should begin our assessment with the more concrete aims of the program before turning to the socialist personality as such.

As a discoverer and developer of new working-class writing talent, the Writing Worker Movement had limited success. The bulk of the literary material produced by writing workers and their affiliated circles was not true literature, but rather such things as Brigade Diaries, articles, agitprop manuals, and the like. What was attempted in the traditional literary genres was, as a rule, decidedly mediocre. Of course there were a few outstanding exceptions, the most prominent being the works of dramatists whose roots can be traced to the movement: Helmut Sakowski, Horst Salomon, and Horst Kleineidam.

The success the writing workers attained as builders of socialist consciousness cannot be determined objectively. Any conclusion reached must be quite general. Through the Writing Worker Movement, a great many workers were exposed to political values and modes of behavior exemplary of the socialist personality. Exposure and incorporation are, as suggested before, distinct or discrete matters. Yet the effort to have people (workers) examine their feelings, attitudes, and perceptions relative to the goals of the political system cannot help but have had an effect upon those participating in the movement. To be a "writer" is to partake of an honored and even exalted status in society. To be a writing worker in a self-styled "workers' and peasants' state" is to be an articulate part of the regime. This is bound to have an impact and a positive one.

In addition, we are convinced that the movement had a demonstration effect in that it encouraged workers to identify with the successes, trials, and problems of others. In this regard it matters less if what was produced was "true literature" than if it "told it like it was." Of course the writing workers were set limits: their realism had to be socialist realism, their criticism of state and society had to be positive criticism, and the conflicts that they portrayed had to be of "nonantagonistic contradictions." All this had a stultifying effect and not only on workers' literature.

Although the Writing Worker Movement was never really terminated, it faded after the Second Bitterfeld Conference of 1964. It was overadministered by officials who had too high expectations and too little faith in the capacity of the working man to produce a usable literature in the service of a socialist national culture and of socialist man in the GDR.

It is interesting and important to our discussion to note that no mention was made of the Bitterfeld Weg in the deliberations of the Eighth SED Party Congress (1971). That this was no simple oversight was confirmed by the currently official statement on the state of the arts in the GDR, *Zur Theorie des sozialistischen Realismus* (1974) [On the Theory of Socialist Realism]. According to the authors, the dropping of the term "Bitterfeld" acknowledged the international aspect of contemporary GDR literature: "internationally the term was not understood." Moreover, the objectives that had been set for Bitterfeld by the Fifth SED Party Congress (1958) had been achieved: literature had been reoriented toward contemporary themes. This having been done, Bitterfeld stood in the way of further development and growth.[36]

GDR Literature and Political Culture since Bitterfeld

The Writing Worker Movement came at a time in the history of the GDR when the regime was faced with the monumental task of securing the identification of its citizenry with the developing political system. This was a difficult task. The prosperity of the FRG was constantly in the minds of the East Germans. The presence of a relatively open path to the FRG through Berlin until August 1961 meant that the GDR citizen could always consider the possibility of leaving. This possibility had a distinctly diminishing effect on the need to come to terms with the "workers' and peasants' state."

After the Berlin Wall eliminated emigration as a viable alternative, more and more people began a process of what might be termed "accentuating the positive." That is, the comprehensive social welfare programs, full employment, and the excellence of the education system in the GDR received more attention than the blandishments of life in the West. Moreover, as indicated in the last section, the economic situation in the GDR began to improve after 1963-1964. The improvements were felt by most in the better quality and greater variety of consumer goods that became available. Disposable personal incomes rose. These developments eased the task of internal integration and strengthened a socialist political culture.

As time passed, more and more young people with a stake in the political system replaced older generations who remembered earlier times and who perhaps harbored greater ambivalence toward the socialist experiment than their juniors. Even the loyal communists of an older generation were finding themselves increasingly out of touch with developments in the GDR in the late 1960s. This was symbolized by the transfer of power from the veteran Walter Ulbricht to Erich Honecker in 1971.

Honecker ushered in a new era, one that was founded on a greater feeling of security and self-assurance than had previously characterized the GDR. Part of this self-assurance among the new leadership no doubt stemmed from the fact that Honecker had served for years in the Free German Youth and knew well the growing resource that young people represented in the cause of socialism.

The cultural part of Honecker's "Report of the Central Committee of the Eighth Congress of the SED" presented a new attitude toward writers and artists. Following some ritual praise, Honecker defined his expectations:

> Writers and artists are themselves best aware of the fact that artistic work is not always good, is at times superficial, deals with externals, and is boring. We are perfectly aware of the fact that it is no easy task to discover great world-transforming actions in the everyday lives of people living under socialism and to make us aware of them through a masterly delineation of our life in its full beauty. Our party will always trustingly support the artists and help them to open up even more effective ways for their work for socialist society.
>
> Success for the writer in the GDR will come to the extent to which our party succeeds in getting artists to center the entire wealth of their writings and powers of expression on coining the image of the socialist personality of our times. This will help them to enrich socialist realist art in the course of their search for new forms of presenting the greatness and beauty of our times in a positive way and also in the critical presentation of the contradictions to be overcome.[37]

Throughout Honecker's remarks there is a tension between the repeated use of terms such as "new forms," "creativity," "objectivity," and "beauty" and the repeated admonition to be aware of "reality," to be "socially effective," and to strive for "agreement between artistic and ideological responsibility." The tension is an old one: the needs of the party and the tendency for writers to express themselves in ways that do not necessarily coincide with party demands and indeed conflict with them. Surely Honecker's remarks were met with some skepticism by GDR writers. Some, familiar with pronouncements of the past, may have felt, "here we go again!"

The tensions and expectations notwithstanding, Honecker's

tenure has seen a considerable upsurge in literary activity and interest. And the West is beginning to "discover" GDR authors.[38]

Indicative of the GDR literary atmosphere in recent years was an article by the deputy minister of culture, Klaus Hoepcke, which appeared in the SED paper *Neues Deutschland.* Hoepcke summarized the tone of party attitudes by saying, "Decisive is that—as Erich Honecker has formulated it—writing is done from socialist standpoints."[39] Hoepcke cited a number of works (Seghers's *Sonderbare Begegnung,* Kant's *Impressum,* Strittmatter's *Wundertäter II,* Braun's *Das ungezwungene Leben Kasts,* and Becker's *Irreführung der Bohörden* among many others) that marked a new stage in the historical development of the GDR and that were accompanied by a good deal of controversy.

Not only have controversial works appeared, they have taken on a new quality. Many of the novels published since the Eighth Party Congress deal with "the way it was" when the Soviet Zone of Occupation became the GDR and the struggle for socialism began. Themes of sacrifice, achievement, loss, and accomplishment are treated with sensitivity, understanding, and even humor. This look at "the way we were in the GDR" can partly be explained by what seems to be a worldwide wave of nostalgia. Even more of these kinds of works represent a new maturity on the part of writers and political leaders in the GDR.

This perceived maturity relates closely to our conclusions about the state of the political culture. In digging into the past, whether out of nostalgia or a desire to find roots, skeletons are unavoidably unearthed. Investigating the past with a socialist, but critical, point of view brings on risks that would have been unthinkable or at least unwise in an earlier era.

Central to the questions Verba asked is the stability of a liberal-democratic political culture. Translating this into a form relevant to a socialist system, we can deal with the questions of how long the GDR political culture is likely to last and in what directions it is likely to change.

The stability of the present-day political culture is encouraged by the increasing self-assurance shown by the regime.

This trend is exhibited in the contrast between the Writing Worker Movement and the current literary scene. Contradictions other than the nonantagonistic are being dealt with in such works as Volker Braun's "Unvollendete Geschichte" [Unfinished Story] (1975).[40] The capacity to deal with the tensions between the individual and the state in a socialist society that is itself "unfinished" indicates a maturity that can only be founded on the knowledge that the SED does not need to be defensive or obsessed with constant streams of undiluted praise.

Interestingly, Braun's story includes a reference to the kind of thing the Writing Worker Movement sought to achieve, but did not quite effect. Braun helps us understand why. The heroine of the story, Karin, is the daughter of a leading SED district functionary. She loves a young man with an asocial background, now reformed, but not fully "with it" from the perspective of the party ("Collective," he says, "is something I have never experienced"). In the course of their unhappy and unresolved affair, Karin works briefly for a district newspaper. When she takes up her work, she reflects that there are two kinds of people: those who are convinced, like her and her family, and those who must be convinced by those already persuaded. (There actually was a third category, the enemy, but there was no dialogue with them.)

In beginning to edit the daily economics section of the paper, Karin sorts texts of speeches from workers. One stack is positive, the other negative. In the process she comes across a highly articulate piece by women describing frankly the work in their department and the manifold difficulties they had encountered with technical and human problems. Karin insisted on publishing the entire speech because it so clearly delineated the strains and stresses characteristic of socialist achievement. The text was not published. Karin protested and was patronizingly put down as "a scrapper" by her departmental head. Of the two GDR "realities" of turmoil and triumph, only the latter was to appear in print. Thus it was in the days of the movement, and Braun's open discussion of the suppression of criticism indicated how considerably the relations between politics and culture have changed. Insecure and immature

systems, overly concerned about "disaffecting large bodies of
. . . constituents" (Neuman) eschew Braun's loyal dissent.

All this does not mean that there will be any "diffusion of
political power and guarantees of basic freedoms" as understood by Verba in his first question. The current literary scene
in the GDR can be taken to show an increasingly meaningful
participation in the constructive criticism of life and politics. If
this trend holds up, we expect the political culture of the GDR
to last as long as the international relations between East and
West remain agreeable to the status quo in Western Europe.
Recent diplomatic activity makes continuance as sure as
anything can be in international politics.

Internally, the trends alluded to in earlier portions of this
chapter and the literary evidence we have examined indicate
that the tendency of writers will probably be wary lest the
German excesses of the 1930s or the Soviet excesses under
Stalin are repeated. This third aspect of Verba's questioning
was also taken up in the issue of *Sinn und Form* containing
Braun's story. Günter Kunert, in his "Pamphlet für K."
[Pamphlet for K.] and "Notwendiges Nachwort zum 'Pamphlet' " [Necessary Afterword to the 'Pamphlet'], deals explicitly with the problem of fascism, its roots and remnants.[41] The
"Pamphlet" had been rejected for an edition of the essays on
Heinrich von Kleist. Now printed in *Sinn und Form,* Kunert
appended an angry afterword. Both pieces dealt with the need
for fascist and bourgeois societies to define what is "healthy"
and "sick" in literary figures and their works. In protesting the
"rude censorship" of his work, Kunert ends with a remarkable
sentence: "So I close in the style of the health and sickness
practitioners cited in the 'Pamphlet for K.,' though remember-
ing the truth that the individual can be mentally sick only to the
extent that society makes him so."

That such sentences can appear and be publicly debated
indicates to us that the political culture of the GDR is gaining a
vitality within its borders that in the gray years of the past
would have sent its cultural figures fleeing either abroad or into
silence. This may change. The mentality and venality of the
functionaries have by no means disappeared. But for now, the
political culture of the GDR is more interesting, more integrat-

ed, and more challenging than ever before.

Notes

1. G. A. Almond and S. Verba, *The Civic Culture* (Boston: Little, Brown, 1965).

2. Ibid., p. 313.

3. S. Verba, "Germany: The Remaking of a Political Culture," in *Political Culture and Political Development,* L. W. Pye and S. Verba (Princeton: Princteon University Press, 1965).

4. Ibid., pp. 134-135.

5. Ibid., p. 170.

6. A. M. Hanhardt, Jr., "Political Socialization in the German Democratic Republic," *Societas* 1, no. 2 (Spring 1971): 101-121.

7. A. M. Hanhardt, Jr., "Political Socialization in Divided Germany," *Journal of International Affairs* 27, no. 2 (1973): 196.

8. J. Starrels, "The Political Culture of the German Democratic Republic," unpublished manuscript, 1973(?).

9. Gebhard Schweigler, *Nationalbewusstsein in der BRD und der DDR* (Düsseldorf: Bertelsmann, 1973).

10. Starrels, "Political Culture," p. 17.

11. Ibid., p. 18.

12. Ibid., p. 24.

13. Schweigler, *Nationalbewusstsein.*

14. Ibid., p. 202.

15. H. S. Park, "Toward a Typology of National Integration," (Paper prepared for the 1976 International Studies Association Annual Convention).

16. S. G. Neuman, "Introduction," in *National Political Integration and the International Political Environment: A Study of Small States and Segmented Societies* (New York: Praeger, 1976).

17. W. Beyreuthers, "Die Aufgaben der Gewerkschaften bei der Entwicklung der Bewegung 'schreibender Arbeiter,' " *Dokumente zur Kunst-, Literatur- und Kulturpolitik der SED* (Stuttgart: Seewald Verlag, 1972), p. 667.

18. Ibid., p. 669.

19. Ibid., p. 670.

20. H. Kersten, "Bitterfeld und die Folgen," *SBZ-Archiv* 12, no. 12 (June 1960): 178.

21. *Dokumente,* p. 671.

22. Ibid.

23. Ibid., p. 665.

24. Ibid.

25. Ibid., p. 670.

26. Ibid., p. 663.

27. H. A. W. Kasten, "Experimente des Ungeistes," *SBZ-Archiv* 11, no. 10 (May 1960): 151.

28. *Dokumente,* p. 663.

29. Ibid., p. 664.

30. "Die Entwicklung der Volkskunst in der DDR," *Dokumente,* p. 774.

31. *Dokumente,* pp. 664-665.

32. Kersten, "Bitterfeld, p. 178.

33. C. Wolf, *Der geteilte Himmel* (Hamburg: Rowohlt, 1968).

34. K. Hager, "Parteilichkeit und Volksverbundenheit unserer Literatur und Kunst," *Beilage zum Sonntag,* 7 April 1973.

35. *Dokumente,* p. 669.

36. Institut für Gesellschaftswissenschaften beim ZK der SED, *Zur Theorie des sozialistischen Realismus* (Berlin: Dietz Verlag, 1974), p. 262.

37. E. Honecker, *Report of the Central Committee to the Eighth Congress of the SED* (Dresden: Verlag Zeit im Bild, [1971], pp. 52-53.

38. There have been several visits by prominent GDR authors since the United States formally recognized the GDR.

39. K. Hoepcke in *Neues Deutschland,* 1 September 1974, p. 2.

40. V. Braun, "Unvollendete Geschichte," *Sinn und Form* 27, no. 5 (September/October 1975): 941-979.

41. G. Kunert, "Pamphlet für K.," ibid., pp. 1091-1094; and "Notwendiges Nachwork zum 'Pamphlet,'" ibid., pp. 1094-1097.

8. The Framework of Foreign Policy

Michael W. Olszewski

Any account of the foreign policy of the German Democratic Republic (GDR) must stress at the outset the inseparability of East German and Soviet foreign policies. Though the treaty signed with the Soviet Union in September 1955 guarantees the GDR freedom "in the resolution of questions of its domestic and foreign policies, including relationship to the FRG as well as the development of relations to other states,"[1] it has not manifested any great independence or deviation from the foreign policy wishes of the Soviet Union.

The dependence of the GDR on Soviet foreign policy receives both explicit and implicit justification. First and foremost among the explicit reasons for GDR dependence is the allegiance of the GDR to the Soviet conception of "socialist (or proletarian) internationalism," which is understood to mean in present-day Soviet ideology "the existence of alleged 'general regular patterns in the development toward socialism' (patterns taken from Soviet developments), the subordination of each Marxist party to a 'united world movement' (under Soviet leadership), and the observance of an 'international general line' (determined by the Soviet leadership)."[2] The GDR has gone so far as to include in the revised 1968 Constitution its fidelity to the Soviet Union and the concept of "socialist internationalism." Article 6 makes it the constitutional duty of the GDR to foster and develop "all-around cooperation and friendship with the Union of Soviet Socialist Republics and the other socialist states according to the principles of socialist internationalism."[3]

The GDR's allegiance to socialist internationalism and the Soviet Union, as stipulated in government statements, is made acceptable by several realities. From a strictly Marxist-Leninist theoretical standpoint, the GDR feels that only through close cooperation with the socialist community (under Soviet leadership) will the international class conflict with the imperialist forces come to a successful conclusion.[4] Thus, it is readily apparent that the GDR does not condone the doctrines of the "renegade" Communist parties (People's Republic of China, Yugoslavia, Italy), because it feels a fractionalized communist movement grossly violates the Marxist-Leninist tenet of socialist internationalism, retards the advent of communism, and only serves the imperialist forces. Of course, the so-called renegade parties counter these attacks with their own arguments: that socialist internationalism is only a facade for Soviet domination of the world communist movement; that "different roads to socialism" are permitted by classical Leninism;[5] and that their ideology is more highly developed or truer to the Marxist-Leninist line and therefore accelerates the coming of communism.

Ironically, the GDR not only agrees with the claim of the "renegades" that socialist internationalism is synonymous with Soviet primacy but it also welcomes it. The reasoning behind the GDR acceptance of Soviet leadership of the world communist movement is primarily based on the acknowledgment and recognition of the vast and lengthier experience of the USSR (CPSU) in the development of socialism both at home and abroad. The logic behind this is that the CPSU, being the oldest governing Communist party—it antedates the second oldest by approximately twenty-five years—possesses twice the "practical experience" in the construction of socialism, and it therefore follows that a relatively neophyte party should learn from Soviet experience.

Erich Honecker, first secretary of the SED, in presenting the Central Committee's report to the Eighth Party Congress of SED, outlined further the reasoning behind the GDR's dependence on the Soviet experience:

> The CPSU has proven itself in more than fifty years of using the theory of Marxism-Leninism in the problems of the revolutionary process and in the practice of building the new social order to be the most experienced and most tested-by-struggle [*kampferprobteste*] party as well as the avant-garde of the international communist and workers' movement. We are adopting the great theoretical and practical experience of the Soviet Union and using it for our own basic conditions.[6]

Another explicit reason given by the GDR for the interlocking of foreign policies is the long history of friendship and cooperation between the peoples of Germany and Russia. To be sure, it is somewhat dubious to base the unity of present-day, Soviet-GDR foreign policy on a heritage of relations that has not always been free from friction and conflict. Nevertheless, the SED leadership has pointed to several positive examples of cooperation and friendship between Germans and Russians. Thus, Peter Florin, current GDR ambassador to the United Nations, in his book on GDR foreign policy[7] traces the roots back to the nineteenth century and the national solidarity between Germans and Russians in the struggle against the foreign rule of Napoleon. He then continues tracing Russo-German cooperation through the workers' movement in the last half of that century to the strong support of German revolutionaries for the struggles of their Russian counterparts in October 1917. Florin next cites the Rapallo Treaty of 1922—which among other things established diplomatic relations between Germany and the Soviet Union—as a model *(Musterbeispiel)* of cooperation. He also mentions the Berlin Friendship and Neutrality Treaty of 1926 and the positive economic benefits for both sides that resulted after its ratification. Finally, Ambassador Florin acknowledges the liberation of Eastern Germany from the yoke of fascism by the Soviet Army and the Soviet ideological and material support for the creation of the GDR in 1949.

When looking into the implicit, or not officially stated,

reasons for the inseparability of Soviet-GDR foreign policies, the most apparent derives from the fact that the GDR was created and nurtured by the Soviet Union. Thus, the GDR's lifeblood came from and continues to come—though less so than previously—from the Soviets. It is not too unreasonable to characterize the Soviet-GDR relationship as that of a parent to a child, for without the continued support of Soviet power over the years, GDR sovereignty would not have survived.

However, it was not a foregone conclusion that the Soviet parent would let the child be born and play with other children. In nonmetaphoric words, the Soviets initially did not in their official pronouncements favor the granting of sovereignty— thus dividing the German nation—to the eastern sector of postwar Germany. They remained steadfast in support of a united Germany (preferably under Soviet hegemony) and only mimicked the fait accompli of the Western powers in their zones of occupation when the GDR was officially established on October 7, 1949. It did not realize sovereignty in foreign policy decision making until March 25, 1954, when the Soviet government published a statement to the effect the "the GDR will possess the freedom to determine according to its own judgment its domestic and foreign affairs, including the question of relations to West Germany."[8] Prior to this time, final foreign and domestic decision making was the sole privilege of the Soviet Control Commission (on 28 May 1953 transformed into the High Commission [*Hohe Kommission*]), which had replaced the Soviet Military Administration after the founding of the GDR in late 1949. Nevertheless, the Soviet Union did reserve for the future the right to maintain definite functions "that are in connection with the acceptance of responsibility to guarantee security (of the GDR) as well as those that are a result of the responsibilities that fall to the USSR from the Four-Power Agreements."[9] The most notable outgrowth of Soviet security guarantees, which is another implicit reason for the interlocking of foreign policies as well, is the permanent stationing of Soviet troops in the GDR. Today there are approximately twenty divisions (180,000 men) in East Germany under the guise of security against Western revanchism.[10] The presence of these Soviet divisions effectively stultifies any possible desire of the GDR citizenry or leadership to "drift away" (as in June 1953) from Soviet tutelage, especially in the realm of foreign policy decision making.

The question of GDR security leads us to one final reason (though in this case not entirely implicit) for the interlocking of foreign policies. Preservation of its sovereignty is the overarching concern of the GDR in both foreign and domestic policy making. In a major foreign policy address in 1968 by Otto Winzer, then the foreign minister, the five basic principles or goals of GDR foreign policy were spelled out:

1. the creation of the most favorable international conditions for the building of socialism in the GDR
2. increasing the political and ideological unity, solidarity, and power of the community of socialist countries by working further on our close and friendly collaboration with the Soviet Union and other members of the socialist family of states, especially of the Warsaw Pact, on the basis of socialist internationalism
3. support for peoples struggling for liberation from the colonial yoke and cooperation with those already liberated, especially if they followed a noncapitalist path of development
4. to develop normal relations with the capitalistic states according to the principle of peaceful coexistence, with the goal of contributing to a European system of collective security and to a stable order of peace in the world
5. to fight the increasingly aggressive and dangerous policies of West German imperialism and its arrogant claim to represent all Germans *(Alleinvertretung)*[11]

In no less than four of the above, the East Germans emphasize a quest for security, i.e., favorable conditions for international socialist development, integration with the Soviet Union and the Warsaw Pact, European collective security, and the fear of FRG imperialism. Thus, the Soviet Union, the strongest member of the socialist bloc, is looked to as the defender of GDR security. Moreover, an adjunct to the GDR's quest for

security has been the struggle against the international isolation sought by the FRG and its Hallstein Doctrine. The Soviet
Union again has been looked to as the superpower buttress and
international lobbyist for the de jure diplomatic recognition of
the GDR. On the other hand, the GDR's faith in the Soviet
Union in this respect has not always been absolute. There was
some not unfounded worry within the GDR ruling circles
during the Beria-Malenkov and early Khrushchev eras that the
Soviets would "sell" them to the West Germans or the West for
the right price or for that matter any price.[12] This worry was
certainly exacerbated with the signing of the Austrian State
Treaty in 1955 and again in the later 1960s, when the FRG was
in the incipient stages of formulating its *Ostpolitik* and was
receiving positive response to her overtures to the Eastern bloc
without first recognizing the GDR, as was stipulated by
agreement between the Eastern bloc and the GDR.[13] These
fears were ultimately laid to rest with the signing of an initiative
by the Warsaw Pact countries on June 22, 1970, to bring about
an all-Europe security conference, which would in effect
completely solidify GDR sovereignty.[14] Although this might
suggest greater freedom of action for the GDR, "the opposite is
the case. Her relationship to her own pact partners is closer"
and will continue to be so.[15]

The foreign policy of the GDR can be broken down into four
basic components, or formats. These formats correspond to
the manner in which the GDR divides the world along political, economic, and ideological-social lines. The four formats
are directed (1) toward the Soviet Union and the socialist bloc,
including such "renegades" as the PRC, Yugoslavia, and
Albania; (2) toward the capitalist states of the West; (3) toward
the FRG; (4) toward the "antiimperialist" states struggling for
national liberation (or already liberated) from the yoke of
colonialism, i.e., the majority of states of Latin America, Asia,
and Africa.[16]

As has already been noted, GDR foreign policy toward the
socialist camp is necessarily based on the principle of proletarian internationalism. Very little need be added except to
reiterate that socialist internationalism requires a bloc of
countries "that are held together . . . by common past expe-

rience . . . , by common ideals, institutions, and aspirations and, furthermore, by the hostility and menace presented by the capitalist world" and that manifest, among other things, a common foreign policy.[17] ⌐

The common foreign policy of the socialist bloc (here excluding only Yugoslavia) toward the capitalist world has for the most part been the same since the early 1920s, when the policy of "peaceful coexistence between states with different social systems" was formulated. Peaceful coexistence as a theoretical and guiding aspect came into being when the hoped-for world revolution failed to materialize after World War I. The repulsion of the Red Army in Poland in 1920 as well as the failures of the Hungarian and Bavarian revolutionary governments made it clear that a spontaneous revolt of the proletariat in countries throughout the developed world was not to be forthcoming and "that the Soviet communists would have to accommodate themselves to a prolonged coexistence between the Soviet Union and the capitalist countries."[18] The peace modifier was added to coexistence as an outgrowth of the nascent Soviet republic's unstable domestic and insecure international positions as well as from the fear that the West might move militarily to oust the new communist order.[19]

Down through the years, peaceful coexistence as a theoretical concept has remained essentially viable. In fact, save for World War II and Stalin's deemphasis—though never a disavowal—of the concept in the incipient stages of the Cold War, it has become more and more salient, not only as a theoretical concept but as a strategic weapon as well. The Khrushchev era saw the codification of the postwar definition of peaceful coexistence. Solid evidence of its renewed emphasis was first manifest at the Twentieth Congress of the CPSU in 1956, where the concept was further developed and brought up to date. It was again reaffirmed by the "Declaration of the Twelve Communist Parties in Power" (including the GDR) in Moscow during 1957 and finally ratified in a document known as the "New Communist Manifesto" by the eighty-one Communist parties that met in Moscow in 1960.[20]

With the coming of détente in the late 1960s, peaceful coexistence became increasingly important, especially for

GDR policy-makers. In August 1968, several GDR diplomats and lawyers took part in a symposium on peaceful coexistence. The symposium basically reaffirmed the principles contained in the "New Communist Manifesto." However, one new principle was added, one that curiously relates to the quest for security, i.e., *das Prinzip der Vertragstreue*.[21] Faithfulness to treaties is vital to the GDR, for its sole raison d'etre is based on treaty. Its sovereignty was established and guaranteed by treaty with the Soviet Union (without whom, of course, there would have been no GDR), and now, with the signing of the Basic Treaty with the FRG, the Four-Power Agreement on Berlin, and the Helsinki European Security Accords, the world has recognized the GDR and its future by treaty. Without the ability to defend its sovereignty militarily, the GDR must rely on the good graces of her treaty partners and for this reason it must rely heavily on the continued observance of the principle of *Vertragstreue*.

Taking the principle of peaceful coexistence at face value, it would seem that the socialist bloc has accepted the world status quo and has given up designs for a communist world revolution. Instead, however, it is considered a strategic maneuver in the international class struggle. World revolution is still called for, though with various alternate methods unlikely to provoke a nuclear showdown. This allows states with different social systems to promote cooperation and compromise, but only in the political (diplomatic), economic (scientific-technological), military (disarmament), and cultural spheres. In the ideological sphere, there can be no compromise on principles; the international class struggle against capitalism continues.

The third and newest format of GDR foreign policy is that toward the other German state—the FRG. It was only with the signing of the Basic Treaty *(Grundvertrag)* between the two Germanies in 1973 that one could speak of an official need for inter-German foreign policies. The Basic Treaty marked a watershed in GDR policy attitude toward the FRG. Upon its signing, the Basic Treaty, for all intents and purposes brought to a successful conclusion the leading policy objectives of the GDR, objectives developed over the course of the first twenty-five years of its existence. In the Basic Treaty, the following

GDR demands *(Ansprüche)* were met: (1) sovereign equality and self-determination; (2) discontinuance of Bonn's claim to *Alleinvertretung* (sole representation of all Germans); (3) a pledge to promote a European Security Conference, arms reduction, and nuclear weapons control; (4) inviolability of state borders and a renunciation of the use of force; and (5) economic, scientific, and cultural cooperation. However, not all of the GDR goals were achieved. The FRG did not yield to the GDR's insistence on de jure recognition of its sovereignty. Instead, relations between the two Germanies are of a "special relationship" *(Sonderbeziehungen),* which is a type of recognition unique in international law.[22] The GRD was forced to compromise on the FRG demand in order to break a deadlock in the negotiations and ultimately to reach an accord. Nevertheless, GDR sovereignty was indeed conceded by the FRG, which opened the floodgates to worldwide recognition of an East German state and created a need for a foreign policy between the states.

The development of the post–Basic Treaty foreign policy of the GDR toward the FRG is only in its incipient stage. As of yet, no new specific goals have been overtly articulated. In general terms, the Pankow regime has publicly announced on innumerable occasions (some before the Basic Treaty) that the FRG will be dealt with in the same manner as all other capitalist countries, i.e., "peaceful coexistence on the basis of international law."[23] However, the principle applies to the FRG in a slightly different manner, for even greater stress is placed on faithfulness to ratified treaties, as can be seen in a statement by Erich Honecker:

In any case our program [foreign policy] stands not for the "cooling" but rather for the warming of the international climate in the interest of peace and mankind. In this regard, we are for the construction of normal relations based on peaceful coexistence even with the Federal Republic. This normalization process will make good progress if both sides show goodwill and political realism and *if they stick to the letter and spirit of the ratified treaties.* In any event, we will do so in the future.[24]

For the present, then, the GDR policy toward the FRG, as Ludz suggests, is one of *Abgrenzung und Attraktion* ("delimitation and attraction"), a policy set for the GDR by the USSR.[25] The primary aim of this policy is to enhance the international position of the GDR for both domestic and foreign political reasons. Domestically, as stated earlier, the legitimacy (voluntary support of the people) of the governing regime still has not been secured, while in the global arena the danger of renewed international isolation is still manifest—though constantly diminishing. The GDR hopes through its *Abgrenzung und Attraktion* policy to secure legitimacy at home by enhancing its international prestige. The Pankow regime feels that the correctness of its new socialist system, in which the working class ostensibly holds the reins of power, will ultimately "attract" more and more progressive individuals alienated from the West German capitalist system, in which the ruling class is the bourgeoisie. With the *Abgrenzung* side of its policy, the GDR wants to sustain the ideological demarcation between the two German states.

Unlike the captialist-oriented and FRG-oriented formats of GDR foreign policy, which can be easily subsumed under a single ideological concept, i.e., peaceful coexistence, the final format (toward the developing countries) does not lend itself to such a precise and concise *Leitdoktrin*. Instead, it comprises a number of carefully articulated ideological concepts that contain strategic and tactical provisions designed to reach a maximum goal of "complete elimination of imperialist influences in all spheres of social life within the developing states"[26] or, in other words, to bring about "full membership [of the developing countries] in the world socialist system."[27] To be sure, full membership does not come overnight; rather it comes only after a carefully orchestrated and gradual process that includes the following generalized steps:

1. elimination of Western influence, especially in the military, political, economic, and cultural fields
2. introduction of the anti-Western and procommunist version of nonalignment (formally nonaligned by palpably leaning toward the socialist bloc; Sukarno's Indone-

sia and Nasser's Egypt [after 1967] are examples)
3. a step-by-step transition to noncapitalist and socialist forms in political, economic, cultural, and social life
4. steady growth and deepening of cooperation with the communist countries and its gradual expansion into an ever closer association in one field after the other, leading ultimately to an associate and then full membership in the world socialist system[28]

Moreover, it is supposed, the developing countries will follow this process one by one until the capitalist West is surrounded and confronted with the overwhelming power of a united socialist bloc, at which time the West would allegedly surrender without a fight. Thus, with the successful conclusion of the process, the way will have been paved for the long-awaited global socialist victory.

Though this ambitious theoretical foreign policy may at first glance appear to be wishful thinking or socialist rhetoric, a more careful look into GDR and socialist bloc writing on this theme will reveal the high degree of salience given to the process and the vital role of the developing states in the world revolutionary scheme. The gravity of the policy is manifested in four primary ways.

1. *Age and longevity of interest:* communist foreign policy toward the developing countries (national liberation movements) dates to Marx and Engels and has been updated and revised (not so much in theory as in strategy) by almost every major communist theorist.
2. *Amount and candor of written material:* compared to the amount of material on the other three formats of GDR foreign policy, it is safe to say that the volume of GDR literature on policy toward developing countries is substantially greater and certainly less obfuscated.
3. *The detail of written material:* while the other formats have only a broad and general strategy, e.g., peaceful coexistence, developing country policy has very specific and elaborate strategic components.
4. *Convening of conferences on the subject:* in Varna,

Bulgaria, in 1971, the socialist bloc on the occasion of the Third Conference of Socialist Africanists met to discuss the "Problems of the Noncapitalist Path of Development" (an integral strategic concept of GDR and socialist bloc foreign policy), "which not only concerned Africa but due to its importance and topicality" was extended to Asia.[29]

Turning to the ideological components that ostensibly explain and justify GDR and socialist policy moves toward these countries, Edward Taborsky has suggested that these policy moves go beyond just ideological reasons based on the Marxist-Leninist "world outlook"; they involve "reasons of primarily strategic and tactical (military and economic) nature, based on the practical necessities and opportunities of the present stage of the anticapitalist struggle."[30]

Although the theoretical justification of the GDR and socialist foreign policy vis-à-vis the developing countries has its roots in the writings of Marx and Engels, the task of developing a communist strategy toward the developing countries fell to Lenin and Comintern theoreticians. In shifting emphasis from Europe to the colonial countries while also legitimizing the Soviet seizure of power, it was important to show that a particular country need not be in the mature stage of capitalism before the communists could move to seize power. Instead, communists in the era of imperialism would have to seize power wherever and whenever the capitalist system was the weakest.[31] Hence, the Comintern's now famous "weakest link in the chain of capitalism" concept was born. The emancipating character of this concept is obvious. The communist movement could now "legitimately" expand anywhere on the globe, and not just into the advanced industrial societies of Europe. The developing countries were then and are now by far the "weakest link" in the capitalist chain, and, for that reason, they are vital to socialist bloc strategic theory.

Lenin also worked out the following concepts: (1) the theory of imperialism and proletarian revolution, (2) the conditions and mechanics of realizing the dictatorship of the proletariat, (3) the mutual relations of the proletariat and peasantry, (4) the significance of the national question in general, and (5) the role of the party.[32] Since Lenin's death, his basic strategic concepts toward the developing countries have been little changed. Any changes that have been made are chiefly variations on his theme to fit the exigencies of a particular point in time.

The Leninist theoretical progression embraces three major stages: (1) colonial, (2) bourgeois or national democratic, (3) proletarian-socialist. With the almost universal liberation from colonialism of the numerous nations around the globe, the "collapse" of the colonial stage of development is considered by the GDR and socialist bloc for the most part to be successfully complete. Save for activity in a few pockets of remaining colonial territory, attention has now shifted primarily to the intermediate stage of development. This "complete collapse of colonialism," which was declared "imminent " by the *1960 Declaration,* has issued in the national liberation movements and is touted by the GDR and socialist bloc as "a development ranking second in historic importance only to the formation of the world socialist system."[33]

The successful end of a war for national liberation, however, does not mean the victory and immediate imposition of a socialist way of life, but only the winning of freedom from imperialism and feudalism. In other words, the war for national liberation is not a true "proletarian-socialist" revolution, such as the Russian revolution of 1917, but only a "bourgeois-democratic" revolution. The end of the struggle for national liberation marks the beginning of the bourgeois, or national democratic, stage of development toward socialism.[34] The initial tasks of the national democratic stage as outlined by the *1960 Declaration* are as follows:

the consolidation of political independence; the carrying out of agrarian reforms in the interest of the peasantry; elimination of the survivals of feudalism; the uprooting of imperialists, the restriction of foreign monopolies and their expulsion from the national economy [to protect against neocolonialism]; the creation and development of a national industry [under state control]; improvement of the living standard; the democratization of social life; the pursuance of an independent and peaceful foreign policy

[leaning in favor of the Eastern bloc]; and the development of economic and cultural cooperation with the
socialist and other friendly countries.[35]

After the completion of these initial tasks aimed at eliminat-
ing political, social, and economic ills, it is theorized that in
most cases social contradictions (class struggle) will grow
between the factions of the revolutionary amalgamation—
especially between the national bourgeoisie, which will be
inclined more and more to compromise "with domestic reaction and imperialism," and the peasant-proletarian alliance,
which will continue to seek the solution of basic social problems.[36] Gradually, the peasant-proletarian alliance will gain
the upper hand and lead the nation to further social reform
with the penultimate goal of complete socialization of life and
the ultimate goal of integration into the world socialist system.

The vehicle or method to be used by the peasant-proletarian
alliance to reach the desired end is the Leninist process of
"noncapitalist development."[37] Noncapitalist development is
viewed as a dialectical relationship between the struggle for the
solution of the antiimperialist and democratic problems and
the gradual transition to socialism. Thus, it is not a third
category, a sort of stable alternative between capitalism and
socialism. Instead, noncapitalist development is a highly
dynamic process, devised either to preempt or cut short the
capitalist stage of development, in order to avoid the misery of
that stage as well as to achieve socialism at a much earlier date.
Whether the capitalist stage is preempted or cut short is
contingent "on the degree of existence of conditions of capitalist exploitation and the resultant power constellation."[38] It is
preempted completely in countries (such as sub-Saharan Africa), where "there is no capitalist class in the sense of a social
force determining the course of development," and cut short in
countries (such as some of the Arab states and Burma) where
"there were essential beginnings of a capitalist development
and there existed a capitalist class, which, however, had not yet
become an autocratic social force."[39]

The foremost task of noncapitalist development, according
to the *1960 Declaration,* is the creation of the state sector in the

national economy, particularly a state industrial base. By developing the state sector, the following benefits would be realized:

1. It would logically continue the antiimperialist struggle and, in many cases, directly attack the position of the imperialist monopolies.
2. It would be an effective means of accumulating national resources and channeling them into the basic sectors of the national economy.
3. It would restrict the area of private capitalism.
4. It would safeguard (especially if there is a monopoly of foreign trade) the country against the pernicious influence of the capitalist world market.
5. It would create and develop productive forces in a manner best suited to their transition to socialist ownership.
6. It would facilitate utilization of the experience gained by the socialist countries in planning, industrialization, and peasant cooperation, etc.[40]

One additional and vitally important advantage of the noncapitalist path is the elimination of the need for another bloody and costly revolutionary struggle, i.e., the proletarian-socialist revolution. With noncapitalist development, the revolutionary demarcation between the capitalist and socialist stages of development is obviated. Instead, the "national-democratic revolution" gradually and *peacefully* "grows over" (or changes) via the noncapitalist path to a "proletarian-socialist revolution."

Finally, the GDR and socialist bloc deem noncapitalist development possibly "the third most important development of our age" (after the socialist world system and the dissolution of colonialism).[41] However, it is also believed that this path can not be followed without the "fraternal assistance" of the GDR-socialist bloc. Here, "fraternal assistance" translates into direct and indirect participation in the domestic developmental patterns of the individual developing countries.

Within the framework of foreign policy thus far described, it is clear that the GDR has to this point enjoyed comparatively little room for independent maneuver, and indeed, that the government has not even sought much room for initiatives. With most initiatives left to Moscow and with such a willing collaboration on the part of the GDR within the socialist camp, the principal task of GDR foreign policy is to assume its assigned function in a Soviet-sponsored division of labor.

Only the relationship with the FRG provides a distinctive accent differentiating the GDR from socialist allies, but even here Soviet leadership is accepted without reservation so long as the GDR feels no threat to its sovereignty and growing international recognition.

Relationships with countries of the developing world may, however, represent an arena for future relative independence in the unfolding of GDR policy. Although this network of relationships is also regulated in broad terms by the Soviet-led regional association, the economic strength and technological eminence of the GDR tend to invite a display of independence and leadership. It would be hard to maintain at this moment, given the small scale of GDR activity in the developing world, that it offers an escape route from an otherwise tightly harnessed policy framework. But the great attention given to developmental problems suggests at least some preoccupation with this dimension of policy, and it may well turn out, as the internal strength of the economy is increasingly fortified, that a continuation of selective and pragmatic ties with developing countries will allow the GDR to carve out for itself a role that corresponds to the one it has already attained as a vital trading partner within the socialist bloc.

Notes

1. Thomas Rüdiger, *Modell DDR; Die Kalkulierte Emanzipation* (Munich: Carl Hanser Verlag, 1972), p. 214.

2. Wolfgang Leonhard, *Three Faces of Marxism* (New York: Holt, Rinehart, and Winston, 1970), pp. 297-298.

3. *The Constitution of the Socialist State of the German Nation* (Dresden: Verlag Zeit im Bild, 1968), p. 76.

4. *Dokumente zur Aussenpolitik der Deutschen Demokratischen Republik 1970,* vol. 18, book 1 (Berlin: Staatsverlag,

1972), p. 320.

5. Lenin himself disclaimed the infallibility of the Soviet communists and the suitability of Soviet rule in Russia as a model for communists in other countries. See his "Report on the Review of the Program and on Changing the Name of the Party to the Seventh Extraordinary Congress of the Russian Communist Party (Bolshevik), *Collected Works* (Moscow: Foreign Language Publishing House and Progress Publishers, 1960-1966) 33: 132, 135.

6. *Dokumente zur Aussenpolitik, 1971,* vol. 19, book 1, p. 58.

7. Peter Florin, *Zur Aussenpolitik der souveränen sozialistischen DDR* (Berlin: Dietz Verlag, 1967), pp. 35-37.

8. *Dokumente zur Aussenpolitik, 1949-55,* vol. 1, p. 281.

9. Ibid., p. 303.

10. Peter H. Merkl, *German Foreign Policies, West & East* (Santa Barbara: ABC-CLIO, 1974), p. 199.

11. Otto Winzer, *Die Aussenpolitik der DDR im Lichte der Lehren von Karl Marx* (Berlin: Dietz Verlag, 1968), pp. 22-23.

12. Walter Osten, *Die Aussenpolitik der DDR im spannungsfeld zwischen Moskau und Bonn* (Opladen: Leske Verlag, 1969), pp. 48-50.

13. Theo Sommer, "Bonn Changes Course," *Foreign Affairs* 45, no. 3 (April 1967): 489.

14. *Dokumente zur Aussenpolitik, 1970,* p. 44.

15. Peter C. Ludz, *Deutschlands doppelte Zukunft* (Munich: Carl Hanser Verlag, 1974), p. 57.

16. Walter Osten, *Die Aussenpolitik der DDR,* p. 48. Osten divides GDR foreign policy into only three categories, omitting a separate policy toward the FRG. Though not so stated, he might have considered FRG-GDR relations at the time he wrote the book in 1969 (prior to the Basic Treaty) to be on a domestic or intranational level.

17. Kermit E. McKenzie, *Comintern and World Revolution, 1928-1943* (New York: Columbia University Press, 1964), p. 243.

18. Leonhard, *Three Faces of Marxism,* p. 118.

19. As stated earlier, domestic instability and international insecurity have been characteristic of the first twenty-five years of the GDR as well, and therefore the GDR, like the early

Soviet regime, has attached great importance to the concept of peaceful coexistence. Peace is especially important to GDR socialism, as the director of the SED Central Committee's Department for International Relations, Paul Markowski, explains: "Peace means maintenance of the productive forces of socialism, protection of the achievements of socialism, and establishing a favorable starting position for its further development." In other words, peace means the preservation of the GDR socialist regime and what it has accomplished so far as well as provides a launching pad for additional socialist expansion to other countries. Paul Markowski, "Common Foreign Policy of the Socialist Community of States and Peaceful Coexistence," *German Foreign Policy* 12, no. 5 (1973): 504.

20. The Communist parties of the world were called to Moscow on the heels of the Sino-Soviet split to discuss relations among themselves, i.e., to profess loyalty to Moscow and not Peking, and to discuss the tactics to be pursued in the future by world communism. Peaceful coexistence with the West occupied a central position in the discussions. For both the declarations of the 1957 and 1960 meetings, see Dan N. Jacobs, *The New Communist Manifesto and Related Documents* (Evanston, Ill.: Row, Peterson & Co., 1961), pp. 11-42, 169-182.

21. *Deutsche Aussenpolitik,* 1968, no. 12, p. 1500.

22. The only other type of recognition possible under international law is de facto. For a complete and exceptionally good survey of the German question from the perspective of international law, see Jens Hacker, *Der Rechtsstatus Deutschlands aus der Sicht der DDR.* (Köln: Verlag Wissen schaft und Politik, 1974), passim.

23. Erich Honecker "Bericht des Zentralkomitees an den VIII Parteitag der Sozialistischen Einheitspartei Deutschlands," *Dokumente zur Aussenpolitik,* vol. 19, book 1, 1974, p. 66.

24. "Es gibt keine Alternative zur Politik der friedlichen Koexistenz," Wortlaut des Interviews Erich Honeckers für die amerikanische Nachrichtenagentur AP, 11 *Neues Deutschland,* 4 June 1974. Emphasis added.

25. Ludz, *Deutschlands doppelte Zukunft,* p. 95.

26. Lothar Rathmann and Helmut Schilling, "The Noncapitalist Development in Asia and Africa: Balance, Problems, Perspectives," *German Foreign Policy* 10, no. 6 (1971): 504.

27. Edward Taborsky, *Communist Penetration of the Third World* (New York: Robert Speller & Sons, 1973), p. 71.

28. Ibid.

29. R. Andexel and H. Kroske, "Problems of the Noncapitalist Path of Development," *German Foreign Policy* 11, no. 1 (1972): 78. The paper presented by the GDR delegation was the previously cited work by Rathmann and Schilling. It is refreshingly scholarly and candid.

30. Taborsky, *Communist Penetration,* p. 3.

31. Bela Kun, ed., *Kommunisticheskii Internatsional v do kumentakh: Resheniia, tezisy: vozzvaniia Kongressov Kominterna i Plenumov IKKI, 1919-32* (Moscow: Partiinoe izdatel'stvo, 1933), p. 9.

32. Shortly after Lenin's death in 1924, the ECCI in 1925 defined the relation between Lenin's theoretical writings and Marxism: "Leninism is Marxism of the era of monopolistic capitalism (imperialism), imperialist wars, and proletarian revolutions." McKenzie, *Comintern and World Revolution,* p. 56.

33. Jacobs, *The New Communist Manifesto,* p. 30.

34. The term "national democratic" is an old Lenin reference to the Asian revolutionary movement in 1920. After a hiatus during the Comintern and early postwar periods, when it was changed back to "bourgeois democratic," the term was reinstituted in the 1960 Declaration and is in vogue today. Cf. Taborsky, *Communist Penetration,* p. 18.

35. Jacobs, *The New Communist Manifesto,* p. 32.

36. Ibid., p. 33.

37. Some socialist bloc theorists are not totally convinced this proletarian-peasant alliance will always win out; they thus make theoretical allowances for temporary "reversals," i.e., when "reactionary elements of the exploiting classes" usurp total power in close allegiance with imperialist forces. "While it is quite appropriate to say that for a large number of Afro-Asian countries the road to socialism will lead via noncapitalist

development, it would be undialectical to derive therefrom a scheme applicable to all countries. It is rather possible that a number of Afro-Asian countries, after an extended period of capitalist evolution and after the seizure of political power by the proletariat and its revolutionary party, will initiate the process of transition to socialism under conditions coming close to the type of antiimperialist and democratic revolution in the developed capitalist countries or the type of revolution aiming at the establishment of a people's democracy." Rathmann and Schilling, "Noncapitalist Development," p. 505.

38. Ibid.

39. Ibid.

40. Taborsky, *Communist Penetration,* p. 23.

41. G. Mirsky, "Developing Nations at the Crossroads," *New Times,* 1971, no. 1, p. 18.

9. Détente and the Military

Dale R. Herspring

How to deal with the gradual movement toward détente in Europe has been one of the most troublesome problems facing East German leaders in recent years. Few areas exist where concern over problems associated with a relaxation of tensions has been more apparent than in the SED's handling of the NVA *(Nationale Volksarmee,* or "National People's Army").[1] The NVA is one of the most modern armed forces in all of Europe.[2] Within the Warsaw Pact, it occupies second place behind the Soviet Union. In addition to a modern air force, it possesses a small, but modern, navy and an army of 90,000 divided into six divisions, four of motorized infantry and two of armor. As a result of high marks earned in past maneuvers and its strategic geographical location, the Soviets view the NVA as an important addition to the Soviet forces stationed in the GDR.[3] Should the great powers agree to reduce their forces and should Soviet, rather than Eastern European, troops bear the brunt of reductions, it is probable that the importance of the NVA within the Warsaw Pact will increase even more. The important position the GDR occupies in the Warsaw Pact, like its economic role in COMECON, is a useful bargaining tool in its relations with the Soviets. As long as the East Germans are able to convince the Russians that the NVA is both militarily prepared and politically reliable, they will be in a good position to bargain with the Soviets for favors in other areas.

From all appearances, the Soviets, at present at least, remain convinced that the NVA fulfills both of these requirements. The Soviets have provided the East Germans with some of the most modern equipment of any of the Warsaw Pact countries, thereby attesting to both its technical competence and its political reliability.[4] Since the Soviet suspicions that a high degree of combat preparedness or ideological purity could be undermined by a relaxation of tensions, which in turn would undermine this beneficial relationship, it is not suprising that the SED has gone to great lengths to assure the Soviets that the NVA continues to be worthy of their trust.

Concern over the effects of movement toward détente on the NVA is not prompted solely by foreign policy considerations. The internal political situation within the GDR also plays an important role. The party has had a tendency to utilize the level of politicization in the NVA as a barometer of party control throughout the remainder of society. Having paid particular attention to assuring a high degree of political reliability in the NVA, the party has long felt that if a deemphasis on ideological factors occurred there, then the situation in the rest of society was probably even more serious.

Unfortunately from the SED's standpoint, the movement toward détente has adversely affected the NVA, both in terms of combat preparedness and ideological purity. There has been a feeling among members of the NVA that since war is becoming less of a danger, perhaps the West Germans and Americans are not as much of a military threat as in the past. If this is so, some ask, then why all of the concern over problems of military preparedness?

The party reacted to this situation by arguing—much like the American and Soviet military—that détente is only possible because of military strength. Nothing in the West has changed, it rejoins. It is only because of the military strength and preparedness of the Soviet Union and other socialist countries, including the GDR, that the West has been forced to recognize the futility of military adventures in Europe. This situation will continue, they argue, only as long as the socialist states remain militarily alert and ready to repel any Western acts of aggression. SED Party Secretary Erich Honecker emphasized this point in an unusually strong speech before members of the NVA on January 7, 1972. In referring to the "Western-imperialist bloc," he stated:

> Nevertheless, it remains aggresssive, malicious, and dangerous. . . . . As a result, we have no reason to let down in our military and political vigilance. Our picture of our enemy *(Feindbild)* is completely accurate. There is nothing in the picture to change, because our enemy has not changed.[5]

Closely associated with the tendency to play down the military threat from the West is the tendency on the part of some to equate peaceful coexistence with ideological convergence. After all, if one can peacefully coexist with the imperialists politically and economically, then why not ideologically? On this point, the party's reaction has been immediate and to the point. The two ideologies are basically incompatible, they argue, as exemplified by Honecker's interview with C. L. Sulzberger of the *New York Times,* an interview in which he stated, "ideological convergence will not come about. We proceed from two different positions."[6]

Party ideology further underlined the incompatibility of military détente and ideological convergence by pointing out that the West, faced with a situation in which the balance of power has shifted to the side of the socialist countries, has merely substituted bourgeois ideology for military power in pursuit of its unchanging goal of undermining the socialist countries. The class struggle has not ceased; it has merely shifted to another area. Consequently, it has become necessary for the GDR and other socialist states to defend themselves by limiting the subverting influence of Western thoughts and ideas.[7] As a result, the party has introduced its policy of *Abgrenzung,* or separation from the West. Contacts with the West, particularly with the NVA, are to be avoided at all costs. Additionally, assuming that some aspects of bourgeois ideology do penetrate, the SED emphasizes factors such as party activities and ideological indoctrination to maintain its hold within the NVA.

Therefore, recognizing the need to maintain a high level of combat readiness and political reliability within the NVA, for both internal and external reasons, the party has taken steps to assure that both remain at a high level. Instead of introducing new procedures or organs, it has tended to rely on established forms of control and increase their effectiveness as the situation warrants. Although the party has been concerned about both combat readiness and political reliability, some of the measures it has emphasized most strongly in these two areas differ.

The Technical Response

A strong indication of the importance attached to a continued high degree of combat readiness is found in the NVA's insistence on technical qualifications. The NVA has long viewed the technical qualifications of its officers and men as the foundation upon which a high degree of combat preparedness is built. As General of the Army Karl-Heinz Hoffmann, the minister of national defense, put it at the Eighth Party Conference:

> When we say we are up to date in fulfilling our tasks, then behind this simple statement is hidden the ability of thousands of the leading officers of our armed forces to engage in combat according to the newest knowledge available to military science, [and] utilize complicated systems. . . ; behind the expert servicing of highly modern technical weapons systems lie well-trained soldiers and NCOs.[8]

In other words, only by obtaining well-educated and trained personnel—particularly officers—is there any hope of maintaining a high degree of combat readiness. Consequently, it is not surprising that the party has placed considerable emphasis on the technical qualifications of its personnel.

Few policies introduced in the NVA indicate more clearly the close association between technical qualifications and career success for an officer in the NVA than the sets of efficiency reports *(Attestation)* originally introduced in 1964.[9]

These early reports, which were supposed to be completed every four years, included information on an individual's technical background and qualifications. For example, what was his highest level of education? If low, particularly if he did not possess the *Abitur,* or even worse the *mittlere Reife,* what had he done to improve the situation? Based on the answer to these and other questions, the individual's military superior, in consultation with the military party organization, would make a recommendation concerning his future. Although these reports were not as well developed at that time as they are today, one thing was made very clear: those who failed to show an interest in improving their technical qualifications might soon find themselves on the outside looking for new employment. The second set of reports was completed in 1968 and closely resembled the first. A third set of reports was introduced in 1972 and a fourth in 1976. Although details concerning the outcome of these reports are not yet known, there is little doubt that they reflect the party's increasing concern over maintenance of a high level of technical competence.[10]

This continuing concern is apparent in changes introduced in 1972 efficiency reports. One of the most important of these changes was the decision to link rank closely with educational qualifications. The use of technology in the NVA has advanced to the point where very few operational positions at the officer level can be carried out by one who has not attended the appropriate school or university. According to East German sources, when filling out an efficency report, the reviewing officer must recommend an officer for attendence at one of the various schools, either civilian or military, if such further education is needed for the next higher rank. In order to be recommended, the individual must be technically qualified. If he is not, he will remain at his present rank and retire upon reaching a certain age. Or, if he is unqualified for this rank also, he may be demoted or released from the service.[11]

Two examples may help to describe this policy. For promotion to major, a captain in the Air Defense section of the Air Force may be required to complete a course at a missile school in order to handle his new responsibilities. Should he be considered incapable or unwilling to apply himself at this school, then in spite of a recommendation for promotion, he is likely to remain a captain; upon reaching the mandatory retirement age (in this case thirty-eight), he will be placed in the reserves. Attendance at special schools is also required for higher-level positions. For example, all regimental-level commanders are now required to attend the Friedrich Engels Military Academy or its counterpart in the Soviet Union or another socialist country for three to four years. As a result, it is very unlikely that those who fail to be recommended for study at the academy will ever command a regiment.

The increasing pressure applied by the party in the form of these efficiency reports has played an important role in producing what must be listed as spectacular increases in the educational qualifications of the East German officer corps. It might be helpful at this point to take a look at some of these advances.[12] In 1956, at the time of the founding of the NVA, 76 percent of all officers had not gone beyond primary school *(Grundschule)*. By 1971 this figure was reduced to 10 percent. Similarly, although only 10 percent and 11 percent of all officers possessed the *mittlere Reife* or *Abitur,* respectively, in 1956, by 1971 the number had risen to 53.9 percent and 37.1 percent. In addition, by 1971, 80 percent of all officers were graduates of three- or four-year officer training schools, while only 10.7 percent had received such training in 1956. One of the most impressive gains was made by the NVA in the area of academic degrees. Although starting from only 2 percent in 1956, by 1973 the NVA had succeeded in raising the percentage of officers with academic degrees to 25 percent. This is particularly noteworthy when one realizes that in the West German *Bundeswehr* in 1971, only 10 percent of all officers possess an academic degree.

In recognition of the increasingly higher level of technology present in the NVA, the Council of State *(Staatsrat)* issued a decree on December 10, 1970, placing officer training schools on a par with civilian universities. This means that, like the civilian schools, they are permitted to award diplomas to successful students (advanced degrees continue to be awarded only by civilian universities or the Friedrich Engels Military Academy). This is the first time in German history that an officer training school has been given this privilege. It is highly unlikely that the East Germans would have granted these schools this status simply as a device to impress the Soviets.The primary reason appears rather to have resulted from a need to attract the best qualified youth of the country to fill military positions demanding a high degree of technical competence. Although not specifically required for entrance to these schools, the military was hopeful of attracting young men with an *Abitur.* This placed them in competition with the universities for the young men holding this passport to German higher education. The military schools were handicapped, however, since youngsters who entered military schools prior to this change were left with nothing more than a certificate classifying them as a technician. The brightest students tended to go to the universities. After all, assuming an individual did not remain in the service for twenty or thirty years, what would he have when he left? Before December 10, 1970, he would have nothing more than a certificate entitling him to work as a technician under the supervision of an engineer with a diploma.

The decision to upgrade the officer schools in recognition of the higher quality of instruction and in order to attract more qualified officer cadets has apparently been successful. According to recent reports, almost all cadets presently attending the NVA's four officer schools[13] now possess the *Abitur,* even though this is still not required by law.

Ever alert to possibilities for raising the combat preparedness of its officer corps, the NVA introduced a directive on January 4, 1969, entitled "Regulations on the classification and awarding of classification medals to members of the NVA."[14] While this order concerned medals that had been issued since 1962, it now awarded the individual qualifying for the distinction a civilian title. The three numerical classification levels introduced in 1961 were made equivalent to the following civilian titles: an individual passing the examination at the first level would be classified as a skilled worker *(Facharbeiter)* in his area of endeavor; those passing it at the second level received the title of master *(Meister)*; while anyone passing the examination at the third level qualified for the title of engineer or technician *(Ingenieur* or *Techniker).*[15] This means that upon leaving the service an individual possessing one of these skill titles can obtain a job commensurate with this title from a civilian place of employment. To pass these examinations, more extensive knowledge is required than mere practical skill. As one naval officer explained,

> An ammunition officer cannot do without a basic knowledge of inorganic and organic chemistry, electronics, and other specialties. Such basic knowledge is unavoidable for a complete understanding of specialized problems. For that reason, these types of demands will be reflected in the tests for classification medals.[16]

Thus from a technical standpoint, the East Germans have utilized the carrot and stick approach. Those who are qualified are rewarded in the form of promotions, medals, and titles. Those who are either not capable or not interested in raising their technical and educational qualifications will either remain at their present rank and retire upon reaching time in grade or, where the situation warrants, face transfer to the reserves.

The Political Response

To assure a continued high degree of political reliability in the face of a relaxation of tensions, the party has sought to reemphasize the importance of the "redness" of NVA officers. According to the Report of the Central Committee to the Eighth Party Conference, the present situation calls for officers who are "class-conscious fighters who master socialist military science from the basis of Marxist-Leninist theory."[17]

Toward this end, the SED leadership adopted two measures of particular interest. First, it forced the regular military officer to continue his close involvement in party activities. Second, the authority and effectiveness of party control mechanisms—particularly the *Politorgane* ("political organs") and the military party organization—to watch over his activities and report on his devotion (or lack of it) to party policies were increased. In order to appreciate fully the role played by these measures and the party's continuing efforts to strengthen their effectiveness, some background information may be useful.

Before the founding of the NVA in 1956, responsibility for party activities in its predecessor, the KVP *(Kasernierte Volkspolizei,* or "People's Police quartered in barracks"), was in the hands of the political officer. Military questions were the regular officer's concern, and political decisions were left to the political officer. As long as the regular officer was at least neutral toward the party, he was left alone. This situation changed, however, when, shocked by the Hungarian Revolution in 1956, the party quickly came to the conclusion that anything less than complete subservience on the part of its military forces was unacceptable. As a result, a large number of former *Wehrmacht* officers who had served in the KVP and newly formed NVA were retired. At the same time, the party's view of the regular NVA officer changed radically. The division between political and technical specialization was no longer satisfactory. From now on, the regular officers would be required increasingly to become "red" as well as "expert."

Two areas are of particular interest in observing the party's attempt to involve regular military officers in political activities; responsibility for political indoctrination and *Massenarbeit* ("work with the masses"). One of the important changes introduced as a result of the Hungarian incident was to make the regular officer officially responsible for both of these activities. Nevertheless, he did share accountability for it with his Deputy for Political Work (or political officer) in practice. This meant that while the political officer might select the topics for discussion or determine the times and speakers for lectures, he did so only after close consultation with the commanding officer. The same was true for *Massenarbeit.* Although the political officer might select which museums to visit and determine the Soviet units with which close contact would be maintained, he did so under the supervision of the commander. Failure to come up to party standards would be entered in the efficiency reports of both individuals. Although formal responsibility for political indoctrination and *Massenarbeit* has remained the same to the present day, changes in the activities of two party control mechanisms, the *Politorgane* and the military party organization, have actually increased the degree of responsibility and involvement by the regular officer with both programs.

Of all the mechanisms the party has on hand to assure a high degree of political reliability on the part of its officer corps, none is more important than the *Politorgane* and military party organization. The *Politorgane* refer to party control units beginning with the Central Committee and extending all the way down to company-level political officers. As presently structured, the *Politorgane* can be pictured graphically as follows:

CENTRAL COMMITTEE OF THE SED
|
DEPUTY OF THE MINISTER, NATIONAL DEFENSE
CHIEF, MAIN POLITICAL ADMINISTRATION
|
LEADER, POLITICAL ADMINSTRATION,
MILITARY "BEZIRK"
|
LEADER, POLITICAL SECTION,
DIVISION LEVEL
|
DEPUTY OF THE COMMANDER FOR POLITICAL
WORK, REGIMENT LEVEL
|
DEPUTY OF THE COMMANDER FOR POLITICAL
WORK, BATTALION LEVEL
|
POLITICAL DEPUTY OF THE
COMPANY CHIEF

The task of the *Politorgane* is to direct all political work within the NVA. This includes, among other things, directing political indoctrination, making certain that all party orders are obeyed, and controlling political cadres. Thus, in theory at least, the *Politorgane* are in a position to report any failure on the part of a regular officer to show proper concern and enthusiasm for his own or his troops' level of political consciousness. The reality of *Politorgane* authority, however, has often differed from the theory.

Before 1958, the *Politorgane* were loosely organized, and although represented by the political officer down as far as the company level, *Politorgane* reports were often sidetracked. Many unsatisfactory reports by the political officer on subjects such as the commander's involvement in political indoctrination never reached the top, where effective action could be taken. Although the 1958 instructions for political work in the NVA created the organizational chart above and provided the *Politorgane* with the responsibilities described above, coordination of activities continued to be a problem. For example, investigations by higher level *Politorgane* into party activities were carried out. However, these investigations were often set up haphazardly, and in many cases, as a result of the loose organizational structure, their findings were never reported.

In 1961, an attempt was made to increase the effectiveness of the *Politorgane* by enlarging and upgrading units at the division and *Bezirk* levels. While helpful, particularly at higher levels, this reorganization still left the *Politorgane* impotent at lower levels, where most political activities occurred. In 1963, another attempt was made to overcome this weakness by making the *Politorgane* responsible for the lowest major unit in the military party organization, the basic organization *(Grundorganisation)*. Their task was to insure that meetings on this level were held and that all party members attended. In spite of this change, problems remained. The political section at the divisional level was expected to coordinate the activities of these basic organizations on the regimental and independent company level. Yet, too many regiments and independent companies existed for anything like an efficient means to coordination to be effected.

Finally, the party moved to correct this problem in 1967 with the creation of a Central Party Directory *(Zentrale Parteileitung,* or ZPL) at the company level to coordinate the actions of not only the basic organization but smaller units as well. As a result, it became possible for the party to watch over the political activities of NVA officers down to a rather low organizational level. Repeated failure of a regular officer to place the proper degree of emphasis on political indoctrination or *Massenarbeit*, for example, would be brought to the attention of the appropriate authorities, and action would be taken to correct the situation. *Politorgane* authorities continued, however, to find one situation unsatisfactory. This involved the reporting of violations or problems in areas such as political indoctrination. Since both the political officer and the regular officer shared responsibility for many of these activities in practice, it is not surprising that they often tended to minimize problems of violations. Recognizing the need for a second mechanism, to be certain that as many violations of the spirit as of the letter of party instructions were reported, the party decided to increase the authority of the military party organization.

Although the military party organization has been involved in the NVA from the very beginning, its activities were often ignored during the early years.[18] For one thing, membership in the SED was not an absolute requirement for service as an officer in the NVA. In 1956, for example, at the time of the founding of the NVA, only 79.5 percent of all officers were members of the SED, a rather low number in view of the fact that 99 percent were members in 1974. In addition, those who were members often missed more party meetings than they attended.

One of the first steps taken by the SED in 1958 that affected the military party organization was the creation of party groups *(Parteigruppen)*. The next highest party unit, the basic organization, existed only down to the regimental level at this time. Most of the party's activities, however, were carried on lower in the organizational structure—primarily at the company level. Consequently, the party was often forced to rely on the political officer for direction and comments on the effectiveness of political activities such as political indoctrination. By creating *Parteigruppen,* which might be composed of four or five members at the company level, however, the party now had an organizational unit to supplement the actions of the political officer.

In 1963, the party moved to strengthen the effectiveness of the military party organization by establishing the basic organization all the way down to the battalion and independent company level. The primary effect of this change was to increase the influence of the military party organization over organized activities such as political indoctrination and *Massenarbeit*. The basic organization made suggestions for improvements in the way these activities were handled. In 1967, however, with the creation of the ZPL mentioned above, the military party organization really began to exert a strong influence. Individuals who failed to attend meetings, made disparaging remarks about the party, or failed to show the appropriate enthusiasm for party activities were reported.

Although there have not been any major structural modifications in either the *Politorgane* or the military party organization in recent years in response to the threat to political fervor presented by a relaxation of tensions in Europe, the party has continued to broaden its areas of authority. This is particularly true of the military party organization.

One indication of just how broad the party's authority is becoming is illustrated by five resolutions adopted at the authoritative Eighth Conference of Delegates of the Party Organization of the SED in the NVA held in 1971. These resolutions, which are binding on all members of the SED in the NVA as well as all components of the party organization, cover just about every aspect of military life.[19]

The first resolution states that it is the most important task of all party organizations as well as each communist in the NVA to further the role of the party in all areas of the armed forces. Specifically, this means that the party organization is to concern itself with the level of combat preparedness. Attention is to be given not only to how well the unit does in combat training exercises, but to ideological matters as well. How many officers and men have qualified in political subjects? Do all attend political indoctrination classes? If not, then who is responsible, and what can be done to correct the situation?

The second resolution deals with questions of order and discipline. Do members of the unit have a good record in this area? If not, why? Is the commander at fault? This resolution goes on to suggest that perhaps if party members spent more time with those who violate regulations, explaining to them the serious effect such violations have on combat readiness, this situation could be improved.

The third resolution deals with relations between subordinates and superiors. Is the commander exercising his authority properly? Is he consulting with the military collective? Or is he one of those commanders who thinks he can go it alone? Any violations of socialist relationships between superior and subordinates are to be uncovered by the party organization and reported to the *Politorgane* immediately.

The fourth resolution admonishes both the military party organization and the *Politorgane* to become more concerned with the selection, development, and placement of military officers, particularly those holding important positions. In evaluating qualifications, they are told to consider not only an individual's technical competency, but his political consciousness as well. In addition, it is important that such individuals, regardless of their educational background, constantly update it by participation in part-time technical and political courses.

The fifth and last resolution directs that more attention be given to increasing the effectiveness of the basic organization. From now on, according to the resolution, the basic organization is to play a more important role in the life of the unit. It must extend its activities beyond merely conducting one meeting per month.

Although adopted in 1971, indications are that these resolutions continue to reflect party policy. Honecker repeated them, for example, in his famous Prora speech cited above. In addition, Colonel General Heinz Keßler also cited them in an article dealing with the contribution of the NVA to the Warsaw Pact.[20] The continuing stress placed by the party on the military party organization, coupled with the increased effectiveness of the *Politorgane* in reporting violations, make it appear very unlikely that members of the NVA are or will be permitted to decrease their involvement in party activities such as political indoctrination and *Massenarbeit*. Indeed, the increasing role being played by the *Politorgane* and the military party organization suggests that rather than decreasing, the level of politicization within the NVA is on the rise.

Conclusion

Recognizing both the internal and external threat presented by a relaxation of tension, the SED has moved quickly within the NVA to minimize its effects. On the one hand, it has continued to stress the importance of combat readiness. This has resulted in an ever-increasing emphasis on both educational qualifications and general technical competency. Perhaps more important than the SED's technical response has been its political one. A decrease in political reliability on the part of NVA members—particularly officers—could create serious problems for the East Germans, not only in their relations with the Soviets but internally as well. To deal with this problem, they have perfected and expanded the authority of their most important control mechanisms in the NVA—the *Politorgane* and the military party organization. In fact, the authority of these organs has increased so much that they pervade almost all aspects of military life, including such vital areas as discipline, promotions, training, and after-duty activities. Every direction he turns, the NVA officer is met by the military party organization. Failure on his part to show sufficient enthusiasm for party policy and activities could mean the end of his career in the armed forces.

While it is too early to tell what the long-term effects of a détente in Europe will be on the GDR, the view from the NVA, at least, suggests that for the present the SED has decided to continue to place great stress on combat preparedness and political reliability. The GDR's military relationship with the Russians and the need for internal stability appear too important at this point to permit "a relaxation of tension" in the NVA.

Notes

1. The views expressed in this article are those of the author and do not represent official State Department policy.

2. This is particularly true of its air force. Eighteen of its twenty-one interceptor squadrons are made up of MIG-21s. International Institute of Strategic Studies, *The Military Balance, 1974-1975* (London: International Institute of Strategic Studies, 1972), p. 12.

3. Thomas A. Forester, *NVA, Kernstück der Landesvertei-
digung der DDR* [The NPA, Heart of the Military Defense of
the GDR] (Köln: Markus Verlag, 1972), p. 88.

4. Only after the construction of the Wall in 1961 did the
Russians really began to trust the East Germans with modern
equipment. Up to that time, there was always the danger that a
disenchanted member of the NVA would walk to West Berlin
with the plans of some piece of modern equipment.

5. Erich Honecker, "Der Sozialismus gewann an Stärke—
der Frieden ist sicher geworden" [Socialism Became
Stronger—Peace Has Become More Secure], *Volksarmee,*
1971, no. 3, p. 40. Although Honecker may have had the
Soviets in mind when he delivered this speech, it is significant
that he chose to make it in front of a military audience. This has
continued to be a frequent theme not only in the civilian press
but within the military as well. See, in particular, Admiral W.
Verner, "Militärpolitische Aspekte des IX. Parteitages der
Sozialistischen Einheitspartei Deutschlands" [Military-
political Aspects of the Ninth Party Congress of the Socialist
Unity Party of Germany], *Militärwesen* (August 1976), p.12.

6. "Antwort auf zusätzliche Fragen von Herrn C. L. Sulzberger" [Answer to Additional Questions from Mr. C. L.
Sulzberger], *Neues Deutschland,* 25 November 1972, p. 3.

7. See Peter C. Ludz, "Continuity and Change Since Ulbricht," *Problems of Communism* 21, no. 2 (March-April,
1972): 61.

8. Heinz Hoffmann, "Remarks," *Protokoll des VIII. Parteitages der SED* [Proceedings of the Eighth Party Conference
of the SED] (Berlin: Dietz Verlag, 1971) 1: 253.

9. For a discussion of these reports, see Generalmajor S.
Weiß, "Alle Voraussetzungen für eine wirksame Qualifizie-
rung schaffen!" [Create All of the Prerequisites for an Effective
Qualification!] *Militärwesen,* January, 1964, pp. 33-45.

10. See especially Generalmajor W. Rothe, "Der Mensch
entscheidet über den wirkungsvollen Einsatz der Kampftech-
nik" [The Individual Decides the Effective Usage of Military
Technology] *Militärwesen,* September 1975, pp. 3-11.

11. This policy is described in Oberstleutnant E. Koepe,
"Ziel der Attestierung—die Förderung der Kader" [Goal of

the Attestation—Advancement of the Cadre], *Militärwesen*, September, 1971, pp. 1188-1196.

12. Most of the statistics that follow both here and under the section dealing with the political response are taken from this writer's full-length study of the NVA. See Dale R. Herspring, *East German Civil-Military Relations: The Impact of Technology, 1949-1972* (New York: Praeger, 1973). Detailed footnotes for these statistics are not repeated here because of the length of the multiple sources used to arrive at many of them.

13. These schools are the Ernst Thälmann Army Officers School, the Rosa Luxemburg Border Troops Officers Training School, the Franz Mehring Air Force Officers Training School, and the Karl Liebknecht Navy Officers Training School.

14. *Zeittafel zur Militärgeschichte der Deutschen Demokratischen Republic, 1948 bis 1968* [Chronological Table of Military History of the German Democratic Republic, 1949 to 1968] (Berlin: Deutscher Militärverlag, 1969), p. 294.

15. The title "technician" or "engineer" puts its holder on a par with a graduate of one of the GDR's technical schools *(Fachschule)*.

16. Fregattenkapitän P. Schubert, "Der Erwerb der Klassifizierungsabzeichen—ein Mittel sur Erhöhung der Einsatzbereitschaft der Bewaffung der Volksmarine" [Acquisition of the Classification Badge—A means of Raising the Readiness for Action of the Weapons of the People's Navy], *Volksmarine,* July, 1969, p. 822.

17. "Bericht des Zentralkomitees an den VIII. Parteitag der Sozialistischen Einheitspartei Deutschlands. Berichterstatter: Genosse Erich Honecker" [Report of the Central Committee to the Eighth Party Conference of the Socialist Unity Party of Germany. Commentator: Comrade Erich Honecker], *Protokoll des VIII. Parteitages der SED* (Berlin: Dietz Verlag, 1971), 1: 88.

18. The SED is the only one of East Germany's five political parties that is permitted to organize in the military.

19. For a complete listing of these resolutions, see "Entschließung der VIII. Delegiertenkonferenz der Parteiorganisationen der Socialistischen Einheitspartei Deutschlands in der

Nationalen Volksarmee am 22. and 23. Mai 1971" [Resolutions of the Eighth Delegates' Conference of the Party Organizations of the Socialist Unity Party of Germany in the National People's Army of 22 and 23 May 1917],*Parteiarbeiter* [Party Worker], special issue, 1971, pp. 6-10.

20. Generaloberst Heinz Keßler, "Der Beitrag der Nationalen Volksarmee zur weiteren Stärkung der sozialistischen Verteidigungsbündnisses" [The Contribution of the National People's Army to the Further Strengthening of the Socialist Defensive Alliance], *Militärwesen*, March 1971, pp. 7-10.

10. International Political Communication

Anita D. Mallinckrodt

Nearly everyone knows that nation-states try to achieve their international goals through diplomacy, or "jaw-jaw," as Churchill said, and when that does not work, through military actions. The organized diplomatic and military efforts of one group of people to influence another have been known since ancient times—the early city-states exchanged emissaries or battled one another to exhaustion to achieve what they conceived of as security. Today these two tools, or instruments, of foreign policy are represented everywhere by the major governmental departments known as the foreign ministry and the ministry for defense or their equivalent.

Slightly less well known is the third instrument of foreign policy, economics. It began to be organized as a state tool following World War I, when interdependence of international economic conditions became strikingly clear. Economic specialists then were added to the political specialists in foreign ministries and also took their place in embassies along with military attachés and political officers. Over the years, the economic tool has become more powerful, visible and understood.

However, the fourth tool, the post–World War II newcomer to the family of foreign policy instruments, is less well known. Specialists cannot even agree on what to call it. Some say simply "international political communication," others "international propaganda" or, more broadly, "psychological operations."

Propaganda as Foreign Policy Instrument

The point, however, is that in the present age of public and mass communications, strictly diplomatic channels, i.e., communications between states, are transcended in the effort to influence the behavior of other states. Foreign policy goals are now articulated over the heads of governments and also often behind their backs, directly to the people.

Because of the mass communications potential of this century, states have become what one specialist calls "other-oriented":

decisions must be explained also internally to allies and friends, to neutrals and to opponents. . . . In international politics explanation plays a particularly important part because much of the behavior is verbal in form; purposes are made articulate and policies are carried out with due regard to the announcements of other states.[1]

When such communications are part of a deliberate national campaign for the purpose of influencing actions abroad that would support the communicator's foreign policy goals, the communications process may be called "psychological operations" or, more simply, "international propaganda." Propaganda, in other words, is

the deliberate attempt by some individual or group to form, control, or alter the attitudes of other groups by the use of the instrument of communication, with the intention that in any situation the reaction of those so influenced will be that desired by the propagandist.[2]

Crucial here is that the attempt to influence be *deliberate* (conscious, planned, organized, a campaign), be intended to produce immediate or future *action* (not just intellectual persuasion for the sake of argument), and be aimed at affecting *attitudes and opinions* (to reinforce, activate, or convert) through external influences of persuasion (communications, not coercion).[3] Another way of putting it is that propaganda aims at shaping expectations, for political decisions are the product of the communications process, of what man *thinks* the world is, not what it *is*.[4] The propagandist communicates to an audience in such a way that it will interpret future events in a manner leading to achievement of the communicator's foreign policy goals.[5]

In the unending controversy over what propaganda is and is not, the above definition has the merit of being value-free. It regards propaganda as a *process of influence*, whose goodness or evil can be seen only in the end goal or the means, but not in the process itself. In this sense, when states moralistically declare, "we do not use propaganda in our overseas radio broadcasts; we only tell the truth about our country," they reflect the semantic confusion and "dirty work" connotation attached to the neutral concept "propaganda."

But regardless of what one calls the process of influencing international political audiences through communications, the fact is that it has become increasingly important in the latter half of the twentieth century. This is due in large measure to (1) increased emphasis on political persuasion in an era where reliance on coercion could mean nuclear suicide, and (2) spreading mass communications media and literacy, which make international communications technically possible.

The result has been that nations have institutionalized and organized their international political communications efforts, especially since World War II.[6] The United States has its U.S. Information Agency, Great Britain its British Information Service, and the Soviet Union has an impressive network of overseas operations directed by the Central Committee's Department of Agitation and Propaganda[7] (implemented largely by the State Committee for Cultural Relations with Foreign Countries).[8]

In each case, the instrument of international political communications is seen as a supplement to the other three. "If there are not good policies," it often is said, "there cannot be effective communications." Another way of illustrating the point might be to suggest that the political acts of granting economic aid or signing treaties achieve optimum impact only if people know about them, i.e., if communicators tell the story.

In addition to becoming more important, the communications tool also is becoming more sophisticated. At first states were seemingly impressed with quantity—all one had to do was print enough brochures or transmit enough broadcasts across national borders, and readers and listeners at once would recognize the "truth" of the message and cheer the foreign policy efforts of the sender. This was often referred to as "the masses approach." Then, however, by applying psychological and sociological insights about how attitudes and opinions are formed and influenced, especially through group associations, the "classes approach" was evolved. Specifically, this means that communicators tailor their messages according to target groups, i.e., appeals to scientists are different from those to workers, and industrialized nations are addressed differently from developing nations.

Insights from psychology also concerned the limitations of communications' influence. "Reinforcement" of attitudes or "modification" of attitudes through awakening latent ones (as by adding to factual information) were found to be feasible goals. "Conversion" was not very likely.

In addition, findings from political science showed that the decision-making process itself—exactly that which the communications sought to influence—is not a matter of masses, but rather of groups. For instance, even in so-called open or democratic societies, there is not a one-way flow of influence directly from "the people" to "the government" or vice versa. Instead, there is a "two-step flow," in which government words are transmitted and interpreted by influential individuals, such as work supervisors, religious leaders, civic club presidents, and journalists. These interpreters are "opinion-makers."[9]

Or the process of communications and decision making may be seen as even more complicated, as a four-step flow: (1) the government speaks, (2) the opinion-makers interpret, (3) opinion-makers report group reaction, and (4) the government hears and decides.[10]

Clearly from this standpoint, in a pluralistic society groups such as educators, journalists, and labor unions are especially important in the information-opinion-decision process of foreign policy formulation. Or, in so-called closed societies, the significant groups obviously include members of the ruling political party and, increasingly, scientists and technocrats.

In short, today's discriminating foreign communicator seeks not only to influence directly foreign policy decision-makers but also opinion-makers, who in turn influence the decision-makers within their own environmental context.

The GDR Context

GDR communications specialists, too, are involved in developing and applying such concepts of effective international communications. In their case, it is especially important, since the GDR, through the absence of diplomatic recognition in many countries of the world, is denied use of the most traditional instrument of foreign policy, diplomacy. In addition, it is clear that as a small country and a subordinate of the Soviet Union, the GDR's military potential is drastically limited. Thus, economics and communications are the two tools on which the GDR must rely in its efforts to achieve its foreign policy goals.

That the GDR is becoming more sophisticated in this regard is clear not only from the quality of its communications output but also its substantive discussions. This undoubtedly is due in large part to the "invitation" of the SED at its Seventh Party Congress "to work out and apply Marxist-Leninist social prognosis to an extent unknown until now."[11] As a result, GDR social scientists are taking a new look at many aspects of politics.[12]

For instance, in a book published in 1968 on the anniversary of Marx's birth, leading figures in the Institute for International Relations in East Berlin called for the development of a sociological method for analyzing international relations, a method that would make use of the groundwork laid in this area by Marx and Engels.[13] One of the authors, a sociologist, acknowledged in another article that systemic aspects of international relations urgently deserving scholarly attention included "the foreign policy purpose formulation and decision making of a state."[14] In that same article on foreign policy,

Professor Lingner further acknowledged the fourth dimension of foreign policy implementation, although he did not call it "international political communication." Rather, he wrote about "the various factors . . . in international relations and foreign policy" as being "for example, the economic, political, military, ideological, etc." That this last factor, the "ideological," also could be labeled "psychological" is clear, for Lingner said it included the

> role and influence of traditionally conditioned perceptions on strategy and tactics as well as on the decision and behavior patterns of classes, groups, and individual personalities.[15]

Similarly, in a later brochure for SED party workers, the means of foreign policy properly are referred to as four, but "communications" again is called something else—"political, economic, cultural, educational, and military means."[16]

In addition to the social scientists generally, communications specialists, too, are discussing their field in increasingly sophisticated terms. Regarding effects, for instance, one writes that

> Through the transmission of information and opinion, as through the power of observation in education and recreation functions, various kinds of influence are exercised on their recipients, on their behavior, their knowledge and ability, their sensitivities as well as their physical condition.[17]

Regarding international communications specifically, Georg Klaus, well-known philosopher, Humboldt University professor, and author of *Die Macht des Wortes* [The Power of the Word], in an interview last year in the newspaper *Sonntag* called for improved quality in the GDR's communications. Especially vis-à-vis West Germany and Western Europe, Dr. Klaus said, not only are the "right ideas" needed, but they must be expressed in ways acceptable and appealing to the different target groups. Words conceptually strange to audiences, for instance, should not be used. Rather, the communicator should have a clear notion of what he wants to achieve, with whom, and what limitations on effectiveness might exist.

It is not surprising that the GDR, as a socialist country, appreciates the value of effective propaganda. That has been a tradition of socialism since the Russian Revolution. However, the Soviet concept of propaganda, on which the GDR's is based, has roots going farther back into Russian history than even 1917.

At least as early as the eighteenth century, the Russian *prosvetiteli* believed that social change could come by means of organized mass persuasion or massive education campaigns. Radishchev, for instance, called for education on a massive scale to uplift the general well-being in Tsarist Russia.

From this idea thinkers moved on to formulate specific means of mass persuasion, i.e., propaganda, agitation, and conspiracy. These tactics, in turn, were adopted by specific *political* organizations, which often made tactics the very essence of their being. A group dedicated to conspiracy could not abide another dedicated to propaganda.[18]

Thus, deep in Lenin's heritage was this history of mass education, or propaganda. He did not distinguish between the two. For him, the word "propaganda" had no negative connotation.

In the prerevolutionary phase of the coming class struggle, Lenin saw propaganda as an essential means of creating "consciousness." He did not view history optimistically. History was not necessarily progressive—iron-willed activists were necessary to make and remake history. Workers had spontaneity but not consciousness—their economic conditions weighed them down. Yet Lenin regarded a consciousness of their condition as necessary for the workers' revolution. Thus, consciousness had to be brought from the outside—it would not result automatically from class conflict, as Marx had said. The necessary outside influence would be that of the party, the professional revolutionaries. The party, in other words, must go ahead of the masses. The party would give the masses "consciousness" through propaganda and agitation. (Writing in *Iskra* in 1900, Lenin criticized those who wanted to use only conspiracy.) All strata were to be reached, with propaganda for the elite and agitation for the masses. The founding of a newspaper would enable the revolutionary vanguard to carry out agitation, propaganda, and organizational aims.

In *What Is To Be Done?* the difference in tactics was clear—propaganda was for the elite, to convert them to the cause through full explanations, presented primarily in printed form. Agitation was for the masses, to persuade them to accept the revolutionary vanguard's concepts and policies, presented in single ideas, usually spoken. Both approaches were to be used with all classes.

The revolution itself, as Lenin saw it, was a matter of power, of seizing it and holding it. It was more than just the development of consciousness. An enlightened general staff was necessary to lead the workers to revolution, but the minority leadership needed mass support. That could be gained only through the party, so it must be the chief means of awakening, through agitation and slogans. Then would follow a victorious popular uprising and seizure of power by the radical wing of the revolutionary movement. The revolution then would spread, as in the "spark theory," to other classes and to other societies.

Thus, today international radio and television propaganda has the same meaning for communism as the press had in the period of preparation for the Russian Revolution.[19] It is one of the most important means of gaining foreign support for political goals. As has been noted, Lenin believed that revolutionary ideology could be formed only through the press.[20] During the Stalin and post-Stalin period, this concept of collective propagandist and organizer was extended to cover all instruments of publicity, especially radio. Then, with the growing importance of the developing countries to the East-West competition in the 1950s, this Leninist concept became especially relevant.

In the Third World, with its shortage of newspapers, its high rate of illiteracy, and its urgent need for trained personnel, radio clearly had an essential function to fulfill. Newspapers were mostly out of the question. Using Africa as an example, Radio Moscow said,

Presently, when many Africans cannot read or write, the radio is especially important. The radio gives all residents of the country the opportunity to experience all events... The radio is a significant medium for overcoming igno- rance; it can disseminate specific political lessons among the people.[21]

Technology, furthermore, made it feasible to meet the need. Intercontinental broadcasting was of relatively good quality, and with the growing production of inexpensive radios, espe- cially transistors, many people in the Third World could receive communications from the communist countries.

In addition, radio could be used in the organizational sense Lenin conceived for his newspaper, i.e., it could be the core around which the communist party would be built. Specifical- ly, as local groups and circles then came together to read (or hear read) the underground newspaper and thus build the skeleton of the Social Democratic Workers' Party of Russia, so in the modern period radio could serve the same purpose. People could come together in listeners' clubs to listen to broadcasts, discuss them, and pass the information along. These groups, organized by the communist radio stations, would thus be the core of a movement sympathetic to commu- nist goals. Formal communications (or propaganda) would in this way be reinforced by informal, or face-to-face, communi- cations (agitation)—considered by Western social scientists to have optimum effectiveness.

In this fashion, the communist countries saw the possibility of using communications to support their foreign policy goals in the developing countries. Their own rapid development of radio and television technology was impressive and could be influential, especially when shared with developing countries building their own mass media systems. By supplying training technicians, transmitters, programs, and films, communist countries could be persuasive. When combined with other short-range communication activities, such as displays, lec- tures, and visits, and with long-range programs of cultural influence or even language instruction, the overall effect could be highly significant.

Thus, little has changed, conceptually, regarding propaganda since Lenin's formulations. His successors always have emphasized that "ideological" or propaganda work is one of the central tasks of the party. A 1960 CPSU resolution suggested that the success and survival of communism as a movement depended heavily on communication skills.[22] Perhaps the most succinct summary of communist usage of propaganda is Harold Lasswell's: "Political propaganda is the management of mass communications for power purposes. In the long run the aim is to *economize the material cost of power.*"[23]

In this effort, communist governments have achieved an extraordinary coordination of policy and practice, or of "word and deed," as some commentators describe it. Indeed, the orchestration of theory and practice is that aspect of politics for which communist governments are known.[24] Studies of the Berlin Blockade,[25] the 1955 Geneva Foreign Ministers' Conference,[26] foreign economic aid and peace campaigns,[27] and the building of the Berlin Wall[28]—all illustrate the coordination of word and deed.

The GDR's increased recognition of the nature and importance of the fourth tool of foreign policy is clear in the new statute of the Foreign Ministry (Ministerium für Auswärtige Angelegenheiten), which went into effect February 18, 1970.[29] In the previous statute,[30] the ministry's permission to use communications to support its efforts toward achieving foreign policy goals was worded rather cautiously:

> 3. (3) The ministry controls the implementation of measures concerning foreign policy and can request the necessary information thereunto.

In the new statute, the relationship of foreign information to foreign diplomatic activities is specifically articulated, as well as the responsibility of the ministry to use such information as a means of implementation:

> 2. (1) The ministry is responsible for the implementation of assignments in the area of foreign policy diplomacy and

state foreign information.

In the old statute, the cultural activities that are part of an international political communications program were coordinated and controlled by a Commission for Cultural Relations Abroad, which was appointed by the Council of Ministers. The commission's resolutions were made binding on state organs through ministry decrees. These activities are now brought more directly under ministry control through the new statute's requirement that

> 2. (3) The Ministry plans, requests, and coordinates the development of relations to other states and international organizations in the area of science, education, and culture, within the context of the relevant stipulations.

Thus, it carries out a host of communications activities coordinated and conceived by the Central Committee's Department for International Relations and implemented by state institutions. The Council of Minsters' State Committee for Radio and Television and ADN News Agency, for instance, are responsible for press activities.[31]

To achieve its goal of diplomatic recognition, the GDR concentrates its communications efforts on five basic targets: the international community of nation-states generally; the Eastern European socialist states; the "enemy," West Germany; the rest of the "West," especially Western Europe; and the developing nations of the so-called Third World.

In general, in all these areas the two overriding themes, or appeals, of GDR propaganda supporting the goal of recognition are "the GDR is good" and "the FRG is bad." Millions of words have probably been used by the GDR to make clear to the world that the FRG is *not* the only German state, despite its years of saying so and its Hallstein Doctrine, which blocked East German recognition for so long. The GDR is, it says, permanent and stable. Thus it is clearly entitled to be accepted officially as an equal into the family of nations.

At the same time, it is a *new* kind of Germany, a socialist, rather than capitalist, country and therefore peace-loving rather than bent on building up a huge army and extending economic control into other countries.[32] At the Thirteenth Meeting of the Central Committee of the SED in 1970, Ulbricht made clear why West Germany is a "foreign state" to the GDR—because the "community" of language, territory, and economic and cultural life that had previously been shared has been split since the early 1950s.[33] Today the GDR is a socialist country, a loyal member of the socialist alliance, and a partner of the Soviet Union. West Germany, on the other hand, is a capitalist country, a member of the NATO alliance, and a partner of the United States. They can coexist, but they remain rivals.

GDR Communications Operations

Target: The World

Among the best known of the GDR's international political voices is its party newspaper, *Neues Deutschland* (ND). Although it is published daily in East Berlin primarily for East German citizens, it also can be considered "international," for it is read throughout the world by persons interested in the official GRD view. Thus it is used regularly by the GDR to support its international goal of diplomatic recognition. Official speeches, reports, and resolutions conveying the East German view of recognition are printed at great length. In addition, greetings, visits, and communiqués from throughout the world are reported, often with great fanfare, to show the international status of the GDR. Editorials from foreign newspapers (from prominent to obscure) are printed (in and out of context) to reflect international support for diplomatic recognition. In addition, letters to the editors from the bourgeois foreign press are sometimes reprinted—as if they were the editorial opinion of the newspaper in which they appeared.

In addition, the "Voice of the German Democratic Republic," or Radio Berlin International (RBI), has been broadcasting from East Berlin to the world for the past fifteen years. It is the GDR's international radio voice, under the guidance of the Central Committee's Departments for Agitation and Propaganda. Transmitting fifty-two hours of programming a day in twelve languages, RBI claims it is heard by coal miners in Sweden, students in India, and trade unionists in Australia. Beginning with a ten-minute broadcast in French in 1955, RBI next added Swedish, Danish, Arabic, and German, then Italian, Swahili, Spanish, and Portuguese. Indonesian and Hindu were added later.[34] RBI also broadcasts for Germans abroad.[35] The themes of all the broadcasts have changed little over the years: attacks on the FRG on the one hand, and support for the socialist system on the other. Its purpose, says RBI, is to broadcast

> The socialist human picture of the GDR, the picture of the new German who is free of national arrogance and racist conceit, who as a socialist citizen not only identifies himself with this state created by him, but rather looks after his social position as a joint owner [*Miteigentümer*] who carries responsibility for the whole, for the development of society.[36]

RBI says it yearly receives tens of thousands of letters from all corners of the world asking questions about the GDR, requesting printed material, or commenting on the programs. RBI very often uses quizzes to win listeners. The questions usually concern the GDR, and the prizes include trips to East Berlin, radio or television sets, or musical equipment. The listeners of RBI have organized themselves into listeners' clubs, often with the help of traveling RBI editors:

> With displays and proposals and meetings celebrating national holidays they spread knowledge about the GDR among their countrymen. With petitions and resolutions to the government of their countries, with collections of signatures for individual officials or parties, they actually involve themselves for GDR recognition.[37]

Books, too, go from the GDR to all areas of the world. The Dresden publishing house Zeit im Bild, specializing in books and newspapers in foreign languages, has been operating at increased tempo in recent years. For the twentieth anniversary of the GDR in 1970, for instance, the publishing house echoed the theme of stability by producing *Die DDR stellt sich vor* [The GDR Introduces Itself] in twenty-two languages, an enlarged and updated version of a standard pocket reference work about East Germany; a new series called *Wissenwertes über die DDR* [Worth Knowing about the GDR]; Marxist-Leninist classics; works of Walter Ulbricht; and, also new, *Realität der DDR* [GDR Reality], with commentaries, reports, and articles from well-known foreign journalists.[38] To further its anti-FRG theme, the GDR published *Anti-faschisten in führenden Positionen der DDR* [Anti-fascists in Leading Positions in the GDR]. It also published, in cooperation with the USSR, *Gefahr am Rhein* [Danger on the Rhine], an "Analysis of the Situation in the West German State." Its *Braunbuch: Kriegs- und Naziverbrecher in der Bundesrepublik und in Westberlin* [Brown Book: War and Nazi Criminals in the Bundesrepublic and in West Berlin] is available in English, French, and Spanish.[39]

Foreign language magazines are important, too, and since about 1967 the GDR has considerably strengthened its offering in this area. The general-audience journals include the *DDR-Revue,* a colorful illustrated journal published in seven languages (German, English, French, Italian, Swedish, Finnish, and Danish) for developed capitalist countries; *Neue Heimat,* a journal for *Bürger deutscher Herkunft im Ausland* ("Citizens of German Background Abroad"); and *Deutsch*, a magazine for German-language instruction for foreigners. Anti-FRG and pro-GDR recognition are favorite themes in such publications. *Rundschau des FDGB,* the monthly publication of the labor unions in eight foreign languages, is circulated among trade unionists in more than one hundred countries. The latest language to be added was Arabic. Ten years old, the magazine deals with union developments in the GDR. It also promises active support to developing countries in return for their support of the GDR's campaign for recognition.[40] For English readers, there is the bimonthly eight-page *Democratic German Report,* which emphasizes foreign affairs. It also makes effective use of reprints from such Western magazines as *Time* (US) and *Stern* (FRG), as well as British-sounding bylines and stories about ex-Nazis in the West German government.

The United Nations is also a forum for the GDR's international communications. While the GDR is not a member of the UN, it does have an official observer there with the rank of ambassador and has voting membership in all the UN's special organizations. It therefore makes adroit use of the communications instrument. Telegrams, position papers, and memorandums expressing the GDR view on problems before the UN are a matter of routine.[41] As an observer has written,

> It would be a mistake to believe that the charges and accusations brought up in these memos against the Bundesrepublik and her Western allies have no impact with the Asian, African, and Latin American diplomats at the headquarters of the world organization. They are read![42]

The purpose, of course, is UN membership, a significant form of diplomatic recognition. While working for its acceptance, the GDR continues to make the world aware—through communications—that it already has many international contacts, so why not UN membership, too?

The GDR also uses organizations to convey its international messages. For instance, the umbrella organization covering Friendship Societies, Friendship Committees, institutions, and the mass organizations (such as the FDGB, FDJ, and National Front) is the *Liga für Völkerfreundschaft der DDR* ("GDR League for People's Friendship"). Founded in 1961 as a coordinating body, it holds conferences, publishes material (4 million copies annually, including brochures in twenty languages), arranges cultural exchanges, operates eleven cultural and information centers,[43] and invites all types of people— from officials and mayors to workers and children—to visit the GDR. Its international conference draws more than 200 delegates from more than fifty countries. All the League's activities serve the cause of recognition. In the Third World, it works through such regional organizations as the Afro-Asian Solidarity Committee, German–Southeast Asian Society, German-African Society, German-Latin American Society, and societies for individual countries which have their headquarters in East Berlin.

In addition, there is the German Peace Council (Deutscher Friedensrat). Begun as a nonparty organization in 1949, the German Peace Council became a party instrument by the end of the 1950s. Today, as an aspect of the communications tool of foreign policy, especially in the Third World, the German Peace Council in the name of peace calls not only for a Vietnam peace but for recognition of the GDR and the convening of a European security conference. It concentrates especially on winning support for recognition among the left intellectuals who often are members of similar peace groups in other countries, as in India or in Latin America. These peace groups, in turn, frequently offer resolutions recommending the recognition of the GDR.[44]

To establish further political contacts in nonsocialist countries, the GDR founded the Interparliamentary Group of the Volkskammer. Invitations from it have prestige but are not directly bound to the SED party. The purpose of such invitations is to impress sympathetic nonsocialist politicians with life in East Germany. It is hoped they then will support the cause of GDR recognition in their own parliaments.

A final communication channel to the world is Neue Heimat [New Homeland]. Founded in December 1964 as an "organization for ties with citizens of German heritage abroad," Neue Heimat evolved from an earlier group called the Arbeitskreis zur Pflege der deutschen Sprache und Kulter ("Workshop for the Cultivation of the German Language and Culture"). Its present purpose vis-à-vis Germans abroad is "to inform, to help them according to their wishes, to keep alive remembrances of the former homeland, and to disseminate informational materials for meetings."[45] Thus, the GDR created a channel for contacting Germans abroad, a channel not possible through earlier organizations such as the Friendship Societies, which sought only to reach foreigners. In this way the GDR has one more possibility for competing with the FRG for influence.

Target: Eastern Europe

An old adage of propagandists is that one is in business to

weaken the enemy, keep friends friendly, and neutrals neutral. In the case of the GDR, the second aim is highly relevant. Without the continued foreign policy support of socialist states for diplomatic recognition, East Germany would stand relatively powerless before Western opposition.

Thus, the GDR cultivates carefully its communications contacts with Eastern Europe. This is not always an easy task, for despite the common communist ties that bind, the GDR is, to some of its neighbors, still German first and communist second. Further, the East Europeans, who in recent years have wanted more flexible relations with the FRG, frequently resent the GDR's intransigence in this area. They also seem to resent the GDR's relative prosperity. Thus, the communication task is unceasingly to assure its allies that it is worthy of their continued support. When they then respond positively, as Poland did in publishing a highly favorable book about the GDR, the GDR's satisfaction seems justified.[46] Especially to the Soviet Union the GDR must communicate total loyalty (as, for instance, through repeated anti-Mao utterances).

It is significant, therefore, that the GDR publishes special magazines for the socialist countries and maintains close radio ties to them.[47] For instance, the GDR was an enthusiastic supporter of the first common communications effort within East Europe, the founding of OIRT, the International Organization for Radio and Television.[48] Examples of the cooperation possible through this organization were the mutual GDR-USSR radio shows produced to celebrate the one hundredth birthday of Lenin and the twentieth anniversary of the GDR. The latter was a natural occasion to stress its recognition theme. This kind of cooperation among the East European countries is according to agreement. However, this has not always been the case, and the propaganda has not always been positive. The GDR's foreign radio, for instance, is believed to have played an unusually significant role in East European foreign policy during the 1968 Czech crisis, i.e., broadcasting covertly for the purpose of putting down the Czech reform movement.[49]

Television, too, is a communications channel to Eastern Europe. In fact, the GDR was one of the first three socialist states to join Intervision, the "Television Bridge of Friend-ship," which now binds the USSR, Czechoslovakia, Poland, Rumania, Hungary, GDR, Finland, and the newest member, the Mongolian People's Republic. Yugoslavia and Austria are observer-members.[50] This impressive network is made possible by a 2,880-kilometer coaxial cable that connects Moscow and Berlin and a Soviet-developed news satellite system called ORBITA, which connects the Asiatic regions. Through ORBI-TA, television broadcasting will be possible not only with Arab and African countries but also with Cuba.[51]

The international radio and television organization that includes the socialist and Third World countries is Intervision, a division of OIRT. Both have their headquarters in Prague. Intervision's purpose is the regular exchange of information, organization of direct transmissions, mutual programming for important events, exchange of programs concerning politics, economics, science, technology, culture, and sports. Further-more, it exchanges programs with Eurovision, its counterpart in Western Europe. Since its founding, the number of direct transmissions, exchanged programs, and relay broadcasts has increased significantly. Most of the last were news broadcasts. As of 1970, GDR television was sending 100 programs per year over Intervision and receiving about 200. Most were from East European countries, with roughly 30 percent being news and 18 percent cultural programs. In 1971, for instance, Czecho-slovakia accepted a weekly program from the GDR, including films as well as documentaries.[52]

The increasing cultural cooperation between the socialist states in recent years has also been clearly visible in the area of movies. In 1970 alone, for instance, the GDR had coproduc-tions with the USSR ("On the Way to Lenin"), Poland ("Signals"), Bulgaria (a film about Dimitrov), and Czechoslo-vakia (a comedy).[53] Another GDR-USSR coproduction in the works is "A Young Man Named Engels."[54] In addition to the coproductions, professional contacts were maintained through the Unions of Film and Television Producers, and films were exchanged among the countries. The East European countries remained the best customers of the GDR's TV films *(Spiel-filme).*[55]

The GDR's Friendship Societies and Cultural Centers obviously are of significance within Eastern Europe. Sometimes, too, they are barometers of inter–East European foreign policy sentiment. A number of visitors appeared at the Czech House of Culture during the "Prague Spring" to read the books and newspapers that were available. Suddenly the House was closed, "for repairs," it was said. In Prague, on the other hand, the Soviet-Czech Friendship Society office was the scene of protest demonstrations after the invasions, and it was not until late May 1970 that a member of the Association for Czechoslovak-Soviet Friendship again ventured to attend a meeting of the German-Soviet Friendship Society, as had been traditional in the past.[56]

Target: West Germany

In addition to the many forms of communications indirectly aimed at West Germany, the GDR also communicates its antagonism directly to citizens of the FRG. Favorite themes are West German "militarism" and "toleration" of Nazis in official positions. Favorite targets are Bundeswehr soldiers as well as private citizens.

To address these groups, the GDR uses a number of radio stations. One is the Deutschlandsender. Broadcasting around the clock, it emphasizes political comment, news and music. Its purpose is to present the East German view to FRG citizens. In addition, it broadcasts special programs in the language of guest workers *(Gastarbeiter)* working in the FRG, i.e., Italian, Turkish, and Spanish. Another station directed at the FRG addresses only one group of citizens, that is, Bundeswehr soldiers. This is the Soldatensender 935. Using modern music to set its tone, this station emphasizes military information, commentary, and news. It aims at undermining the Bundeswehr and defaming the West German government. Exposés of the Nazi past of present FRG officers is a favorite theme, as are the alleged wish of the FRG for atomic weapons and current public opinion differences regarding the military. One tactic of the Soldatensender 935 is to use exact detail of daily Bundeswehr operations, hoping thereby to create a sense of uncertainty through its "inside" information. In addition, the GDR also has a special radio station that broadcasts to West Berlin. It is Berliner Welle, a division of Berliner Rundfunk for the GDR.[57]

Brochures, too, play an important role in communications to West Germany. Every year thousands of brochures, pamphlets, and leaflets are rocketed several kilometers across the border. After one such barrage, for instance, FRG border police reported to the press that they collected thirteen kilograms of paper from the border area around Lücho/Dannenberg. In addition to the rockets, some aluminum containers were used to float propaganda material to Bavaria via the rivers and streams flowing out of Thüringen.[58] Sometimes, too, it is said that packages simply are thrown over the border or hidden in inter-German trains, picked up by middlemen in the FRG, and distributed. According to press reports, if the materials are to be mailed, the GDR supplies the postage, either in the form of stamped envelopes or cash.[59] In 1970, on the anniversary of Lenin's birth, the West German press reported that the GDR used a balloon to float fliers across the border calling for recognition of the GDR, signing of permanent treaties, and maintenance of peaceful coexistence. Featured was a citation from Lenin calling for peace.[60] Typical, too, was said to be a yellow flier for soldiers; it read:

There are three possibilities for peace in Europe:
1. Diplomatic recognition of the GDR
2. Diplomatic recognition of the GDR
3. Diplomatic recognition of the GDR[61]

Propaganda is also mailed to West Germany directly from the GDR or through other European countries. It includes brochures, letters, illegal newspapers, and pamphlets. The volume of such material is estimated by the press at 750,000 to 800,000 pieces per month. Signatures of students and organizations are often used as "covers."

Displays, lectures, and travel invitations are additional media. During the GDR's twentieth anniversary in 1970, its propaganda activities in the FRG became especially evident. Displays, for instance, were used to tell the story of GDR stability and strength and its right to recognition. The display

"Die DDR—dein Nachbar, Bilanz von 9000 Tagen" ("The GDR—Your Neighbor, Balance of 9000 Days") was shown in many West German cities. GDR Weeks, emphasizing the right to recognition, were held in Freiburg, Kassel, Wolfsburg, and Cologne. Similarly, GDR clubs, as the one in Mannheim called DDR Objektiv, sponsored lectures and speakers featuring the subject of recognition. Sometimes such events are arranged and sponsored by student groups.[62] Invitations to West German citizens to travel in the GDR are a favorite form of propaganda. GDR trade unions, for instance, have through the FDGB invited West Germans, as has the FDJ.

Target: Western Europe

In Western Europe, the GDR is not diplomatically recognized anywhere (although it has economic representation), and so it relies heavily on the fourth tool of foreign policy. The possibilities it has found for creative communications are astonishingly numerous. These many activities have been detailed in a series of studies based on original GDR and West European sources.[63] Examples presented here have been chosen from those detailed studies, as well as other sources, to indicate the range of communications activities. These efforts are especially intensive in Scandinavia. Finland, under strong Soviet influence, is a good possibility for recognition. So is Sweden, which has maintained its policy of neutrality for 150 years.

Official receptions are a favorite communications channel in Western Europe. Although the GDR does not have embassies and consulates in Western Europe, it frequently manages to create a quasi-diplomatic atmosphere by holding receptions at GDR trade missions. A favorite time is in October, on the anniversary of the founding of the GDR. In Paris, for instance, about 200-300 persons from the world of French economics, politics, and culture, as well as diplomats from the socialist states, are invited.[64]

Trade union contacts, too, are significant. These oldest of international contacts are concerned not only with union problems. They also take up foreign policy problems and arrange travel, support youth work, and offer adult education.

At each of these levels, the GDR's contacts to Western European trade unions are used to articulate its case for recognition.

Parliamentary delegations have apparently proved to be useful as well. The GDR strives for official multiparty delegations of visitors in order to establish contacts with noncommunist parties. The British group, for instance, visits the GDR frequently and is especially firm in support of recognition.

Parliamentary Friendship Groups are similar. In Belgium and Italy, and probably France, such groups have been formed across faction lines among peoples sharing an interest in intensive parliamentary contact with the GDR. They also travel and attend meetings and voice support for recognition within their parliaments.[65]

A bit more unusual is the Rostock–Baltic Sea Week. Called by one specialist "the most spectacular instrument of the GDR for its foreign policy vis-à-vis the Nordic states," the Rostock Ostseewoche was begun in 1958 as a forum for displaying the economic and cultural achievements of the GDR as well as its peaceful intentions. It offers the thousands of official and private visitors displays, music, demonstrations, discussions, photo displays, and youth programs. Conferences of trade unionists, youth, jurists, women, and local-level politicians also are held:

> the propaganda assumes an economically and politically stable state whose natural symbol of excellence is the overseas port (Rostock). Therefore because the state is stable it must be recognized by the Nordic states as soon as possible. . . .
>
> The GDR leadership skillfully permits the foreigners at the Rostock-Baltic Sea Week to intercede in favor of the GDR's interest. . . . As a rule the GDR brings it about that all committees and individual conferences attending the Baltic Sea Week recommend to their governments direct recognition of the GDR."[66]

Communications at the personal, face-to-face level, as in exchanges and visits, is also a favorite medium of the GDR in

Western Europe. One of the most interesting such campaigns is that focused on the 70,000 Germans who live in France (most of them since they were imprisoned there in World War II). They are concerned about their old-age security, the fact that their children do not speak German, and what has happened to their hometowns (many of which are on GDR territory). To such persons the GDR sends letters or personal representatives saying that they can receive their pensions even though they live in France and that their children are invited to vacation in the GDR (at minimum cost). Such intensified cultural work in France in recent years is supported by the French Communist party and communist trade union organizations, as well as by leftist social groups, the Society for German-French Exchange, and the German-French Study Society.[67] The resulting accumulation of voices for recognition is not difficult to imagine.

On the personal level, it is reported that letters, too, are used to communicate the GDR propaganda messages into Western Europe. The Belgian Post Ministry estimated that about 70,000 propaganda letters per year are sent into Belgium. Their contents are described as "propaganda materials from various state organizations."[68] GDR recognition is a frequent theme. In England, the campaign is one of personal letters to British politicians. The appeal is for recognition in return for increased British trade possibilities and strengthening the labor union movement and the cause of world peace.[69] For Britons, invitations to the various scientific congresses sponsored by the GDR are also of special interest, as well as international celebrations such as Marx's or Hegel's birthday.

More formal means are, of course, also used by the GDR in its communications to Western Europe. For instance, its radio stations exchange many cultural programs with other European stations. Its closest contacts are with Finland, followed by Sweden, Denmark, and France.[70] The GDR also encourages film weeks throughout Western Europe. Austria, for instance, held its first such event in January 1971—it opened with the film "Meine Stunde Null" [My Zero Hour], attended by prominent public figures.[71] Even advertising is used to present the case for recognition to Western Europe. Ads calling attention to the GDR's growing importance appeared in the London *Times, Le Monde,* and other papers.

In Western Europe, the GDR also emphasized sister-city relations *(Partnerschaftsstädte),* especially with large numbers of French cities (e.g., Dunkirk and Rostock), as well as with Scandinavian cities.[72] One of the most interesting pairs is Coventry and Dresden, both targets of controversial and destructive World War II bombing raids. Local-level political contacts concentrate largely on communications through meetings, conversations, and discussions among local politicians and representatives of the sister-cities.

Culture, too, is a communications medium. In Rome the GDR's cultural institute, "Centro Thomas Mann," was founded by Italian intellectuals with the support of the CPI.[73] In Helsinki the Cultural Center is ten years old and includes an extensive library, film collection, and language instruction for more than 1,000 persons.[74] In Stockholm the center has close contacts to university institutes and student organizations and arranges dozens of displays and programs. In short, "of all the instruments the GDR uses in its foreign competition, the cultural institutes or cultural centers are the most effective" as voices for recognition.[75] Guest performances, concert tours, and art exhibits are also important. For instance, the GDR sends its famous Berliner Ensemble (Brecht Theater) into Central Europe to carry the unspoken message of the GDR's cultural *niveau.* Youth choir appearances in Scandinavia help make firm the concept of the GDR as an individual entity, as well as readings by writers Hermann Kant, Anna Seghers, and Christa Wolf.[76] In Britain the Leipzig Bach Orchestra and the Berlin State Orchestra serve the same purpose.

Target: The Third World

In the Third World, the GDR has won embassy-level recognition from seventeen states (Cambodia, Iraq, Sudan, Syria, Republic of South Vietnam, Yemen, Egypt, Congo-Brazzaville, Somali, Central African Republic, Algeria, Republic of Maldives, Ceylon, Guinea, Chile, Equatorial Guinea, and Chad). In addition it has consulates-general in Burma, Indonesia, Yemeni Arab Republic, Tanzania, India, and Kuwait. In some countries there are trade representations on governmental levels (*Handelsvertretungen auf Regierungse-bene*)—Lebanon, Ghana, Tunisia, Mali, Morocco, Cyprus, and Libya. In others there are trade representations on the basis of bank agreements (*Handelsvertretungen auf der Grundlage von Bankenabkommen*)—Brazil, Ecuador, Columbia, Mexico, and Uruguay. Thus the Third World is an especially fertile area in which to disseminate communications regarding the need for recognition from nonsocialist countries.

The GDR acknowledges that its cultural relations often are an indirect first step to diplomatic recognition: "The taking up of first political contacts to individual countries was in most cases connected to economic, and not least to cultural, agreements."[77] The scope of such cultural relations is wide and legally agreed to by both countries.[78] Cultural agreements are in effect with about a dozen countries of the Third World (Algeria, Chile, Dahomey, Guinea, India, Indonesia, Iraq, Cambodia, Congo-Brazzaville, Mali, Sudan, South Yemen, and the UAR).[79] Regional friendship societies often are used to coordinate cultural activities in such countries. For instance, there is the German-Arab Society, the DAG. Central to its work are the cultural and information centers the GDR has in Cairo and Alexandria, Damascus, Baghdad, and Sudan. Here displays are arranged, German-language classes held (or arranged for television), scientific and practical lectures scheduled by GDR citizens working in the Arab lands, cultural presentations of visiting artists held, and movies shown. Printed material, too, is prepared by the DAG, such as the illustrated forty-eight page monthly *Al-Matschalla*. Sponsorships between cities as well as seminars for local politicians are also arranged. Friendship societies, too, exist in many countries, as in Iraq, the UAR, and Sudan. In each case they implement the program of DAG. The purpose is achievement of diplomatic recognition:

Through a very active information program, whose core is the dissemination of knowledge about the GDR and her antiimperialistic policy, and through its consequent intercession for the diplomatic recognition of the GDR, it in recent years has won an always increasing circle of friends for the GDR and significantly prepared for the establishment of normal state relations.[80]

Educational and technical exchange is a favorite form of propaganda of all nation-states, especially student exchanges. The communications medium can have a positive influence not only on present attitudes and opinions, but also on those of future leaders as well. Experience has shown that young citizens of developing countries who have the advantage of training in industrialized lands often rise quickly to leadership positions in their own nations. When they do, they are often favorably disposed toward the country that gave them their education. Thus, the GDR, in its search for developing nation diplomatic support now and in the future, emphasizes education. Students from around 100 nations today study at GDR institutions. The Herder Institute in Leipzig provides such students with a thorough knowledge of German so that they may derive optimum benefit from their studies. In addition, the universities have founded special institutes that teach subjects of interest to the developing nations, such as the Institute for Tropical and Subtropical Agriculture and the Department for Tropical Veterinary Hygiene at the Karl Marx University in Leipzig.[81] Conferences of teachers, too, are important forums. The GDR, for instance, sponsors an International Pedagogic Colloquium attended by representatives from Arab, African, and Southeast Asian states. The GDR also prints polytechnical texts in foreign languages, exchanges educational delegations, sponsors informational travel, assists in designing educational systems in the developing countries, and sends advisors and educational displays throughout the Third World.[82] Exchange of journalists also is important. Agreements for the exchange of programs, training, and experience exist between the Union of German Journalists (VDJ) and a number of journalist organizations in the Third World.[83] Typical of such cooperation is the 1970 agreement with South Yemen to train television and radio communications engineers and to exchange news between the GDR's ADN Agency and the Aden News Agency.[84]

The electronic media are favorite channels to the Third World. In developing countries, for example, cinema is a significant form of education as well as entertainment. As a result, the GDR is active in the area. From 1958 until 1970, for instance, about sixty "film weeks" featuring GDR movies were held throughout the world, many in the developing countries. In recent years, increasing numbers of film festivals are also being held in the Third World. Coproductions are becoming more popular, too, such as the short film "Hirde Dyamma" [People's Festival] that the DEFA Studio made in cooperation with Guinea.[85] Unique as well as significant among film activities are the children's movies the GDR is making for the Third World. It held its first Festival for Children's Movies in the UAR in 1967 and since then has been supplying films for youngsters.[86] Radio is, of course, also important. RBI uses twelve languages to reach the developing nations of the Third World and reinforces its communications through more than 200 listeners' clubs. These are organized among RBI hearers who listen in groups to the broadcasts and later discuss their contents. They organize film evenings and public forums "to demand full diplomatic recognition of the GDR."[87] The GDR, through the main Department of International Relations of the German Democratic Radio, maintains contact with 144 radio stations and organizations in seventy-six countries. Legal agreements for mutual cooperation in radio work exist with twenty-eight countries. In 1969 about 1,600 hours of programming, mostly music, were available to foreign stations.[88] German-language courses are broadcast, for instance, to South Yemen, Iraq, and Sudan.[89] Three new radio series to Vietnam during 1970 are of special interest: their themes are the development of a socialist economy in the GDR and the evolution of military training in that country.[90]

In the Third World other, less conventional, media also have apparently proved useful. For example, a regular feature of the GDR's international propaganda is the use of contests that stimulate people to inform themselves regarding the GDR in return for an opportunity to win a prize. During the celebration of its twentieth anniversary, for instance, the GDR conducted a contest through the Beirut newspaper *Al-Shaab.*

It ran an advertisement consisting of twenty questions concerning the GDR's "history, socialist achievements, and most significant sights." First prize for the participants, who included trade unionists, intellectuals, and students, was a trip to Berlin.[91] Graphic appeals are not neglected, and displays are often used to communicate special messages. Among the displays that have been shown at cultural centers in the Third World in recent years are "Berlin—Capital of the GDR," "The Germans and the Arabs" (featuring the FRG's anti-Arab stand), "Imperialism Without Mask" (anti-FRG and anti-US), "Experienced Africa" ("neocolonial brutalities"), and one concerning the rebuilding of East Berlin. Others featured education, books, and photos about life in East Germany.[92]

Special conferences have their place in communications to the Third World, as well as more formal channels. The GDR occasionally sponsors special regional conferences, such as one in Sierra Leone in 1969 attended by more than a hundred Africans fron twenty-five states. The diplomatic recognition of the GDR was a major topic during the three-day event, which emphasized African-GDR friendship. Among the resolutions passed were those

> for a still closer cooperation between the African states and the GDR in different areas of social, scientific, and cultural life.
> In addition the conference participants have approached in writing the state and governmental heads of every one of the six states that recently took up full diplomatic relations with the GDR. A letter conveyed congratulations for this step as "convincing expression of a far-sighted policy, a real and consistent policy of neutrality and bloc freedom."[93]

Representatives of the GDR abroad also work with already sympathetic groups to organize public events that call attention to the demand for diplomatic recognition, such as a convention of "Friends of the GDR." In Chile, for instance, more than a hundred delegates from Chilean organizations, institutions, and public life organized a meeting that "would prove to what extent there exists in our country a recognition of the necessity to recognize the GDR."[94]

Fairs, too, are used as instruments of international political communication. In 1968 the GDR founded the Interwerbung GmbH, or Society for GDR Advertising and Foreign Fairs. Previously such activities had been organized by the GDR's Chamber for Foreign Trade. Clearly the major activity of this group is the internationally known Leipzig trade fair in spring and fall. Not only are there economic benefits to be gained, but the prestige conferred by this fair, which communicates stability and prosperity, cannot be overestimated. As a result, the GDR holds press conferences and arranges receptions in the developing countries to entice visitors to the fair. About twenty official delegations from such countries usually attend the fairs.

Summary

The foregoing examples illustrate the skill with which GDR propagandists have conceived an international political communications program for their state. All possible modern media are used: newspapers, books, magazines, brochures, letters, official communiqués, radio, television, movies, organizations, cultural centers, lectures, displays, contests, advertisements, travel, exchanges, education, training, and art.

Appeals for diplomatic recognition are made directly or indirectly on the basis of common language, political beliefs, legal grounds, national prestige, and the like. Targets include friends, "enemies," and neutrals.

Concentration in the Third World is on electronic and cultural media, based on the experience that communications investments pay off in the long run in the form of diplomatic recognition. In Western Europe, too, the goal is long-range, with concentration on cultural and quasi-diplomatic communications media, such as the Baltic Sea Week and parliamentary groups. Among the allies of Eastern Europe, the emphasis is both short-range and long-range to assure present and continued diplomatic backing, with communications channels being those underlining the GDR's dependability and cooperation. Vis-à-vis the FRG, favorite channels in the past understandably have been relatively subversive, e.g., rockets, hidden brochures, and covert radio stations, with an increasing shift to open and official contacts. On the whole, the GDR addresses the world frequently and widely through all possible modern formal and informal communications. Where conventional channels are not available, the GDR creates others to serve its long-range purpose.

But the GDR undertakes its present activities within a schizophrenic international communications context.

The West reluctantly accepts the need for psychological influence (because it is "manipulatory"), covers its embarrassment in continued assertions that what it does is not really "propaganda" (but rather "information"), separates its long-range propaganda activities (so they will not be contaminated) and applies an acceptable term ("cultural relations"), implements the whole range of activities on a relatively hit-and-miss basis, and studies to death social science findings regarding effective communications while applying few.

The East eagerly accepts the need for psychological influence (because it is "educational"); usually calls it properly "propaganda" (but sometimes also "Kulturpolitik");[95] carefully coordinates its many aspects with political actions;[96] gives the instrument a top political priority; attacks (1) those Western statesmen who accept a similar coordination of the instrument and (2) the operations of the "enemy" as immoral "ideological diversion" (because of scientific manipulation rather than "truthfulness");[97] becomes increasingly "scientific" about its own operations; and carries on the same activities as in Western international political communications work.

The West sees an international threat in the one-sidedness, coordination, and high priority of the East's communications, yet it seeks to coordinate and elevate its own efforts. The East sees a threat in the subtlety of such Western communications concepts as "subliminal stimulation" yet seeks to increase the scientific quality and sophistication of its own effort.

Notes

1. Joseph Frankel, *The Making of Foreign Policy* (London: Oxford University Press, 1963), p. 216.

2. Terence Qualter, *Propaganda and Psychological War-*

fare (New York: Random House, 1962), p. 27.

3. Propaganda is to be distinguished from *psychological warfare,* which implies military operations, and *subversion,* which usually includes a good measure of coercion. Some specialists include these two aspects in the general phrase "psychological instrument" but exclude them from the concept "propaganda" in the sense used by Qualter. Others put "psychological warfare" within the category of the "military tool" and do not accord subversive operations the rank of "foreign policy tool."

4. Robert T. Holt and Robert W. Van de Velde, *Strategic Psychological Operations and American Foreign Policy* (Chicago: University of Chicago Press, 1960), p. 15.

5. Hans Speier, "Psychological Warfare Reconsidered," in *The Process and Effects of Mass Communication,* ed. Wilbur Schramm (Urbana, Ill.: University of Illinois Press, 1955), p. 461.

6. Kalevi J. Kolsti, "The Instruments of Policy: Propaganda," in his *International Politics* (New York: Prentice-Hall, 1967), pp. 247-278.

7. Frederick C. Barghoorn's *Soviet Foreign Propaganda* (Princeton: Princeton University Press, 1964) describes the USSR's activities, and W. Phillips Davison's *International Political Communication* (New York: Praeger, 1965) covers the field generally.

8. Jan F. Triska and David D. Finley, *Soviet Foreign Policy* (New York: Macmillan Co., 1968), p. 43.

9. Elihu Katz and Paul F. Lazarsfeld, *Personal Influence: The Part Played by People in the Flow of Communications* (New York: The Free Press, 1955).

10. James N. Rosenau, *Public Opinion and Foreign Policy* (New York: Random House, 1961).

11. Walter Ulbricht, *Die gesellschaftliche Entwicklung in der Deutschen Demokratischen Republik bis zur Vollendung des Sozialismus* [Social Development in the German Democratic Republic until the Completion of Socialism] (Berlin, 1967), p. 92.

12. The development of political science as a whole in the GDR is discussed in two well-documented articles by Hermann Weber. "Ansätze zur Herausbildung einer Politikwis-

senschaft in der DDR," *Deutschland Archiv* 3, no. 11 (1970) and no. 12 (1970).

13. Herbert Kröger and Klaus Lingner, "Wege zu einer marxistisch-leninistischen Methodologie der Analyse in internationaler Beziehungen" [Means to a Marxist-Leninist Methodology for International Relations Analysis], in *Karl Marx: Begründer der Staats- und Rechtstheorie der Arbeiterklasse* (Berlin: Staatsverlag, 1968), pp. 339-372.

14. Klaus Lingner, "Die Anwendung der methodologischen Grundlagen der Marxschen Gesellschaftsprognostik in der Aussenpolitik der DDR" [The Application of the Methodological Basis of Marxist Social Prognosis to GDR Foreign Policy], in *Die Aussenpolitik der DDR in Lichte der Lehren von Karl Marx* (Berlin: Dietz Verlag, 1968), p. 82.

15. Ibid., p. 350.

16. Walter Krausse, "Erfahrungen der Parteiarbeit im Staatsapparat bei der Verwirklichung der Beschlüsse der VII. Parteitages der SED" [Experiences of Party Work in the State Apparat During Application of the Resolutions of the Seventh Party Congress of the SED], *Der Parteiarbeiter* (Berlin: Dietz Verlag, 1969), p. 6.

17. Frank Knipping, *Monopole und Massenmedien* (Berlin: VEB Deutscher Verlag der Wissenschaften, 1969), p. 11.

18. The development within Russian intellectual history of the concept of propaganda is traced in an unpublished paper of the author entitled, "The Concept of Propaganda in Marxism-Leninism," May 1965.

19. Harald Ludwig, "Rundfunk und Fernsehen in Dienst kommunistische Auslandspropaganda" [Radio and Television in the Service of Communist Foreign Propaganda] *Deutsche Welle Dokumentation*, December 1967, pp. 280-285.

20. "In our opinion the starting point of our activities, the first step toward creating the desired organization, or, let us say, the main thread which if followed, would enable us steadily to develop, deepen, and extend that organization, should be the founding of an All-Russian political newspaper. ... the role of a newspaper, however, is not limited solely to the dissemination of ideas, to political education, and to the enlistment of political allies. A newspaper is not only a

collective propagandist and a collective agitator, it is also a collective organiser." V. I. Lenin, "Where to Begin," *Collected Works* (Moscow: Foreign Languages Publishing House, 1961), 5: 17-24.

21. Radio Moscow Swahili, 27 January 1965, 10.00 MET.

22. "Resolution on the Tasks of Party Propaganda in Present-Day Conditions," *The Current Digest of the Soviet Press* 12, no. 37 (1960): 11-15.

23. Harold Lasswell, "The Strategy of Soviet Propaganda," in *Process and Effects of Mass Communication,* ed. Wilbur Schramm (Urbana, Ill.: University of Illinois Press, 1955), p. 538.

24. W. Schramm, "Soviet Concept of Psychological Warfare," in *A Psychological Warfare Casebook,* ed. William E. Daugherty and Morris Janowitz (Baltimore: The Johns Hopkins Press for Operations Research Office, 1960), pp. 779-788.

25. W. Phillips Davison, *The Berlin Blockade* (Princeton: Princeton University Press, 1958).

26. E. M. Kirkpatrick, ed., *Target: The World* (New York: Macmillan Co., 1956).

27. Barghoorn, *Soviet Foreign Propaganda,* pp. 210, 114-121, and 260-270.

28. Anita Dasbach Mallinckrodt, *Propaganda Hinter der Mauer* (Stuttgart: Kohlhammer Verlag, 1971).

29. *Gesetzblatt der Deutschen Demokratischen Republik,* pt. 2, no. 23, 14 March 1970, pp. 173-175.

30. *Gesetzblatt der Deutschen Demokratischen Republik,* pt. 1, no. 18, March 1960.

31. Federal Republic of Germany, Bundesminister für innerdeutsche Beziehungen, *Materialien zum Bericht zur Lage der Nation 1971* (Bonn, 1971), p. 16.

32. Werner Hänisch, "Probleme der international Stellung der DDR" [Problems of the GDR's International Position], *Deutsche Aussenpolitik,* 1970, no. 2, p. 185.

33. Walter Ulbricht, "Bemerkungen zu den Beziehungen zwischen der DDR und der BRD" [Comments on the Relations Between the GDR and the FRG], *Protokol der 13. Tagung des ZK der SED 9/10.6.70* (Berlin: Dietz Verlag, 1970).

34. "Hier Spricht Radio Berlin International," *Horizont,* 1970, no. 23, p. 3.

35. *RBI Journal,* October 1970.

36. *Horizont,* 1970, no. 23.

37. Ibid.

38. For a detailed account of the books published especially for the GDR's twentieth anniversary, see *Einheit* 24, no. 1 (1969): 119-128.

39. *Deutsche Aussenpolitik,* 1969, no. 5, p. 626.

40. *Tribüne,* no. 166, 26 August 1960.

41. Harold Rose, "Die Deutsche Demokratische Republik und die Organisation der Vereinten Nationen" [The German Democratic Republic and the United Nations Organization], *20 Jahre DDR: 20 Jahre Friedenspolitik. Deutsche Aussenpolitik Sonderheft* (Berlin: 1969), p. 144.

42. Manfred Rexin, "Aussenpolitik der DDR" [Foreign Policy of the GDR] (Paper presented to Study Group for German Politics, International Political Science Association Conference, Munich, August 31, 1970).

43. *DDR Report Archiv,* 4.8 (Würzburg: Gesellschaft für Politische Bildung).

44. Harold Ludwig, "Der 'Deutscher Friedensrat,'" *Deutsche Welle Dokumentation,* 26, September 1969, 160/69.

45. *Neue Zeit,* 4 December 1964.

46. "Polnische Literatur über die Entwicklung der DDR" [Polish Literature Concerning the Development of the GDR], *Deutsche Aussenpolitik,* 1969, no. 4, p. 482.

47. "Im Dienste der Völkerfreundschaft: Verlag Zeit im Bild" [In the Service of Friendship Among Peoples: Publishing House Time in Pictures], *Horizont,* 1971, no. 9, pp. 3-4.

48. *Junge Welt,* 5 February 1970.

49. Author's unpublished study "Radio Vltava—the Warsaw Pact's Covert Radio," September 1970.

50. *Junge Welt,* 5 February 1970.

51. Ibid.

52. *Sonntag,* 10 January 1971.

53. *Neues Deutschland,* 1 February 1971.

54. *Neues Deutschland,* 18 March 1970.

55. *Neues Deutschland,* 26 April 1970.

56. Radio Free Europe, *Research Report: Communist Area.* 0602, 4 June 1970.

57. *Bonner Rundschau,* 3 November 1970.

58. *Frankfurter Allgemeine,* 30 December 1968.

59. *Ost-West Kurier,* 13 July 1968.

60. *Christ und Welt,* 21 August 1970.

61. *Die Welt,* 21 October 1970.

62. See Robert Steigerwald, "Die 'Frankfurter Schule' im Lichte des Marxismus," *Einheit* 25, no. 10 (1970): 1355-1360; and G. Krasanow, "Beim Institut für Marxistische Studien und Forschung zu Gast," *Probleme des Friedens und des Sozialismus,* 1970, no. 8, pp. 1052-1057.

63. "Die Tätigkeit der DDR in den nichtkommunistischen Ländern," Forschungsinstitut der Deutschen Gesellschaft für Auswärtige Politik. Sibylle Reime, IV, EWG-Staaten (ohne Bundesrepublik); Friedrich Eymelt, II, Die Nordischen Staaten, and V. Grossbritannien.

64. Reime, p. 14.

65. Reime, p. 66.

66. Eymelt, II, pp. 28

67. *Frankfurter Rundschau,* 26 March 1968.

68. *Frankfurter Allgemeine,* 11 August 1970.

69. Eymelt, V, p. 8.

70. Ludwig, "Rundfunk und Fernsehen."

71. *Neues Deutschland,* 27 January 1971.

72. Eymelt, II, p. 47.

73. Reime, p. 92.

74. Harald Ludwig, "Erfolgloses Werben um europäische Neutrale" [Unsuccessful Competition for European Neutrals], *Deutschland Archiv* 4, no. 2 (February 1971): 166-170.

75. Eymelt, II, p. 36.

76. Eymelt, II, p. 38.

77. *Geschichte der Aussenpolitik der Deutschen Demokratischen Republik: Abriss* (Berlin: Dietz Verlag, 1968), p. 433.

78. Typical are the activities in the agreement signed with the Republic of Mali in 1964 and reprinted in ibid.

79. *Materialien zum Bericht,* p. 16.

80. Paul Scholz, "20 Jahre DDR—20 Jahre Freundschaft und Solidarität mit den arabischen Volk" [20 Years GDR—20

Years Friendship and Solidarity with the Arab People], *Deutschen Aussenpolitik Sonderheft "20 Jahre DDR,"* July 1969, pp. 132-142.

81. *Geschichte der Aussenpolitik: Abriss,* pp. 435-438.

82. *Presse-Informationen,* 20 September 1968.

83. *Neue Deutsche Presse,* 1970, no. 2, p. 10.

84. *Middle East and Maghreb Topics,* December 1970.

85. *Neues Deutschland,* 16 September 1970.

86. *Neues Deutschland,* 19 April 1968.

87. "Besuch bei RBI-Hörerklubs in Indien" [Visit with RBI Listener Clubs in India], *Neue Deutsche Press,* 1971, no. 9, p. 24.

88. *Neue Deutsche Presse,* 1970, no. 12, pp. 8-9.

89. *Middle East and Maghreb Topics,* December 1970.

90. *Neue Deutsche Presse,* 1970, no. 17, p. 2.

91. *Neues Deutschland,* 8 August 1969.

92. Harald Ludwig, "Messen und Ausstellungen als Aushängschild der DDR in der Dritten Welt" [Fairs and Displays as Advertising Signs for the GDR in the Third World], *Deutsche Welle Dokumentation,* 17 September 1969, 159/69.

93. *Neues Deutschland,* 19 July 1969.

94. Ibid.

95. *Deutsche Aussenpolitik,* 1969, no. 6, p. 734. Descriptions of the cultural and scientific foreign relations of the GDR appear in a cultural-political dictionary, *Kulturpolitisches Wörterbuch* (Berlin: Dietz Verlag, 1970).

96. For a striking example of such coordination and priority, see accounts of the GDR's internationally orchestrated "Kampfwoche" (2-9 May 1970) for diplomatic recognition in *Horizont,* 1970, no. 22, pp. 2, 4, 5, and *Dokumentation der Zeit,* 2 September 1970, pp. 3-12.

97. For GDR criticism of FRG international political communications see: Armando Lupescu, "Goethe Institut dient Bonns Expansionstreben," *Deutsche Aussenpolitik,* 1968, no. 1, pp. 76-86; Joachim Schmidt, "Bonns Kulturpolitik gegenüber der deutschsprachigen Bevölkerung Südwestafrikas," *Deutsche Aussenpolitik,* 1968, no. 3, pp. 310-317; Klaus Ziermann, "Kultur für die psychologische Kriegführung,"

Einheit 24, no. 1 (1969): 101-109; Amandus Wulf, "Funktion und Konzeption der Bonner auswärtigen Kulturpolitik," *Deutsche Aussenpolitik,* 1969, no. 7, pp. 831-845; Otfried Dankelmann, "Sprache und Expansion," *Deutsche Aussenpolitik,* 1969, no. 8, pp. 975-982; Walter Hänel, "Die 'vierte Gewalt'—Rundfunk und Fernsehen in Westdeutschland im Dienste imperialistische Meinungsdiktatur und geistiger manipulation," *Neue Deutsch Presse,* 1 October 1970, pp. 24-26; Hans Walter Callenius, "Aggression mit schöner Worten— zum Mechanismus bundesrepublikanischer Auslandspropaganda," *Sonntag,* 11 October 1970, p. 9; Kurt Zeisler, "Zur Genesis der psychologischen Kriegsführung—Ein überblick," *Dokumentation der Zeit,* 1971, no. 6, pp. 3-14; Gerhard Dengler, "Psychologischer Krieg—ideologischer Diversion," *Horizont,* 1971, no. 21, pp. 8-9.

11. Continuity and Change Since Ulbricht

Peter C. Ludz

May 1972 marked the first anniversary of the sudden, but surprisingly peaceful, transfer of power from East Germany's veteran communist chieftain, Walter Ulbricht, to a successor regime headed by Erich Honecker. At this moment, it is too soon to offer any definitive analyses or firm prognostications concerning how this first shift at the apex of power in the history of the GDR will affect its future course, its society, or its ruling party, the SED (German Socialist Unity Party). It is, however, possible to examine a number of trends and developments that suggest—at least tentatively and for the time being—lines of continuity and lines of departure from the policies and attitudes of Herr Ulbricht. Perhaps the best way to preface a discussion of what is going on in the GDR today is to examine the reasons why that stalwart and seemingly irremovable strong man of the Soviet bloc finally stepped down from the top leadership of the East German State.

Ulbricht's Last Hurrah

Walter Ulbricht's resignation from his position as first secretary of the Central Committee of the SED—officially tendered on 3 May 1971, at the sixteenth SED conference—came as a surprise to many observers. To be sure, he was within two months of the age of seventy-eight, and advancing years were a factor—as well as a face-saver—in his acceptance of a much less important role in the regime (besides his party post, he gave up his chairmanship of the important National Defense Council, remaining only chairman of the Council of State). Yet the very fact that for twenty-five years he had guided the destiny of East Germany—first as the Soviet Occupation Zone and after 1949 as the German Democratic Republic—made it strange that there was no advance preparation or announcement of his impending "retirement" as party secretary; it strongly suggested that his relinquishment of the leadership was less than voluntary. Ulbricht was seemingly at the peak of his prestige at home and in the communist world; in particular, he had been accorded a large share of credit for the development of the GDR into a dynamic, performance-oriented state—the second strongest industrial society (after the USSR) in the Eastern bloc. Moreover, he had long been famous for his adeptness at neutralizing political rivals. Yet once the surprise was sprung and Ulbricht was out of the top spot, it was easy to perceive a number of reasons why pressures may have been brought to bear, from inside and outside the GDR, to force him to pass on the leader's mantle.

For most of his career, Walter Ulbricht was regarded, by friends and foes alike, as the very epitome of the authoritarian, pro-Muscovite communist leader; on the domestic front, he insisted on strict controls over East German society even while he showed flexibility in launching the GDR on a reformist course after 1963; in bloc affairs, he unquestioningly supported the Kremlin in its pressure for "integration" and its fight against the liberalizing trends generated by "polycentrism" and "revisionism" in broader international issues, he was again Moscow's staunchest ally—at least until late 1969, when, for the first time, a divergence developed between Soviet objectives and Ulbricht's view of East German interests.

Yet despite his reputation as a servant of Moscow who had ruthlessly pushed the "Sovietization" of East Germany and opposed polycentric trends in other bloc countries, the ironic fact is that in the last eight years of his rule Ulbricht increasingly came to emphasize the importance of independent German achievements in the economic, political, and ideological spheres and to underscore their departure from the Soviet model of development. Indeed, dating from the introduction of East Germany's program of economic reform—the so-called New Economic System—in July 1963, Ulbricht took the lead in making "national interest" and "national economy" common phrases in the lexicon of East German officialdom. To cite an early example, in a speech to the Sixth SED Congress in 1963, he declared:

> The unity of peace, national interest, democracy, and socialist order determines the historical function of our German Democratic Republic.[1]

Not long afterward, in a speech to the Central Committee in February 1964, Ulbricht clearly differentiated between the East German and Soviet reform efforts in the following terms:

> Our new economic system . . . could be described as the concrete application and continuation of the Leninist principles of the management of socialist economy, [an application] consistent with our conditions in the German Democratic Republic, which is a highly developed industrial country. We in the German Democratic Republic are conscious of the fact that we have carried out and are continuing to implement the transition from capitalism to socialism in accordance with our national conditions. These conditions are different from those obtaining when the Soviet Union carried out the transition from capitalism to socialism.[2]

More recently—especially after the failure of reformist efforts in Czechoslovakia in 1968—Ulbricht spoke up on a number of occasions to recommend the GDR's course of development to other Communist parties in both Eastern and Western Europe as a model worthy of imitation. He was well aware that the successful development of "his" GDR had gradually caught the attention and interest of many observers in the West as well as in the East, and he seldom missed an opportunity to emphasize the independent ideological basis on which the GDR had found its own "right" road to socialism. Among his favorite topics were the distinct ideological and cultural demands of the East German working class; the GDR's recent contributions to Marxist-Leninist theories of education and to the growth of a "socialist ethic," and the East German communists' successful molding of a socialist national culture as a result of concrete progress in such areas as scientific endeavor and educational reform.[3]

Over the years Ulbricht's pronouncements must have become increasingly irksome and disturbing to the Soviet leaders. In a certain sense, he was projecting himself as a potential rival of Moscow in its claim to ideological leadership; beyond that, by stressing the GDR's independent achievements, he was obviously trying to strenghten its position and influence in the international political arena. Yet as long as the strengthening of East Germany could be reconciled with Soviet goals, the GDR's role as Moscow's most important political economic junior partner made it possible for Ulbricht to pursue his course without challenge. What vitally changed his situation was a shift in the international climate precipitated in large part by the foreign policy initiatives of Willy Brandt during and after his successful bid to become chancellor of the Federal Republic of Germany in 1969, initiatives that contributed decisively to a new effort at rapprochement between the Soviet Union and the United States and to progress toward international agreement on a number of long-standing issues, including, most importantly in the current context, the status of Berlin and the broader problem of the future of the two Germanies.

To review the trend of events in barest outline, Brandt—having decided that the only road to a solution of the problems posed by a divided Germany lay through Moscow—undertook negotiations with the Soviets in which he (1) offered on the part of the FRG, a nonaggression treaty that included implicit recognition of the long controversial Oder-Neisse line as the boundary between East Germany and Poland,[4] (2) opened the door to attractive agreements for increased trade and industrial cooperation between the USSR and the FRG; (3) suggested a new approach to the "German question" that endorsed a concept of two German states within one German nation and thus downplayed the idea of unification; but (4) insisted, as a reciprocal condition of these offers, that quick and concrete progress be made toward an agreement regularizing West Berlin's independent status and its ties to the FRG.

The possibility of a new phase of détente held attractions for the leaders of most of the powers involved— but emphatically not for Walter Ulbricht, at least insofar as the Federal Republic was involved. For a number of years Ulbricht had been willing and even eager for better relations with other West European countries, with the aforementioned aim of strengthening the GDR's position and enhancing its legitimacy; while for the most part his efforts were rebuffed, in the case of France he had shown great flexibility and astuteness in building up ties that led that country quite far along the road to formal recognition of the GDR. On the German question, however, Ulbricht's position was rigidly uncompromising: it amounted to absolute and unconditional insistence that the German Democratic Republic be recognized by the Federal Republic of Germany under international law prior to any negotiations between the two governments. On the Berlin issue, he had steadfastly professed the conviction that the enclave of West Berlin constituted the "base of operations for a neofascist and imperialist policy of expansion" on the part of the FRG and the Western powers and thus represented an intolerable threat to the GDR.[5] Ubricht had never swerved from this position and, if anything, was even more adamant in his stance in the decade after the erection of the Berlin Wall in 1961. Very probably it was above all his unwillingness to modify his rigid posture on these issues that precipitated his downfall. As late as three months before his "resignation," at a meeting of the SED Central Committee on January 19, 1971, he reiterated his demand for recognition of the GDR by the FRG as a precondition to intra-German relations, even though a softening of the Soviet attitude on this question was clearly perceptible by that time.[6] Meanwhile, his unyielding posture on West Berlin was creating an impediment to progress in new negotiations among the United States, Great Britain, France, and the Soviet Union to reach a Berlin Settlement (a four-power agreement was eventually concluded in September 1971; it reaffirmed West Berlin's ties with the Federal Republic, in disregard of the

Ulbrichtian view of East German interests[7]).

While there is no way to tell what went on behind the scenes, the circumstances outlined make it a highly reasonable assumption that the Soviet leaders finally intervened to force Ulbricht to step down (if so, the deal could well have been arranged at the thirty-fourth CPSU Congress, which met from March 30 to April 9, 1971). From their point of view, Ulbricht—in his prime a master maneuverer for political gain—had become so inflexible that he simply could not adjust to the change in the international climate and the consequent shift in Soviet objectives. Besides the renewed Soviet interest in arriving at certain international agreements with the United States, Moscow obviously seemed ready to establish a dialogue with the FRG and to explore Herr Brandt's tempting prospects of West German credit allowances and future industrial collaboration. Beyond these considerations lay the broader question of future relations and balances between Eastern Europe and the European Economic Community—a matter of increasingly vital interest to the Soviets in view of West Europe's impressive progress toward economic integration; in this situation, the Soviet leadership could not afford to run the risk of allowing Ulbricht's rigid attitudes—equated with GDR policies so long as he was at the helm—to spoil the show. It was time to downgrade Ulbricht and call the East German junior partner to heel.

Shifts in Foreign Policy

Against this background, it should not be surprising that the most important policy shifts initiated by the Honecker regime have involved the GDR's external relations—in the first instance, with the USSR and the Soviet bloc. Very quickly the new party chief indicated his intention to move toward greater dependence on Moscow both politically and economically. In a major address to the Eighth SED Congress, convened in mid-June 1971, he strongly reemphasized the GDR's ties with the Soviet Union and projected a course of foreign policy that was geared to accommodate Moscow.[8] On this occasion and in subsequent developments, it became clear that the GDR would give the USSR full backing on all issues related to the Soviet

"Friedenspolitik"—literally "peace policy"—used to depict Moscow's present inclination, within definite limits, to move toward détente. Honecker's policy on the "German question" will be taken up shortly. Insofar as the broader issues involved in East-West relations are concerned, East German statements and sources have echoed nearly every nuance or shift in the Soviet attitude on such complex issues as the need for a European Security Conference or the prospect for eventual agreement on U.S.-USSR troop reductions in Europe.[9] For example, the Soviets' long-standing emphasis on the desirability of convening an all-European Security Congress seemed to abate somewhat in the summer of 1971 and then to pick up again later in the fall—an oscillation that was faithfully reflected in the coverage given the issue in the East German daily and weekly press. The GDR has also echoed the Soviet policy line on the People's Republic of China; in one instance, commentaries published in *Pravda* and *Neues Deutschland* resembled each other almost verbatim in many passages.[10]

The GDR's closer relations with the USSR have been paralleled by closer ties to the other bloc countries. In his speech to the Eighth SED Congress, Honecker declared that the GDR stood next in line after the USSR in its support of the process of strengthening the "uniform basic interest of the socialist countries." His acceptance of Moscow's bloc policies has been underscored by complete freezing of the trend, observable under Ulbricht after 1968, toward the emergence of independent GDR policies vis-à-vis Poland, Hungary, and Rumania. Thus the GDR under Honecker is reasserting what constituted its basic posture for most of the 1960s and earlier, during the process of the integration of the bloc countries under COMECON (Council for Mutual Economic Assistance)—the only modification, if any, being that the GDR's own "national" interests may initially be relegated to the background more than they were under Ulbricht.

The trend toward closer ties was confirmed at the twenty-fifth COMECON Conference, which took place in Bucharest in July 1971. Prime Minister Willi Stoph, who represented the GDR at the conference, reported that its main purpose was to coordinate the long-range plans of the member countries for the years 1971-1975, and the final communiqué spoke of the "organization of a new type of economic cooperation" among members.[11] Just before the conference, an East German economic journal elaborated on what it called the "new quality" of future cooperation within COMECON in terms of the following objectives:

1. perfection of the coordination of national economic plans
2. effective and lasting international specialization and production cooperation, especially in branches crucial for technical progress
3. expansion of the collaboration between scientific, technological, and research institutes
4. establishment of international scientific-technical and other organizations
5. expansion of reciprocal trade
6. active application of currency and financial relationships and of international credit
7. comprehensive development of ties between ministries, economic agencies, associations, and enterprises[12]

While one may be permitted some skepticism about the feasibility of a number of these ambitious goals, in the case of intrabloc trade, the GDR, at least, is firmly committed to efforts to expand its foreign trade with the Soviet Union and the other COMECON countries. In discussions of the new five-year plan presented at the Eighth SED Congress[13] and adopted in December 1971, frequent reference was made to the regime's intention to increase the proportion of the GDR's trade with socialist countries (meaning predominantly the COMECON bloc) from an already heavy 72 percent to 75 percent of total trade by 1975. While this increment is not dramatic, its significance has to be weighed in terms of the projected expansion of the volume of trade. In brief, total East German trade is to increase from 9 to 10 percent annually, reaching a peak of 63 billion marks in 1975; of this figure, 47 billion is scheduled for trade with COMECON countries and only 16 billion for trade with the West and with developing countries. Over the five-year period, these figures represent an increase of

70 percent in trade with the socialist countries, as contrasted to 42 percent with the West.[14]

Honecker's German Policy

Perhaps most important among the new regime's moves to align its foreign policy with that of the Soviet Union was its decisive shift on the "German question."

Honecker's course vis-à-vis the Federal Republic could be best described as a double-track approach. On the one hand, he quickly made it clear that he would continue and even intensify the policy of "demarcation" pursued under Ulbricht—i.e., the systematic differentiation of the two Germanies and the ideological "diabolization" of Bonn as the "agent of imperialism" and "class enemy" (a line reflecting the East German communists' recognition of their own, and consequently the GDR's political instability). Yet at the same time, he took the steps necessary to facilitate an East-West détente—either because of a pragmatic reassessment of East German interests, or because of Soviet pressures, or because of a combination of both.

In short, while still demanding recognition of the GDR by all countries (especially the Western nations) and admission of the GDR to the United Nations, Honecker abandoned Ulbricht's key condition that such recognition must be extended by the Federal Republic as a prerequisite to any dialogue with Bonn. On the Berlin issue, he discarded the tired Ulbrichtian clichés of the past, admitting for the first time (in his Eighth Congress speech) that West Berlin has a "special political status." This crucial change in policy—together with the aforementioned FRG-USSR nonaggression treaty, which had been signed on August 12, 1970, and the four-power agreement on Berlin reached on September 3, 1971—opened the door to the first formal East–West German talks in the history of the two polities.

In the four-power agreement, the Soviets formally agreed—for the first time since the partition of Germany—to share the responsibility for the expeditious handling of traffic and communications into and out of West Berlin. In practical terms, the USSR's assumption of this responsibility obviously impinged on the control rights of the GDR authorities over the access routes to Berlin, rights the Soviets delegated to them in 1955. The indication was that Moscow had sought and obtained the compliance of the SED leadership in this important particular. In the meantime, there had been hints during the summer of 1971 that the East Germans were prepared to enter into cooperation with Bonn in certain specific areas, including environmental protection, the opening of additional border crossings, and improvement of tourist travel, handling of freight, and technical cooperation between the railroad administrations of the two Germanies.[15] Actual negotiations got underway soon after the signing of the four-power accord, and by December three agreements were reached—one between the GDR and the FRG easing the movement of people and goods between the FRG and West Berlin, and two between the GDR and the city government of West Berlin, on liberalizing the rules for travel between West Berlin and East Germany and the other paving the way for the elimination of enclaves within Berlin itself through territorial exchanges.[16]

Meanwhile, East Germany's domestic propaganda machine pressed on with its ideological crusade against Bonn and the FRG. Since Brandt's accession to the top leadership in West Germany, the claim most frequently reiterated has been a variation on the theme that "the imperialist state of the FRG is . . . a dictatorship of the monopoly bourgeoisie, irrespective of whether the government is headed by representatives of the CDU/CSU or rightist SPD leaders" (a reference to the West German coalition parties now out of power, the Christian Democratic Union and the Christian Socialist Union, and Brandt's Social Democratic party).[17] The rise of the SPD to power as the dominant party in the present SPD-FDP (Free Democratic party) coalition government was a special thorn in the side of the East Germans, owing to the SED's immense antagonism toward the SPD in decades of struggle by the social democratic movement against communism in general and Stalinist communism in particular. For the SED, all Social Democratic parties—and especially the SPD—are enemies and agents of imperialism; the SPD in turn charges the SED with having betrayed the basic democratic principles of socialism. Thus there remains an all but unbridgeable gulf between the two parties, at least in the ideological sector, a gulf that finds expression in a wide variety of propaganda themes.[18]

For example, throughout 1971 a major target of attack and complaint in the GDR mass media was the choice of Munich as the site for the 1972 Olympic games. Not only was the city of Munich branded as a "main base of counterrevolutionary radio transmitters" (a reference to Radio Free Europe and Radio Liberty), but the games themselves were represented as instrumentalities of Bonn's "reactionary foreign and domestic policy." When an Olympic medal was put on the market in the Federal Republic, its inscription—"Games of the XXth Olympiad 1972 in Germany"—was denounced in the East German press as an arrogant slogan and proof that in the pursuit of its new *Ostpolitik,* Bonn was attempting to exploit the Olympic Games to further the revanchist aims of "West German imperialism," i.e., to push for the reunification of Germany on the FRG's terms.[19] In the case of this particular campaign, it is of course possible that the SED leadership was laying the ground for a boycott—or at any rate a drastic curtailment—of East German attendance at the Games, for fear that too many GDR athletes or visitors might decide to avail themselves of the opportunity to remain in the West.

This consideration aside, the Honecker regime's ideological line should be viewed as an understandable and, from the East German viewpoint, even necessary stance. Aside from the traditional hostility of the respective ruling parties, the creation of a negative "image" of the Federal Republic as the external enemy is obviously deemed a crucial exercise to offset the appeal of the richer—and freer—West German state and to give the new regime a chance to strengthen the still weak political system of the GDR and thus the leadership role of the SED. On the other hand, the new contacts with the FRG are probably considered just as necessary—among other reasons, because Honecker needs to demonstrate his acquiescence to the wishes of the Soviet ally as a means to strengthen his own political position.

These two strands of policy, which at first glance seem contradictory, are by no means irreconcilable, and both can be rationalized in ideological terms. Indeed, the body of Marxist-

Leninist "ideology" has grown fat with an array of formulas that can be used to justify just about any course of action. Consider, for example, that the concept of "peaceful coexistence" has come to have three distinct shades of meaning since its formulation by Lenin; it has been applied to denote (1) a form of class struggle, (2) the ongoing nonmilitary contest with imperialism, and (3) a positive effort at cooperation. These definitions can be used in a great variety of combinations and weights to fit any specific political situation, turning the notion of "peaceful coexistence" into a magic umbrella. In the East German situation, paradoxical as it may seen, it is perfectly possible for the SED leadership to combine the waging of "class struggle" (connotation 1) with an increasing readiness of "cooperation" with West Germany (connotation 3); thus the propaganda way may be expected to go on, even if East–West German relations continue to improve.

While Honecker has firmly committed East Germany to closer links and increased trade with the COMECON countries, this does not mean that he will abandon Ulbricht's long-standing efforts to improve relations with the West European states. It should be noted that Ulbricht's policies in this respect generally had Moscow's endorsement, and in the current phase of East-West relations, East German efforts at rapprochement would presumably be right in line with Soviet wishes.

GDR Relations with Western Europe

East German policy vis-à-vis Western Europe has involved a combination of political and economic motives. The overriding objective has been to upgrade the international status of the GDR by whatever means and in whatever way possible, toward the end of achieving formal recognition of its legitimacy under international law. While this ultimate goal eluded Ulbricht during his rule, he was able to forge a number of links with various countries through such tactics as the establishment of city partnerships, cultural exchanges, visits to West Europe by representatives of labor unions and other mass organizations, participation in sports events, and—last but not least—foreign trade. For a number of complex domestic and international reasons that are beyond the scope of this chapter,

Ulbricht's efforts to upgrade the GDR had more success in France than elsewhere; thus it may be useful to touch in briefest outline on the course of relations between the two countries as a clue to the tactics that Honecker will doubtless continue to pursue in the future.

The first direct contact of significance occurred in 1959, when a French parliamentary delegation visited the GDR. During the 1960s, a series of sister-city relationships were established between French and East German cities, and the GDR became an active member of the "World Federation of Partner Cities," which has headquarters in Paris. In 1967, factions in the French National Assembly and in the French Senate organized parliamentary "friendship groups" to promote the cause of closer Franco-GDR ties, thereby giving relations between the two countries something of a semiofficial sanction for the first time. Meanwhile, efforts on nongovernmental levels to promote economic contacts of mutual benefit constantly intensified over a number of years, climaxing in the establishment by the French Manufacturers' Association of its own office in East Berlin in 1970. In October 1970 several members and candidates of the SED Politburo (including Kurt Hager, Hermann Axen, Werner Jarowinsky, and Werner Lamberz) visited France as a party contingent and used the occasion of a press conference in Paris, organized by the French Communist party, to reiterate the demand for recognition of the GDR.[20] Most recently, in June 1971, the first official delegation of the GDR Volkskammer went to Paris and was received by, among others, Jean Broglie, chairman of the Foreign Policy Committee of the French National Assembly.[21]

The visit of the SED Politburo contingent highlighted an increase in open activity between the East German and French Communist parties—a pattern that has also emerged in the case of SED relations with the CPs of Italy, Norway, and Denmark. This stepped-up pace on Communist party relations has followed upon a similar increase of activity and contacts among the Social Democratic parties of Western and Northern Europe since 1969. In the latter development, the West German SPD has played a major role, expanding and cementing its relations with most Social Democratic parties and making friendly overtures to several of the Communist parties as well. In this light, the upsurge in SED party contacts in the West suggests a second political objective on the part of the East German leadership: beyond its basic aim of achieving recognition for the GDR, it may wish to assume the leading role in the ongoing struggle against West European social democracy. Certainly, the profound animosity of the East German communists for all social democrats, and especially West German social democrats, makes the SED a likely candidate for the role of arch-opponent.

Insofar as East German economic objectives in West Europe are concerned, it has already been pointed out that the Honecker regime plans a sizable increase in trade with the noncommunist world in the next five years, though the total falls well below the projected targets for trade within the COMECON bloc. In discussing East German trade with West Europe, it is necessary to point out that the GDR, without ever having engaged in any formal negotiations, has long had indirect access to the markets of the countries in the European Economic Community through unique circumstances that evolved basically out of two international accords. First, the Potsdam Concord of 1945 stipulated that all Germany was to be treated as a single economic unit, paving the way for later agreements allowing GDR products to enter the Federal Republic without being subject to international customs regulations.[22] Later, the Treaty of Rome, which set up the Common Market in 1957, implicitly recognized the FRG's position that East–West German trade was an internal matter and thus gave the Federal Republic—as a member of Commart—a controlling voice in the movement of East German goods within the EEC.[23] This arrangement has represented a mixed bag of political and economic advantages and disadvantages for all concerned. In the present context, the important point is that if the Western states did come to extend recognition to the GDR, it would have to sacrifice its indirect ties with the EEC. On the other hand, this would seem to be less of a problem to the GDR than in the past, since it has been increasingly successful in pursuing the alternate route of bilateral trade relations conducted through semiofficial channels.

The interest of the GDR (and USSR) in all questions

touching on the EEC has been indicated by the increasing amount of analytical research and literature being published on the subject. Communist analysts used to tend toward negative forecasts of the possibility of EEC's future progress toward union, but they now accept the probability of the eventual integration of the economies and currencies of the Common Market countries (recently grown from six to ten).[24] The communists' interest in this ongoing process is more than academic: as one East German source put it, the detailed investigation of the processes of "state-monopoly economic integration and the increasing internationalization of economic life" in Western Europe is ". . . of special importance for working out and perfecting an effective GDR foreign trade strategy in economic relations with capitalist industrial countries."[25] Statements such as this suggest that with respect to its trade and economic activity outside the Soviet bloc, the GDR is moving away from its one-sided concentration on the countries of the Third World and toward an all-European foreign trade strategy.

Developments on the Home Front

When we turn to the East German domestic scene, perhaps the single most striking fact is the smoothness with which the switch in the top leadership was accomplished and the lack of repercussions—at least in public—in the months that have since passed. Thus, only a few weeks after Ulbricht's resignation as party secretary, the Eighth Party Congress conducted its business with very few signs of confusion or reaction over the changes taking place. (Even the firmest of Ulbricht's former supporters did not seem to raise an eyebrow over the fact that Honecker barely mentioned the former leader in his address to the Congress—which Ulbricht, incidentally, did not attend.)

Ironic as it may sound, this surface serenity may well be explained by the essential instability of the East German political system—or, more accurately, by the recognition of that instability on the part of the party leadership that dominates the system. That there have long been tensions and rivalries within the SED is well known: in fact, in an article published several years ago, the present author analyzed in some detail the tendency of the SED leadership to divide into three basic groupings of reform "technocrats," hard-line "dogmatists," and pragmatic political "centrists."[26] These rivalries certainly did not suddenly dissipate with Ulbricht's fall; but there may well have been tacit (or explicit) agreement among all elements of the SED leadership that they must pull together for the time being or else take the risk of triggering reactions that could imperil the party itself.

The SED's long preoccupation with the problem of its own political legitimacy and security is underscored by the background of its new top leader. Erich Honecker can best be described as a professional "political specialist." He established an early reputation for organizational ability in the years 1946 to 1955, when he was responsible for directing and building up the Free German Youth (FDJ), East Germany's communist youth corps. Subsequently, in the central SED apparatus, he became the expert on all questions having to do with party organization, control, and security. As CC secretary for security affairs, he was the one man most responsible for the insulation of the SED from internal and external "contaminating" influences.[27] As Ulbricht's successor, he now has the responsibility for the similar ideological and political insulation of the whole GDR.

In the past, Honecker's political concerns have inclined him toward alliance with the hard-line elements in the party, though he is also a pragmatic politician. For many years his position as Ulbricht's heir-designate was unquestioned; yet with the progress of economic reform, there was increasing speculation that he might have to share power in a collective leadership with the centrists (notably Politburo member Willi Stoph, who is also the GDR's prime minister) and the technocrats (possibly Günter Mittag) in any successor regime. The fact that he has instead emerged as top man—with decisive control over the machinery of governance, at least for the time being—seems to indicate that the prevailing pressures within the party, and no doubt from Moscow as well, favored priority emphasis on the internal security and order of the East German state.

The internal trends of regime policy over the past several

months tend to support this interpretation. On the one hand, there has been an effort to reinforce the ideological claims and to strengthen the political controls of the SED over East German society. The intensification of the policy of "demarcation" with respect to the FRG has already been mentioned—a policy that Honecker must hope will fortify his own position as well as that of the GDR by systematically instilling fear of the West German "enemy." Another development in the ideological area was the adoption of a directive giving increased weight to the political attitude, as opposed to the performance record, of applicants for admission to GDR universities, colleges, and technical schools.[28] In the area of economic performance, the new regime has been able to step up control through the "growing responsibility" of the Workers' and Peasants' Inspectorate (ABI), which organizationally is under the direction of both the SED Central Committee and the Council of Ministers and which has been assigned key responsibility for checking on the implementation of party resolutions affecting the East German economy and society.[29]

At the same time, the regime has tried to increase domestic political stability by taking steps to improve the morale of the East German people. The most important feature of the Honecker course in this respect is a planned rise in the living standard of the population. At the Eighth Congress, the SED adopted special resolutions to this effect, patterning them after similar resolutions that had been adopted at the twenty-fourth Congress of the CPSU. Willi Stoph reiterated the regime's intentions in his speech on the new five-year plan, emphasizing the its "primary task" was to raise the "material and cultural living standard" of the East German population. The plan itself set forth the prospect of a considerably greater volume of consumer goods and services over the next five years. Housing construction is also supposed to be increased and improved: for example, the plan calls for the erection of 500,000 new apartment units by 1975—representing an annual rate of increase that is considerably higher than that planned for either industrial output or investments.[30]

Probably this stress on meeting the people's needs was triggered in large part by the widening gap between the living standards of the GDR and those of the FRG.[31] While the economy of the GDR has made significant strides forward under the reform program, East Germans have still had to endure the role of poor relations vis-à-vis the West Germans, who have literally galloped along the road to prosperity. While the SED leadership could not fool itself about closing the gap in living standards in the immediate future, it apparently felt it had to offer the people some reassurance that conditions would improve and that they would soon have more of the amenities of life.

Interestingly, the East German leadership expects to achieve these improvements by restructuring priorities and inputs even while reducing the rates of expansion in overall industrial output and investments. Thus, industrial production, which increased at an average annual rate of 6.5 percent in the last five-year-plan period, is to be increased only 3.9 to 6.4 percent over the next five years; similarly, investments, which increased annually by 9.7 percent in 1966-1970, are planned at a lesser growth rate of 5.1 to 5.4 percent for 1971-1975.[32]

Internal Politics

There remains the pivotal—and politically the most interesting—question of whether Erich Honecker has enough influence to retain his present dominating role in the leadership.

Certainly there can be no doubt that Honecker has a significant power base that he built up during his years of control over the party security apparatus. An initial sign of the extent (as well as the limits) of his influence was provided by the personnel changes announced at the Eighth Congress.[33] His hand was evident in certain appointments to the Politburo, more pronouncedly in shifts on the Central Committee, and finally in the appointments of some first secretaries to the SED Bezirk Committees (the party overseers in the seventeen basic administrative divisions of the GDR). Honecker showed a definite preference in these appointments for younger party functionaries (generally in their forties) whose careers have reflected a combination of political pragmatism, ideological activism, and organizational capabilities, as opposed to the equally pragmatic but nonideological technocrats whom Ulbricht tended to lean on in the last years of his leadership.[34] In a number of cases Honecker promoted personal associates from his years with the FDJ and the SED Secretariat.

Insofar as the Politburo is concerned, relatively few changes were made in the overall membership, giving the impression of continuity with the past. The composition was slightly altered to comprise sixteen members and seven candidates, a rise of one in each category. To the surprise of some observers, none of the Old Guard party faithful (including, e.g., Friedrich Ebert and Herbert Warnke[35]) was retired. In this respect, the East Germans again imitated the Soviets, who similarly kept their older functionaries on the new CPSU Politburo elected at the Twenty-fourth Party Congress. From the point of view of Honecker's interests, two men promoted from candidates to full members of the Politburo—Werner Lamberz and Werner Krolikowski—could be considered his supporters and were probably selected at his bidding. Lamberz, born in 1929, epitomized the relatively new and relatively young party ideologist who has eschewed the hard-line dogmatism of the past in favor of more flexible "scientific" and "strategic" approaches to Marxism-Leninism. Significantly enough, his interest has concentrated on the ideological aspects of the so-called Western matter—in other words, on the ideological-propagandistic conflict with the Federal Republic. His intellectual dexterity, as demonstrated in his published analyses,[36] would seem to make him an ideal collaborator for Honecker in the latter's double-track course vis-à-vis the FRG. It also seems possible that Lamberz might develop into a serious rival for the now sixty-six-year-old Albert Norden, a hard-line Politburo member who has long had dominant control over SED agitation and propaganda. The second newcomer to the Politburo, Werner Krolikowski, is another member of the forty-plus age group (he was born in 1928) who has risen in the party apparatus; he has been first secretary of the Dresden SED Bezirk Committee since 1961, and he is considered a Honecker confidant. Two new candidate members of the Politburo are also regarded as Honecker appointments. Erich Mielke (born 1907) has been minister of state security since 1957, and his elevation within the party no doubt reflects the regime's current emphasis on internal security. Harry Tisch (born 1927) has been first secretary of the Rostock SED Bezirk Committee since 1961; his allegiance to Honecker became evident at the Eighth Congress when he delivered a speech that indirectly but unmistakably criticized Ulbricht.

The trend toward promotion of "Honecker-type" functionaries was revealed in sharper focus in the composition of the new SED Central Committee approved by the Eighth Congress (whose 189 members and candidates again represent a slight enlargement over the previous CC).[37] Of the eleven former candidates raised to full membership on the CC and the eight new men appointed directly to membership, almost all came from the central SED apparatus or the Bezirk party administrations; almost none came from party members manning the economic agencies or directly participating in the economy. A similar tendency could be observed in the case of the twenty-eight new candidates to the CC, although the stress was not so pronounced. Conversely, among the fifteen members who lost their seats on the Central Committee, there was a striking preponderance of party members directly involved in economic and agriculture management. While it is beyond the scope of the present chapter to provide a complete breakdown of age levels and backgrounds here, it is certainly valid to claim that the forty-year-plus group of professional party workers has been given special weight in the new Central Committee.

Finally, Honecker had an obvious voice in the appointment of at least three new first secretaries of the Bezirk party committees, all in important areas of East Germany (most other appointees were incumbents). In all three cases, the appointees had been top-level officials of the FDJ and had worked with Honecker during the decade that he built up the youth organization, in the process providing the "cadre reserve" of the SED. In East Berlin, the man chosen was Konrad Naumann; in Frankfurt/Oder, Hans Joachim Hertwig; and in Halle, Werner Felfe (all born in 1928). It might be noted that a colleague of these men—Horst Schumann, Honecker's successor as chief of the FDJ for many years—had already been appointed first secretary of the Leipzig Bezirk Committee in 1970, upon the death of the incumbent, Paul Fröhlich.

Honecker's ability to place a number of his supporters in key positions was certainly an indication of his considerable strength within the party. To all appearances, his influence among party functionaries is not due simply to the power of his position but reflects their genuine respect for the special talents he has demonstrated in dealing with intraparty organizational and cadre problems. According to reports, he has built up good relations with leading officials at all levels of the SED apparatus, and he has made a point of being personally accessible to minor and local party officials.[38] Besides his following in the SED and the FDJ, he is said to have good contacts in the National Volksarmee ("National People's Army"). In terms of personal leadership style, he is reported to lean toward directness and informality and to have a hearty dislike for bureaucratic pretense and red tape. So far he has shown none of Ulbricht's disposition to be authoritarian and dictatorial; in fact, he has gone out of his way to pay lip service to the principle of "collective leadership," even though he obviously has the final power of decision in all matters so long as he remains both first secretary and chairman of the National Defense Council (the second most important position in the GDR power structure).

Despite these many factors in Honecker's favor, the fact remains that he by no means possesses the authority and prestige, either within the SED or in East German society at large, that Ulbricht enjoyed for many years. While his role in the party has given him an inside track in establishing a personal following, the narrowness of his specialization in matters of party organization, control, and security could work to his disadvantage over time. The debit side of the coin is that he has played no part whatever—so far as is known—in overall economic and social planning or more particularly in the crucial reorganization and modernization of the East German economic and educational systems since 1963. Nor has he distinguished himself in any significant way in the field of ideology. Thus he is in the position of having to rely for help in a number of areas on men who have been real, or who are now potential, rivals.

It thus seems entirely possible that a succession crisis might still develop in the GDR. As mentioned earlier, the very smoothness with which Ulbricht was eased out of the top spot suggests the probability that in the minds of at least some of the leaders, Honecker's assumption of power was an interim necessity subject to possible challenge when time and circumstances should permit. For years Honecker's chief rival in and out of the Politburo has been Prime Minister Willi Stoph, whose professional specialty is economic organization—a field in which Honecker cannot personally compete. A second, younger rival is the aforementioned Günter Mittag, who in Ulbricht's last years was the leading light of the faction of technocrats who guided the course of economic reform. If a power struggle should develop within the Politburo at some future date, it could conceivably see an alignment of Stoph and Mittag—and possibly also Alfred Neumann as a source of conservative support—against Honecker.

The harder question is to determine who would stand by Honecker in the face of such a challenge. Besides Lamberz and Krolikowski, one probable supporter is Horst Sindermann, a tough-minded but capable ex-chief of the Halle Bezirk party organization, a man who has been on the Politburo since 1963 and who, in the wake of Ulbricht's ouster, was elevated—seemingly at Honecker's behest—to the post of deputy chairman of the Council of Ministers, making him a potential successor to Stoph. A clear sign that Sindermann has joined the "inner circle" of the Politburo leadership was the fact that he—together with Honecker, Stoph, and Hager (but not Mittag)—made up the top SED delegation that visited Moscow in mid-May 1971, obviously to coordinate future Soviet–East German strategy. Sinderman was noted for his total loyalty to Ulbricht; whether he will show the same fealty to Honecker remains to be seen.

Another Politburo member owing his promotion to the new party chief is Paul Verner, appointed Honecker's successor as CC secretary in charge of security, organization, and cadre questions. Verner, whose experience with matters of internal security and order derives from many years as chief of the

Berlin SED Committee, could probably be counted in Honecker's corner in the case of a struggle, but there is no way to be sure.

Summary

The latest developments at this time seem to indicate that Honecker is in no immediate danger of such a political challenge and in fact has managed to strengthen his hand in the state apparatus as well as in the party.[39] Still, he is a political man attuned to all political possibilities, so no doubt his main order of business for the present and the foreseeable future will be to rally further support for himself within the SED and in the GDR at large, as well as among communist leaders in other Soviet bloc countries.

The importance of the latter fund of support probably means that he will hew rather closely to the lines of policy established when he took over from Ulbricht and will refrain, at least for the time being, from stepping forward with any dramatic innovations of his own, especially in the field of foreign policy. To repeat, then, the GDR can be expected to continue along a course of closer ties to the COMECON countries and firm support for Moscow's line on such international issues as the Sino-Soviet confrontation and the conflicts in the Middle East, Southeast Asia, and other areas of the globe. In its policy toward the Federal Republic, the Honecker regime will continue to put great stress on the ideological differentiation of East and West Germany, even while moving in certain limited areas along the paths of possible cooperation with the FRG.

Concomitantly, the new regime will continue to pursue all possible tactics to upgrade the international status of the GDR. In this area it has rather good prospects for some success in the near future. There has been widespread sentiment favoring the admission of the GDR to membership in a number of organizations affiliated with the United Nations, including the Economic Commission for Europe (ECE), the UN Economic and Social Commission (UNESCO), and the World Health Organization (WHO). Moreover, a number of states, including Sweden, India, and Japan, have indicated an interest in expanding their official relations with the GDR. Finally, if a European Security Conference should ever be convened, as a number of states in both East and West would like, it is widely expected that the two German states would participate on a basis of equality.

At home, Honecker has a long way to go to match the image that Ulbricht managed to project of himself as the "father of his country." For the long run, it remains an open question whether Honecker will be able to assert and stabilize his authority in the face of potentially formidable—if presently latent—competition. All that can be said at the moment is that he has established a very good lead.

Notes

1. Ulbricht speech entitled "The Program of Socialism and the Historical Mission of the SED," published in *Protokoll der Verhandlungen des V. Parteitages der SED: 15. bis 21. Januar 1963* [Record of the Proceedings of the Sixth SED Congress, 15-21 January 1963], 4 vols. (Berlin, Dietz Verlag, 1963), 1: 53.

2. Quoted in Walter Ulbricht, *Zum neuen ökonomischen System der Planung und Leitung* [The New Economic System of Planning and Management] (Berlin, Dietz Verlag, 1966), p. 398.

3. See, e.g., Ulbricht's speech at the Fifteenth Plenum of the CC-SED, in *Neues Deutschland,* 30 January 1971, p. 4.

4. This treaty was signed by Bonn and Moscow on 12 August 1970. For the text, see *Deutschland Archiv* 3, no. 9 (1970): 956-960.

5. See, e.g., his speech to the Seventh SED Congress, published in *Protokoll der Verhandlungen des VII. Parteitages der SED: 17. bis 22. April, 1967,* 4 vols. (Berlin, Dietz Verlag, 1967), 1: 61 ff.

6. See Ulbricht's speech in *Neues Deutschland,* 30 January 1971, p. 4.

7. The agreement was signed on 2 September 1971; an official German translation was published in *Die Welt* (Hamburg), 4 September 1971, pp. 6 ff.

8. Honecker's speech was published in *Neues Deutschland,* 16 June 1971, pp. 5 ff.

9. See, e.g., Peter Florin, "The Foreign Policy of the Working Class in the Foreign Policy of the GDR," *Horizont,* 1971, no. 24, pp. 3 ff.

10. Cf. I. Aleksandrov in *Pravda,* 24 July 1971; and "M.A.," in *Neues Deutschland,* 29 July 1971.

11. Stoph's interview and the communiqué were both published in *Neues Deutschland,* 30 July 1971.

12. Edlegard Göhler et al., "Socialist Economic Integration—a Law of Socialist Construction," *Wirtschaftswissenschaft* 19, no. 7 (1971): 949.

13. "Directive of the Eighth SED Congress on the 1971-1975 Five-Year Plan for the Development of National Economy of the GDR," special supplement published in *Neues Deutschland,* 23 June 1971.

14. See "Is the GDR Stifling Western Trade?" *Frankfurter Allgemeine Zeitung* 24 July 1971, p. 15.

15. On the question of ecological cooperation, see *Der Tagesspiegel* (West Berlin), 21 July 1971, p. 5; see also "Bonn Striving for Two Treaties with East Berlin," in *Frankfurter Allgemeine Zeitung,* 22 July 1971, p. 3.

16. Texts of these agreements were published in *Presse und Informationsamt der Bundesregierung* [Bulletin of the Press and Information Office of The Federal Government—Bonn], no. 183, 11 December 1971.

17. Quoted from Otto Reinhold, "The Imperialism of the FRG," in *Einheit* 26, no. 6 (1971): 765.

18. See, e.g., *Die Westdeutsche Sozialdemokratie in der gegenwartigen Etappe der Auseinandersetzung zwischen Sozialismus und Imperialismus* [West German Social Democracy during the Present Phase of the Conflict between Socialism and Imperialism], official publication of the SED (East Berlin, 1970).

19. See, e.g., "The SED Zeroes in on Munich," *Süddeutsche Zeitung* (Munich), 20 July 1971, p. 4.

20. See the later interview of Hager published in *Horizont,* 1970, no. 46, p. 3.

21. See interview of Klaus Sorgenicht, a member of the GDR Council of State (Staatsrat) in ibid., 1971, no. 25, p. 6.

22. The accord now in force is the so-called Berlin Agree-

ment on Interzonal Trade (IZT) of 1960.

23. See Secretariat of the Interim Committee for the Common Market and Euratom, "Protocol Relating to German Internal Trade and Connected Problems," in *Treaty Establishing the European Economic Community and Connected Documents* (English language) (Brussels, 1957), annex 2, p. 261.

24. See e.g., H. D. Kuhne, "Disputes over the Development of Two Imperialist Currency Areas," *Sozialistische Aussenwirtschaft* (East Berlin), 1971, no. 5, pp. 30 ff.

25. G. Hofmann, "Tendencies of Capitalist Concentration in the EEC Countries," *Sozialistische Aussenwirtschaft,* 1971, no. 1, p. 18.

26. Peter C. Ludz, "The SED leadership in Transition," *Problems of Communism* 21, no. 3 (May-June 1970): 23-31.

27. For details of Honecker's background, see Peter C. Ludz, *The German Democratic Republic from the Sixties to the Seventies,* Harvard "Occasional Papers" Series (Cambridge, Mass.: Harvard University Press, 1970), pp. 48 ff.

28. "Directive on Application Procedure, Selection, and Admission to On-Campus Study at Universities and Colleges—Admission Regulations," 1 July 1971, published in *Gesetzblatt der DDR,* pt. 2, 1971, p. 486.

29. On the role of ABI, see Heinz Matthes, "Reliable Popular Control—Principle of Socialist State and Economic Management," *Einheit* 26, no. 6 (1971): 715 ff.

30. "Directive of the Eighth SED Congress on the 1971-1975 Five-Year Plan."

31. For comparative statistics on living standards, see *Deutschland 1971: Bericht und Materialen zur Lage der Nation* [Germany 1971 Report and Materials on the Situation of the Nation] (Köln-Opladen, Westdeutscher Verlag, 1971), especially chap. 5.

32. "Directive of the Eighth SED Congress on the 1971-1975 Five-Year Plan."

33. Party personnel actions taken at the Eighth SED Congress were published in *Neues Deutschland,* 20 June 1971.

34. See Ludz, "The SED Leadership in Transition."

35. Ebert also remains on the Presidium of the Volks-

kammer; Warnke continues as chairman of the National Board of the 7 million member Free German Trade Union Association (FDGB), East Germany's largest mass organization, which he has headed since 1948.

36. See, e.g., his articles, "New Demands on the Ideological Work of the Party," in *Der Parteiarbeiter* (East Berlin, Dietz Verlag, 1969); "The Leninist Principles of the Scientific Management of Socialist Construction and Their Application in the GDR," in *Der Leninismus und der Revolutionare Prozess: internationale theoretische Konferenz . . . vom 19. bis 21. November 1969 in Prag* [Leninism and the Revolutionary Process: International Theoretical Conference . . . November 19-21, 1969, in Prague] (East Berlin, Dietz Verlag, 1970), pp. 67 ff; and "A Quarter-Century of Victorious History," *Neuer Weg* (East Berlin), 1971, no. 3, pp. 99 ff.

37. The CC was increased from 131 to 135 members and from 50 to 54 candidates; see *Neues Deutschland,* 20 June 1971.

38. See Harald Ludwig, "The SED before the Eighth Party Congress," *Deutschland Archiv* 4, no. 6 (1971): 596.

39. At the end of November 1971, Honecker, Paul Verner, and several presumable allies were appointed to the Council of State, the third most important ruling body in the GDR (after the SED Politburo and the National Defense Council, both headed by Honecker. While Ulbricht remained chairman of the Council, his intimate associate Otto Gotsche—long head of the Staatsrat Secretariat—was removed. Günter Mittag also lost his seat on the Council, though he remains on the Politburo. For the composition of the new Council, see *Neues Deutschland,* 27 November 1971.

Selected Bibliography

The three standard, and fairly recent, sources of bibliographical information on the German Democratic Republic, in order of appearance, are:

Price, Arnold, comp. *East Germany: A Selected Bibliography.* Washington, D.C.: Library of Congress, 1967.

Horecky, Paul L., ed. *East Central Europe: A Guide to Basic Publication.* Chicago/London: University of Chicago Press, 1969. East Germany, pp. 361-440.

Hersch, Gisela, comp. *A Bibliography of German Studies: 1945-1971.* Bloomington/London: Indiana University Press, 1972. The German Democratic Republic, pp. 374-498 and passim.

For periodical literature, the best single source of references, aside from journals published in the GDR, is the West German *Deutschland Archiv.* Also useful for periodical literature not covered by the above sources is *ABC Pol Sci* (Santa Barbara: American Bibliographical Center–Clio Press, 1969–).

The following list, consisting of books only (or whole issues of journals), is a selection of items that have appeared in English since the period covered by the aforementioned bibliographies.

Area Handbook for East Germany. Washington, D.C.: Government Printing Office, 1972.

Baylis, Thomas A. *The Technical Intelligentsia and the East German Elite.* Berkeley: University of California Press, 1974.

Bender, Peter. *East Europe in Search of Security.* Baltimore: Johns Hopkins University Press for the International Institute for Strategic Studies, 1972.

Birnbaum, Karl E. *East and West Germany: A Modus Vivendi.* Lexington, Mass.: Lexington Books, 1973.

Flores, John. *Poetry in East Germany.* New Haven: Yale University Press, 1971.

Hancock, M. Donald. *The Bundeswehr and the National People's Army: A Comparative Study of German Civil-Military Polity.* Denver: University of Denver Monograph Series in World Affairs, 1973.

Herspring, Dale R. *East German Civil-Military Relations: The Impact of Technology, 1949-1972.* New York: Praeger, 1973.

Krisch, Henry. *German Politics under Soviet Occupation.* New York: Columbia University Press, 1974.

Lippmann, Heinz. *Honecker and the New Politics of Europe.* New York: Macmillan Co., 1972.

Ludz, Peter C. *The Changing Party Elite in East Germany.* Cambridge, Mass.: M.I.T. Press, 1972.

Ludz, Peter C. *The German Democratic Republic from the Sixties to the Seventies.* Cambridge, Mass.: Harvard University, Center for International Affairs, 1970.

Ludz, Peter C. *Two Germanys in One World.* Paris: Atlantic Institute for International Affairs, 1974.

Merkl, Peter H. *German Foreign Policies, West and East.* Santa Barbara: Clio Press, 1974.

Schnitzer, Martin. *East and West Germany: A Comparative Economic Analysis,* New York: Praeger, 1972.

Schweigler, Gebhard L. *National Consciousness in Divided Germany.* Beverly Hills: Sage, 1975.

Sontheimer, Kurt, and Bleek, Wilhelm. *The Government and Politics of East Germany.* New York: St. Martin's, 1976.

Starrels, John M., and Mallinckrodt, Anita D. *Politics in the German Democratic Republic.* New York: Praeger, 1975.

Wettig, Gerhard. *Community and Conflict in the Socialist Camp: The Soviet Union, East Germany, and the German Problem 1956-1972.* London: C. Hurst, 1975.

The German Democratic Republic. Special issue of *East Central Europe,* Spring, 1977.
The German Democratic Republic. Special issue of *New German Critique,* Spring, 1974.